# THE POLICY PROCESS
# AND
# SUPER-OPTIMUM
# SOLUTIONS

# THE POLICY PROCESS AND SUPER-OPTIMUM SOLUTIONS

## Stuart S. Nagel
### University of Illinois

Nova Science Publishers, Inc.

Art Director: Christopher Concannon
Graphics: Elenor Kallberg and Maria Ester Hawrys
Book Production: Roseann Pena, Tammy Sauter,
              Barbara Byrne, Ludmila Kwartiroff
              and Michelle Lalo
Circulation: Irene Kwartiroff and Annette Hellinger


*Library of Congress Cataloging-in-Publication Data*

Nagel, Stuart S., 1934-
    The policy process and super-optimum solutions /
    Stuart S. Nagel.
        p. cm.
    Includes bibliographical references and index.
    ISBN 1-56072-135-9 : $53.00
    1. Policy sciences. I. Title.
    H97.N334  1993                                  93-14235
    320'.6--dc20                                    CIP


© *1994 Nova Science Publishers, Inc.*
  *6080 Jericho Turnpike, Suite 207*
  *Commack, New York 11725*
  *Tele. 516-499-3103  Fax 516-499-3146*
  *E Mail Novasci1@aol.com*

*Printed in the United States of America*

Dedicated to the people who have pioneered in the fields of policy formulating, adopting, implementing, and facilitating.

# Detailed Table of Contents

# THE POLICY PROCESS AND SUPER-OPTIMUM SOLUTIONS

**INTRODUCTION** ................................................................................ *1*

    I. The Political Process of SOS.............................................*2*
        A. Arriving at SOS Solutions ......................................*2*
        B. Adopting SOS Solutions.........................................*4*
        C. Implementing SOS Solutions ................................*6*
        D. Political Facilitators ..............................................*8*

    II. The Economic Process of SOS........................................*9*

    III. The Psychology-Sociology of SOS Solutions ...............*9*

**PART ONE: THE POLITICAL PROCESS OF SOS SOLUTIONS**

Chapter 1. <u>WAYS OF ARRIVING AT SUPER-OPTIMUM SOLUTIONS</u>......*15*

    I. Expanding the Total Resources.....................................*15*
        A. The Alternatives.....................................................*15*
        B. The SOS Table.......................................................*16*
        C. The Causal Arrow Diagram...................................*18*
        D. The Compromise Position .....................................*19*
        E. Broad Implications ................................................*20*
        F. Increasing Productivity ........................................*20*
        G. Analysis and Advocacy.........................................*21*
        H. Summarizing the Example ....................................*22*

    II. Raising Goals Above What is Considered the Best....................*22*

    III. Big Benefits for One Side, Low Costs for the Other....................*23*
        A. Litigation Situations..............................................*23*
        B. The SOS in the Migrant Labor Case ...................*26*
        C. The Computer Analysis.........................................*28*
        D. Some Conclusions.................................................*30*

    IV. Third Party Benefactor .................................................*34*
        A. Housing for the Poor.............................................*34*
        B. Food Prices in China.............................................*39*

  V.   Combining Liberal and Conservative Alternatives..................43

 VI.   Removing or Decreasing the Source of the Conflict.................45
       A.  Points Favoring Capital Punishment...........................45
       B.  Points Disfavoring Capital Punishment........................47
       C.  SOS Murder Reduction.........................................47
       D.  Other Examples...............................................47

VII.   A Package of Alternatives.......................................48
       A.  General......................................................48
       B.  Pretrial Release of Arrested Defendants......................50

VIII.  Redefining the Problem..........................................53
       A.  Traditional Alternatives and Goals..........................53
       B.  An SOS Solution..............................................54
       C.  Factors Interfering with Adoption...........................56
       D.  The Importance of Problem Definition
           and SOS Awareness...........................................58

 IX.   Reducing Costs and Increasing Benefits..........................58
       A.  Computer-Assisted Instruction...............................58
       B.  Other Examples..............................................61


Chapter 2. CAUSAL ANALYSIS IN SOS ADOPTION
           AND IMPLEMENTATIONS.........................................71

  I.   Thinking About the Concept of SOS Prediction....................71

 11.   Causal Analysis of SOS Adoption.................................72
       A.  Up the Ante.................................................72
       B.  Representatives.............................................73
       C.  Regardless How Well the Other Side Does.....................74
       D.  Suspicion That a Trap is Involved...........................74
       E.  Removing versus Adding Goals................................74
       F.  Vested Jobs and Property as an Obstacle
           to SOS Adoption.............................................75

III.   Causes of Successful and Unsuccessful
       SOS Implementation..............................................76
       A.  Clarifying SOS Success......................................76
       B.  Some Experiences of the Reagan Administration...............78
       C.  Some Experiences from Great Society Legislation.............81
       D.  Successful SOS Experiences..................................84

**PART TWO: THE ECONOMIC PROCESS OF SOS SOLUTIONS**

Chapter 3. INCENTIVES, GROWTH AND PRODUCTIVITY......................89

   I.   Introduction .........................................................................89

   II.  In Incentives Perspective .................................................90
        A.  Encouraging Socially Desired Behavior in General.........90
        B.  Some Aspects of Well-Placed Subsidies............................92
        C.  Incentives for Encouraging Socially
            Desired Behavior .......................................................93
        D.  Necessity-Invention......................................................94

  III.  A Growth Perspective ......................................................95

  IV.  Incentives Related to Growth ..........................................96
        A.  Outline......................................................................96
        B.  U.S. Is Still the Richest Country in the World
            in Terms of Total Assets ...........................................97
        C.  Debt Really Hurts.......................................................97
        D.  Budget Deficit and the International Trade
            Deficit Look Like Good Things....................................98
        E.  Ironies in This Debate................................................99
        F.  Using Incentives to Increase Productivity.....................99
        G.  The Upward Spiral .....................................................100
        H.  Why Has It Not Been Done Already ...............................100
        I.  Things to Watch Out For.............................................101
        J.  Obtaining Incentives Money from Reduced
            Defense Spending......................................................102
        K.  Separate Segments .....................................................102
        L.  Subunits on Relating Incentives and Productivity ........103
        M.  New Developments and Summary................................104

   V.  Some Comparisons Between Japanese
       and American Productivity .............................................105

  VI.  How Increased Productivity Tends to Lead
      to Increased Productivity................................................106

 VII.  Council on International Competitiveness............................107
        A.  What Is Wrong with the American Economy..................107
        B.  Position of the Council on Competitiveness ..................108
        C.  How That Institution Could Be Changed.......................109
        D.  Asking How Come Japan is Doing So Well
            in Terms of Economic Growth and the United
            States is Not Doing So Well........................................111
        E.  The Phrase Super-Optimizing......................................112

Chapter 4. <u>COMPETITION IN THE PUBLIC
            AND PRIVATE SECTORS</u> ............................................117

   I.  Competition in the Private Sector.................................117
       A.  Competition and Cooperation Simultaneously............117
       B.  Competition Contrasted with Monopoly,
           Rather Thanwith Cooperation......................................118
       C.  Encouraging Competition and Cooperation
           in the Workplace, Marketplace, Academia,
           and the World.................................................120
       D.  Other and General Aspects ...................................123

   II. Competition in the Public Sector..................................126
       A.  Consolidation versus Competition Among  Agencies....126
       B.  Competition Among Public Schools, Police
           Departments, and Political Parties............................129

   III. The Public and the Private Sectors...............................132

**PART THREE: THE PSYCHOLOGY-SOCIOLOGY OF SOS SOLUTIONS**

Chapter 5. <u>THE POSITIVE PSYCHOLOGY
            OF SUPER-OPTIMUM SOLUTIONS</u> ..............................139

   I.  Methods for Generating Alternative Policies
       and Decisions.....................................................139
       A.  Pushing Factors..............................................140
       B.  Facilitators...................................................141
       C.  Pulling Factors: Rewards ...................................142
       D.  Balancing Fact-Learning with Stimulating
           Creativity and Reasoning Powers..............................143

   II. Combining Pessimism and Optimism...............................147

   III. Relations Between High Societal Goals
        and Societal Happiness..........................................149

   IV. Risk Taking.......................................................152
       A.  Relevance to Technological Innovation.......................152
       B.  A Better System of Liability...................................154

   V.  Socialization and Public Policy ...................................158
       A.  In General ...................................................158
       B.  Specific Policy Problems ....................................158
       C.  Preschool Education ........................................162

VI. Balancing Positive and Negative Discretion............................165
    A. The 30% Tax Cut as Too Little Discretion.......................165
    B. Some HUD Subsidies as Too Much Discretion ...............166
    C. Opposite Trends................................................................168
    D. Criteria for Granting Discretion.....................................169
    E. The Example of Requiring Overly Precise Addresses.....170
    F. The Example of New Pharmaceuticals ...........................172
    G. Being Flexible to Adopt an SOS Solution .......................173

VII. The Psychology of Benefits, Costs, and Efficiency..................175
    A. Undue Cost Sensitivity.....................................................175
    B. Three Key Criteria ...........................................................177
    C. Two Kinds of Efficiency...................................................177
    D Three Typical Situations .................................................179
    E. What Really Counts .........................................................180
    F. Psychology of Efficiency..................................................182
    G. Miscellaneous Points.......................................................182

VII. The Psychology and Legal Obligation of Helping Others........183

Chapter 6. INSTITUTIONALIZING SOS ANALYSIS ..............................189

  I. Five Policy Analysis Activities and Three Institutions.........190

  II. Trends, Developing Nations, and SOS....................................192

  III. Appendix: Allocating $100 Million to Policy
     Analysis Activities and Institutions.......................................195

BIBLIOGRAPHY ...................................................................................198

# THE POLICY PROCESS AND SUPER-OPTIMUM SOLUTIONS

## LIST OF TABLES

| Table # | TITLE | Page |
|---|---|---|

1. ARRIVING AT SOS SOLUTIONS

| | | |
|---|---|---|
| 1-1 | Dealing with Deficit | 17 |
| 1-2 | The Upward Spiral of Well-Placed Subsidies in Facilitating Increased Government Services and Reduced Tax Rates | 18 |
| 1-3 | The Asian Labor Shortage Criteria | 24 |
| 1-4 | Super Optimizing Litigation Analysis | 31 |
| 1-5 | Resolving Litigation Disputes through Super-Optimum Solutions | 34 |
| 1-6 | An SOS Analysis of Housing for the Poor | 36 |
| 1-7 | Pricing Food in China and Elsewhere | 41 |
| 1-8 | Combining Public and Private Higher Education | 46 |
| 1-9 | Evaluating the Policy of Capital Punishment | 49 |
| 1-10 | Evaluating Alternative Ways of Handling | 51 |
| 1-11 | 6-Person v. 12-Person Juries | 57 |
| 1-12 | Reducing Costs and Increasing Benefits In Education | 60 |
| 1-13 | An SOS Analysis of Some Aspects of Federal Aviation Administration Policy | 62 |
| 1-14 | Dealing with the Pollution of Archer Daniels Midland | 64 |

2. CAUSAL ANALYSIS IN ADOPTION AND IMPLEMENTATION

3. PRODUCTIVITY, INCENTIVES AND GROWTH

| | | |
|---|---|---|
| 3-1 | Evaluating Alternative Positions onTariffs | 114 |

4.  COMPETITION IN PUBLIC AND PRIVATE SECTORS

    4 1    Political and Econimic Competition
           as Key Causes of Prosperity                    *133*
    4-2    Competition as an SOS Economic Solution        *135*


5.  PSYCHOLOGY OF SOS SOLUTIONS

    5-1    Alternatives for Product Liability             *157*
    5-2    Evaluating Policies toward Preschool Education  *163*
    5-3    Using Benefits and Costs in Measurement        *178*


6.  INSTITUTIONALIZING SOS ANALYSIS

    6-1    Institutions for Policy Studies Activities     *191*
    6-2    Allocating World Bank Funds to Policy
           Analysis Activities and Institutions           *196*

# INTRODUCTION

This book deals with the process of super-optimizing. That refers to generating, adopting, implementing, and facilitating solutions to policy problems whereby conservatives, liberals, and other major viewpoints can all come out ahead of their best initial expectations simultaneously.

The book is divided into three parts. The first part refers to the political process of SOS solutions. The phrase "political process" is used in a broad sense to refer to the total political or policy cycle covering agenda-setting, formulating policy, adopting it, implementation, evaluation, and termination. The most important stages in that cycle are formulating, adopting, and implementing, which are discussed in Chapters 1 and 2. Evaluating alternatives is an important subject covered in the companion volume entitled *Policy Analysis Methods and Super-Optimum Solutions*.

The second part is the economic process of SOS solutions. It is concerned with such economic variables as incentives, growth, productivity, competition, the public sector, and the private sector. Incentives refer to encouraging socially desirable behavior by increasing the benefits of doing right, decreasing the costs of doing right, increasing the costs of doing wrong, decreasing the benefits of doing wrong, increasing the costs of doing wrong, and increasing the probability of the appropriate benefits and costs occurring. Growth refers to increases in the gross national product, education level, and longevity as the three key national growth indicators designated by the United Nations. Productivity refers to increasing the quantitative or qualitative national output while decreasing costs, or at least holding constant on outputs or inputs while improving on the other. Competition refers to having multiple suppliers, buyers, firms, political parties, or other entities all seeking to do the best job in order to receive higher rewards. The public sector refers to government agencies that are supported mainly out of taxes. The private sector refers to business firms that are supported mainly out of selling products.

The third part is the psychology-sociology of SOS solutions. It deals first with the positive psychology of SOS solutions. That covers generating creating policies, being appropriately optimistic, taking risks, socializing children into societal values, balancing positive and negative discretion, and showing relevant consent over benefits and costs. The third part also deals with a kind of sociological regard for the building of relevant institutions and institutional activities. The most relevant institutions in the SOS process are government agencies, policy institutes, and universities. The most relevant activities are training, research, publishing, funding, and networking.

## 1. THE POLITICAL PROCESS OF SOS

### A. Arriving At SOS Solutions

There are approximately eight different ways of arriving at super-optimum solutions. They consist of the following:

1. Expanding the resources available. An example might include well-placed subsidies and tax breaks that would increase national productivity and thus increase the gross national product and income. Doing so would enable the tax revenue to the government to increase even if the tax rate decreases. That would provide for a lowering of taxes, instead of trying to choose between liberal and conservative ways of raising them. It would also provide for increasing both domestic and defense expenditures, instead of having to choose between the two.

2. Setting higher goals than what was previously considered the best while still preserving realism. An example might include the Hong Kong labor shortage with unemployment at only 1%. Hong Kong is faced with the seeming dilemma of having to choose between foregoing profits (by

not being able to fill orders due to lack of labor) and opening the floodgates to mainland Chinese and Vietnamese (in order to obtain more labor). A super-optimum solution might involve adding to the labor force by way of the elderly, the disabled, and mothers of preschool children. Also by providing more and better jobs for those who are seasonally employed, part-time employed, full-time employed but looking for a second job, and full-time employed but not working up to their productive capacity.

3. Situations where one side can receive <u>big benefits but the other side incurs only small costs</u>. An example is in litigation where the defendant gives products that it makes. The products may have high market value to the plaintiff, but low variable or incremental cost to the defendant, since the defendant has already manufactured the products or can quickly do so.

4. Situations involving a <u>third party benefactor</u> which is usually a government agency. An example is government food stamps which allow the poor to obtain food at low prices, while farmers receive high prices when they submit the food stamps they have received for reimbursement. Another example is rent supplements which allow the poor to pay low rents, but landlords receive even higher rents than they would otherwise expect.

5. <u>Combining alternatives</u> that are not mutually exclusive. An example is combining government-salaried legal-aid attorneys with volunteer attorneys. Doing so could give the best of both the public sector and private sector approach to legal services for the poor. Another example is combining (1) tax-supported higher education plus democratic admission standards with (2) contributions from alumni and tuition plus merit standards. Doing so results in universities that are better than pure government ownership or pure private enterprise.

6. Removing or <u>decreasing the source of the conflict</u> between liberals and conservatives, rather than trying to synthesize their separate proposals. An example would be concentrating on having a highly effective and acceptable birth control program to satisfy both the proponents and opponents of abortion, since abortions would then seldom be needed. Another example would be concentrating on a highly effective murder-reduction program to satisfy both the proponents and opponents of capital punishment. Such a murder-reduction program might emphasize gun control, drug medicalization, and reduction of violence socialization.

7. Developing a <u>package of alternatives</u> that would satisfy both liberal and conservative goals. An example is pretrial release where liberals want more arrested defendants released prior to trial, and conservatives want higher rate of appearances in court without having committed a crime while released. The package that increases the achievement of both goals includes better screening, reporting in, notification, and prosecution of no-shows, as well as reduction of delay between arrest and trial.

8. Increasing benefits and reducing costs through new technologies or procedures. An example might be computer-assisted instruction in the elementary schools. It can reduce the cost of teachers if one teacher can supervise more than one class through the use of CAI. It can increase the learning experience if software is used that children find both enjoyable and educational. Other examples involve improved technology for simultaneously (1) increasing air traffic safety while reducing the payroll, or (2) increasing the cleanliness of manufacturing processes while reducing manufacturing costs.

## B. Adopting Super-Optimum Solutions

Merely arriving at a suggested policy that is capable of enabling conservatives, liberals, and other major viewpoints to all come out ahead of their best expectations simultaneously does not guarantee that the policy will be adopted or that it will be successfully implemented even if it is adopted.

Since SOS policies enable all sides to be better off than their best expectations, one would think that merely developing such policies would get them adopted. There are, however, at least four factors that can interfere with successful adoption. Their presence should be watched for, and one should plan accordingly in order to deal with them.

1. Upping the ante. Suppose one side says we must have a minimum of 500 units, and the other side says we will not pay one unit more than 400 units. Suppose further an SOS solution is developed to enable the first side to obtain 501 units and the second side to only have to pay 399 units. One would think such a solution would be instantly adopted. The first side might, however, say that it has now changed its mind and wants 600 units after seeing how easy it is to get 501 units. To deal with such a problem and many other SOS situations, it is helpful to have a third party mediator (or one or both of the parties) make clear that if the initial demands are more than satisfied, that the dispute should be considered resolved. It should also be made clear that if the gap widens from an original gap of 500 versus 400 to 600 versus 400, then it may be impossible to provide an SOS solution because the cost to one of the parties or a third party may become too great.

2. Satisfying the mediator. Mediators and representatives of the conflicting parties or viewpoints can often be helpful in developing super-optimum solutions because they are trusted by each side more than the other side is trusted. However, an SOS solution might sometimes be developed that does not get adopted because the mediator or the representative of one side or the other needs some satisfaction other than knowing that both sides are pleased. This can be the situation where each side is represented by one or more lawyers who want to be paid substantially for their services. The agreement may involve one side getting something that is worth 501 units to it, with the other side paying something that is worth only 399 units to it. An example is where

the second side gives products that it makes. The lawyer may not be happy with receiving one third of the 501 units, and may therefore discourage such an SOS settlement unless adequate provision is made for covering the lawyer. That can be done by the receiving side agreeing to convert some of the 501 units into cash to pay the lawyer or obtaining cash from other sources available to the receiving side. This problem does need to be explicitly recognized because the lawyer may otherwise have a conscious or subconscious tendency to disrupt the settlement for reasons that are supposedly for the client's benefit.

3.  <u>The revenge factor</u>. This can occur where the receiving side in the above example is pleased to receive 501 units, but is displeased that the giving side is only paying 399 units, as measured by the giving side's benefit-cost assessment. It can also occur where the giving side is pleased to have to give only 399 units, but is displeased that the receiving side is getting 501 units, as measured by the receiving side's benefit-cost assessment. Under those circumstances, it helps to have a third party mediator emphasize to each side how well off it is even beyond its initial best expectations. There may be some special circumstances where it is necessary for the other side to suffer in order to provide specific deterrence to him or general deterrence to discourage others from engaging in similar undesirable behavior. In non-criminal situations, a revenge factor may be the equivalent of cutting off one's opportunity to greatly benefit in order to spite the other side as well as oneself.

4.  <u>Suspicion that a trap is involved</u>. If one side demands a minimum of 500 units, and the other side says I will give you 501 units, it is reasonable for the receiving side to be suspicious that there is a trap or catch involved. Again, a third party mediator (or the giving side that wants adoption) can present the SOS solution in such a way that both sides can see the results are mutually beneficial and that it makes sense to accept them. This kind of suspicion is likely to be reduced if from the start all sides are instructed or directed toward finding a super-optimum solution. That kind of orientation not only lessens suspicion, but it also becomes a self-fulfilling prophecy that leads to finding super-optimum solutions.

5.  <u>Vested jobs or property</u> A big problem in replacing a traditional compromise with an SOS solution is that there may already be vested jobs or property in the previous decision that need to be taken into consideration. An example is that both conservatives and liberals strongly endorse rent supplements over public housing projects. Conservatives do so partly because rent supplements represent a marketplace solution to housing for the poor. Liberals do so partly because rent supplements facilitate integration along economic and racial lines. The rent supplement program has, however, not replaced public housing. A big part of the explanation is the vested jobs and property in the previous solution. Public housing was previously supported by liberals as a form of equitable socialism. It has been tolerated by conservatives as an approach to housing for the poor which

would not involve integration at a time when integration was less acceptable. Neither of those original purposes have much explanatory value for the retention of public housing over a rent supplements program, but the existence of vested jobs and property does.

The key question is not what explains why the SOS solution has not been fully adopted, but rather what to do about the kind of interfering factor. The traditional compromise approach is a variation on grandfathering or a tolerated zoning use. Such a solution means that no new public housing projects are built but the old ones are allowed to die of old age. It also means that people holding jobs under the old system are allowed to retain them but a minimum of replacement occurs when the former jobholders die, retire, or resign. An SOS solution that relies more on well-placed subsidies would phase out the property as quickly as possible, rather than wait for natural obsolescence. A fast phase-out though would not mean a wasteful dynamiting of the public housing projects as was done with the Pruitt-lgoe Homes in St. Louis. Instead, the projects could be made available along with appropriate subsidies for use as factories, warehouses, or other buildings as part of an inner city Enterprise Zone Project which is an SOS in itself. The jobholders could also be provided with well-placed subsidies for retraining, buying small businesses, or other alternative activities that fit their skills. This problem of what to do about vested jobs and property comes up in many SOS situations, such as tariff reduction which can be highly mutually beneficial internationally. Adequate provision needs to be made for people and property that have a vested interest in the previous, less beneficial activities.

## C. Implementing Super-Optimum Solutions

One would think that arriving and adopting an SOS solution would produce mutually beneficial results. That is not necessarily the case. An SOS solution may be arrived at using the checklist of eight approaches previously mentioned, or other approaches. The solution may be successfully adopted by a legislature, court, administrative agency, business firm, or other entity, after overcoming the four factors mentioned above that sometimes interfere with successful adoption. Yet, the SOS solution may fail to achieve its mutually beneficial results for at least the following five reasons.

1. No strings attached. SOS solutions to public policy problems often involve subsidies or tax breaks, such as the 30% across-the-board tax break given by the Reagan administration in the early 1980s. That was meant to be an SOS solution which would so stimulate the economy that the gross national product would increase and thereby provide more money for government spending at lower tax rates than before the 30% tax break. It would enable an SOS increase in government spending and a reduction in taxes simultaneously without adding to the deficit. The idea was arrived at by supply-side economists and adopted by Congress. It

failed in practice because there were no strings attached to the tax breaks to provide for any retooling of the economy that would have resulted in the productivity increases needed to increase the GNP. Instead, the money went disproportionately to real estate, luxury goods, and high CEO salaries.

2. <u>Insufficient funding</u>. The Enterprise Zone idea of the Reagan administration was well conceived and adopted with bipartisan enthusiasm. It also had strings attached by way of offering subsidies to business firms only if they would partly locate in inner city neighborhoods. Doing so would provide employment opportunities that would reduce welfare expenditures and anti-social behavior, while improving role models, productivity, multiplier effects, and tax paying by people who otherwise would be heavy tax recipients. The program failed in practice mainly because the amount of money was not enough to do much attracting of business firms to inner city neighborhoods, and relaxing regulatory legislation was not acceptable as a substitute by Congress.

3. <u>Competent personnel</u>. The housing programs of the Reagan administration had many strings attached (at least on the books) regarding the kind of housing that should be provided by private contractors. There was also big money available. The program could have been an SOS program in the sense of exceeding the best expectations of landlords, tenants, and the general public. A key reason the program failed was that it was placed in the hands of people who were largely political appointees, rather than specialized, experienced civil servants. The contracts as a result tended to be awarded too much on the basis of partisan considerations and campaign contributions, rather than on the basis of merit.

4. <u>Proper sequencing of events</u>. The subsidy for developing an electric car embodied in the 1972 Air Pollution Act is an example of Democratic legislation that was well-intended, successfully adopted, well-funded, competently administered, and had detailed specifications for what would constitute an acceptable electric car. As of 1992, it has produced no significant results. If an electric car had been developed, we would have less expensive and better quality transportation simultaneously, especially in terms of air pollution as well as energy independence. A key explanation for the failure of the legislation is that it did not provide for a step-by-step incremental development of an electric car through a series of numerous grants to try out various component ideas. Instead, the legislation provided for a massive reward after a whole electric car had been developed at high-cost, high-risk expense to private sector individuals. The reward was to be that the government would replace its internal combustion automobile fleet with those electric cars. What was thought of as a well-placed subsidy failed to take into consideration the numerous implementation problems that had to be provided for along the way.

5. Imaginative personnel. Point 3 above refers to competent personnel, which means people in that context who will comply with federal rules concerning nonpartisan government procurement. Avoiding fraud and corruption is a minimum regarding qualified personnel. More imagination than that is needed in order to successfully implement SOS solutions, as well as to develop them in the first place. For example, even if the National Science Foundation were given large sums of money to award grants to develop components for an electric car, the implementation of that well-placed subsidy might still fail. The reason might be that the NSF would rely on peer review to determine who should get those grants for developing innovative ideas. Peer review probably works well for funding conventional research. If one wants to develop breakthrough unconventional ideas, however, then review by well-credentialed people in the field may result in an undue rejection of ideas which they find disturbing to what they are accustomed to in their conventional wisdom. It may be necessary to resort to non-peer review in the sense of including imaginative humanities people and social scientists to evaluate the proposals from physicists, chemists, and engineers who are likely to submit the grant proposals. SOS innovation and implementation is too important in terms of its implications and opportunities to be left to the subject-matter experts.

### D. Political Facilitators

Competitive political parties. This is the key facilitator since the out-party is constantly trying to develop policies (including possibly SOS policies) in order to become the in-party. The in-party is also busy developing new policies in order to stay the in-party. New policies are developed largely as a result of changing domestic and international conditions, not just for the sake of newness. Without the stimulus of an out-party, the in-party would have substantially less incentive to be innovative. More important, without the possibility of becoming the in-party, the out-party would lose its incentive to be innovative. More innovation generally comes from the out-party than the in-party (all other factors held constant), including the possibility of SOS innovations.

Better policy analysis methods and institutions. SOS solutions are likely to be facilitated by policy analysis methods that deal with multiple goals, multiple alternatives, missing information, spreadsheet-based decision-aiding software, and a concern for successful adoption and implementation. Better policy analysis institutions refer to training, research, funding, publishing, and networking associations. Those institutions can be part of the activities of universities, government agencies, and independent institutes in the private sector. The extent to which those policy institutions deal with super-optimizing analysis will make them even more relevant to facilitating SOS solutions.

## II. THE ECONOMIC PROCESS OF SOS

Competitive business firms. Competition among business firms may be essential for facilitating a prosperous economy and a prosperous world through international business competition. Numerous examples can be given of nations that failed to advance and collapsed due largely to a one-party system, such as the Soviet Union. Likewise, numerous examples can be given of business firms that failed to advance and virtually collapsed due largely to lack of substantial competition such as the American steel industry. The American automobile industry has not collapsed, but it did fail to develop small cars, cars that resist style changes, safer cars, less expensive cars, and more durable cars in comparison to the international competition that was not taken seriously until almost too late.

Well-targeted subsidies and tax breaks. In the context of super-optimum solutions, this tends to mean subsidies and tax breaks that increase national productivity and international competitiveness. Such subsidies and tax breaks are the opposite handouts which provide a disincentive to increased productivity on the part of either welfare recipients or big business. Good targeting in this regard especially refers to upgrading skills and stimulating technological innovation and diffusion. A dollar invested in those kinds of subsidies is likely to pay off many times over without necessarily having to wait very long for the results.

Increased national productivity. All these facilitators are important. Economists might rightfully consider increased national productivity to be especially important. It leads to an increased gross national product or national income, which means an increased tax base to which the tax rate is applied. If increased productivity increases the tax base, then tax rates can be lowered and still produce more tax money for well-targeted subsidies that produce further increases in national productivity. Those increases, however, are not an end in themselves. The increased national income can facilitate finding and implementing SOS solutions that relate to employment, inflation, agriculture, labor, business, poverty, discrimination, education, families, the environment, housing, transportation, energy, health, technological innovation, government structures, government processes, world peace, international trade and every other public policy field. In other words, with more money and resources available, SOS solutions are facilitated, but SOS solutions often draw upon creativity that is associated with doing much better on relevant goals with constant or decreasing resources.

## III. THE PSYCHOLOGY-SOCIOLOGY OF SOS SOLUTIONS

Childhood socialization. In the SOS context, this refers to creating a frame of mind that causes adults to do what is socially desired because the alternative is virtually unthinkable. This can be contrasted with a less effective emphasis on a deterrence whereby socially desired behavior is achieved through threats and bribes. Examples include childhood socialization to reduce adult behavior that is violent, alcoholic, drug addictive, and hostile toward constitutional rights.

Innovative risk taking. This is an important SOS facilitator because many SOS solutions involve technological fixes. In order to develop those new technologies, many people usually had to risk substantial amounts of money, time, effort, and other resources. There may have been a strong possibility that it would have all been wasted. An SOS society needs more people who are willing to take such chances. Classic examples include Marie and Joliet Curie who sacrificed about 30 years of work plus their health to develop radium and thus radioactivity which is part of the basis for nuclear energy. Thomas Edison frequently not only risked his resources but his whole reputation by announcing inventions before he had developed them in order to give himself an ego risk as a stimulus to quickly inventing what he falsely said he had already done.

Sensitivity to opportunity costs. This means either through socialization or an appropriate incentive structure trying to get decision-makers to be more sensitive to the mistake of failing to try out a new idea that might work wonders, as contrasted to being so sensitive to sins of commission rather than omission. Both wrongs are undesirable. One can, however, say that a police officer who wrongly beats a suspect is doing less harm to society than a president who wrongly fails to adopt a new health care program that could save numerous lives or a new education program that could greatly improve productivity and the quality of life. A person who is sensitive to opportunity costs tends to say "Nothing ventured, nothing gained"; whereas an insensitive person tends to say "Nothing ventured, nothing lost." We need more of the former in order to facilitate the generating, adopting, and implementing of SOS solutions.

An SOS combination of pessimism and optimism. This does not mean a balance or a compromise between being pessimistic and being optimistic. It means being 100% pessimistic or close to it regarding how bad things are and how much worse they are going to get unless we actively do something about it including developing SOS solutions. It simultaneously means being 100% optimistic or close to it regarding how good things can get in the future if we do vigorously work at it including developing SOS solutions. This is in contrast to those who say the present is wonderful and needs little improvement. It is also in contrast to those who say the present may be wonderful or not so wonderful but some invisible hands or automatic forces of Adam Smith, Karl Marx, or God will automatically improve the future.

Constantly seeking higher goals. This list is in random order. Some of the items overlap or interact, but it is better to overlap than leave gaps in this context. It is appropriate perhaps to have the last facilitator relate to constantly seeking higher goals. Traditional goal-seeking leads to compromises. Worse, it can lead to one side trying to win 100% and the other side losing 100%, but the war, strike, litigation, or other negative dispute resolution leads to both sides losing close to 100%. Obviously seeking higher coals is more likely to result in higher goal-achievement than seeking lower goals, including SOS goal-achievement. The counter-argument that is sometimes made is that higher goals lead to frustration because of the gap between goals and achievement. There may be more frustration in fully achieving low goals that provide a low quality of life when others are doing better. High societal goal-seeking (including SOS solutions) is facilitated by all of the above factors, but it is a factor in itself because high goal-seeking tends to become a self-fulfilling prophecy.

# PART ONE:

# THE POLITICAL PROCESS
# OF SOS SOLUTIONS

# CHAPTER I

## WAYS OF ARRIVING AT SUPER-OPTIMUM SOLUTIONS

### I. Expanding the Total Resources

#### A. The Alternatives

The four basic alternatives for dealing with the deficit are:

1. The <u>liberals</u> want to increase taxes on the rich, hold constant taxes on the poor, decrease military spending, and hold constant domestic spending. One might say they want to decrease taxes on the poor, but the poor pay very little taxes right now and there is not much possibility for decrease. One might say they want to increase domestic spending. That might be unrealistic if we are talking about traditional ways of dealing with the deficit. One does not increase spending or decrease taxes.

2. The <u>conservatives</u> want to hold constant taxes on the rich, increase taxes on the poor by way of sales taxes and other regressive taxes, or a value added tax. They want to hold constant military spending and decrease domestic spending.

3. The <u>compromise position</u> wants to do a little bit of everything. It would have a medium increase of taxes on the rich and on the poor, and a medium cutting of military spending and domestic spending.

4. The S̲O̲S̲ wants to decrease taxes on both the rich and the poor, especially by way of tax breaks that will stimulate increased productivity. The main way, though, in which the tax decrease occurs is by way of decreasing the tax rate, not the quantity of dollars taxed. The rate goes down and the quantity of dollars taken in goes up if the GNP goes up by way of well-placed tax breaks and subsidies. The SOS wants to increase spending in the form of subsidies, but more importantly the increased spending comes from the increased GNP as a result of the well-placed subsidies the GNP allows for more spending. If we had more room to write something on the alternatives display, it would read like the following: "SOS - subsidies and tax breaks to increase productivity which increases GNP and thus allows tax rates to fall while tax intake increases, thereby allowing more government spending." [1]

## B. The SOS Table

Table 1-1 shows those alternatives in the context of an SOS table. The first goal listed is to increase the gross national product. That means the same thing as increasing gross national income and gross national consumption or spending. This is an effectiveness measure. The second goal is to decrease taxes or the amount or percentage of the GNP that people spend on government activities. That is an efficiency measure.

The conservative alternative constitutes at least a mild reduction in goal achievement on both increased national spending and decreased taxes since the conservative alternative decreases domestic spending and increases taxes at least on the poor. The liberal alternative also constitutes a mild reduction on both goals since the liberal alternative decreases defense spending and increases taxes at least on the rich. The compromise alternative decreases both kinds of spending and increases both kinds of taxes, although not as much as the conservatives or liberals would do. The SOS alternative has at least a mildly positive effect on increasing the gross national product and decreasing taxes.

The neutral totals are calculated by summing the raw scores after doubling each one. That reflects the idea that a neutral weight is a 2 on a 1-3 scale, where 1 is relatively low importance, 2 is middling, and 3 is high importance. The liberal totals reflect a high weight for the relatively liberal goal of increasing spending and employment, and a relatively low weight for the goal of increasing spending and employment, and a relatively low weight for the goal of decreasing taxes. The conservative totals reflect a relatively low weight for increasing national spending, and a relatively high weight for decreasing taxes. Both liberals and conservatives, however, give positive weight to increased GNP and decreased taxes. The bottom line of Table 1-1 thus shows the SOS alternative as a clear winner on both the liberal totals and the conservative totals, as well as the neutral totals. A key question is how is that possible?

TABLE 1-1.  DEALING WITH THE DEFICIT

| Alternatives | Criteria | | | | |
|---|---|---|---|---|---|
| | C Goal <br><br> Defense and <br> Investment | L Goal <br><br> Domestic and <br> Consumption | N Total <br><br> (Neutral <br> Weights) | L Total <br><br> (Liberal <br> Weights) | C Total <br><br> (Conservative <br> Weights) |
| C Alternative <br><br> - Domestic Spending <br> + Taxes Poor | 4 | 2 | 12 | 10 | 14* |
| L Alternative <br><br> Defense Spending & <br> + Taxes Rich | 2 | 4 | 12 | 14* | 10 |
| N Alternative <br><br> - Both Spend <br> + Taxes Both | 3 | 3 | 12 | 12 | 12 |
| SOS Alternative <br><br> + Spending <br> - Taxes | 5 | 5 | 20 | 20** | 20** |

*NOTES:*

1.  *A fuller statement of the conservative goal might be (1) have a strong national defense, and (2) stimulate investment through low taxes on the relatively rich.  A fuller statement of the liberal goal might be (1) have strong domestic policies like education and housing, and (2) stimulate consumption through low taxes on the relatively poor.*

2.  *The SOS involves a reduction of taxes in the form of tax breaks designed to stimulate greater productivity.  Likewise, the SOS involves an increase in spending in the form of well-placed subsidies designed to stimulate greater productivity.  The increased productivity means an increased gross national product which means an increased base on which to apply the national tax rate.  Thus, the tax rate can drop and still bring in increased tax revenue and thereby have more money available for government spending including defense, domestic policies, deficit reduction, and more well-placed subsidies.*

## C. The Causal Arrow Diagram

This is better shown with a system of arrows plus Table 1-1 instead of verbally. The arrows would look like what is shown in Table 1-2.

TABLE 1-2. THE UPWARD SPIRAL OF WELL-PLACED SUBSIDIES

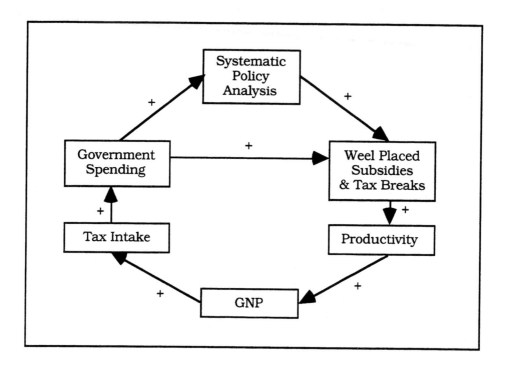

1. In verbalizing that arrow diagram, a couple of points might be especially mentioned, the first one of which is that the increased GNP results in increased tax revenue even if the tax rate remains constant at approximately 20%. However, we are talking about a decreased tax rate.

We should give a simple example. If the GNP is $4 trillion in the before period and is $8 trillion in the after period, then with a constant 25% tax rate, the tax intake will double. Even if the tax rate drops below 25%, the tax intake will still increase so long as it does not drop below 12.5%. At 25% tax rate with $4 trillion, the income to the government is $1 trillion. At 25% tax rate with $8, the income is $2 trillion. Thus, so long as the tax rate falls to anything above 12.5%, the tax intake will still increase.

2.  We could add a circle, although maybe just verbally without it being in the diagram, to say that in order to have the right kind of subsidies and tax breaks, systematic public policy analysis is necessary. Without such analysis, subsidies could wind up supporting inefficient, unproductive activities in a kind of bail-out dole system rather than a system designed to provide incentives. That is what has happened in China. Its system of subsidies decreases productivity rather than increases it because the subsidies go disproportionately for what amounts to charitable purposes to keep inefficient firms and individuals from going bankrupt. They do not do much with tax breaks, but bad tax breaks could have the same effect.

3.  Another point that can be mentioned verbally that would clutter up the graph is that the increased government spending feeds back on the subsidies and tax breaks since that is a form of government spending. Well-placed subsidies increase productivity. GNP, tax revenue, and money available for well-placed subsidies.  It becomes the opposite of a vicious circle. There is a word needed to modify the word circle that is the opposite of vicious. It could be called a SOS Circle, although that has a specialized meaning of being better than the best expectations of both sides to a dispute, or all sides to a dispute.

4.  Showing it as a hexagon with a six-pointed star underneath it to get things in the right place provides a good picture. But not good enough because it looks too much like a kind of around and around treadmill. It is like an expanding pie, with each time around the circle getting bigger, meaning the GNP gets higher. It is an expanding-pie circle (rather than a vicious circle) where things get better with each round.

### D. The Compromise Position

Another aspect of this that may need some kind of explanation or adjustment is why the compromise does not do better than either the liberal or the conservative position. It should do better in order to explain why compromises are usually adopted. The compromise can do better if it taxes the rich and the poor, but does not do so in such a way as to add up to as much tax as the liberal alternative alone or the conservative alternative alone. And likewise on the spending side. Thus, we would not want a split right down the middle.

Instead, we would say the compromise position taxes the rich somewhere between the liberal position on taxing the rich and the conservative position on taxing the rich. It is a little closer to the conservative position in order to get adopted. And likewise, a little closer to the liberal position on taxing the poor in order to get adopted. It compromises by undertaxing the rich slightly to make the conservatives happy, but not going to far as the conservatives would. It undertaxes the poor slightly to make the liberals happy, but not going so far as the liberals would.

Likewise, on cutting military spending it stands between the liberals and the conservatives but a little less than the middle to make the conservatives happy. Then it cuts domestic spending somewhere in about the middle, but not as far as the conservatives would, in order to make the liberals happy. By knocking a smidgen off on each of those compromise relation scores, the compromise position comes out the winner among the traditional positions.

Thus, the compromise position is the best of those three traditional choices, but just barely the best. It is like the lesser of three evils or undesirable positions. Liberals would not consider the liberal position to be evil, but it is an evil if it reduces spending to the point where defense is jeopardized. Likewise, conservatives would not consider the conservative position to be evil, but it is if it reduces domestic spending to the point where housing, shelter, education, pollution, and other domestic policies are jeopardized. It is not necessary to say that liberals, conservatives, and compromisers are evil in any absolute sense. It is just necessary to recognize that by definition and by realistic analysis, they are not as good as working for an SOS.

### E. Broad Implications

This is a very general example because increased government spending affects every public policy problem. It is also very general because it puts systematic policy analysis in a favorable key position. It is also general because it deals with positive incentives and the importance of productivity. The computer is used as a visual aid to display and manipulate alternative decisions, goals, and relations.

### F. Increasing Productivity

We want to increase national productivity. We ask what are all the ways we could do it. We come up with alternatives like the following:

1. Better child care to allow mothers of preschool children to be able to work.
2. Subsidies to move unemployed people to places where increased job opportunities are available.
3. Subsidies to business firms to move where there are pockets of unemployment.
4. Subsidies to business firms to move where there are pockets of unemployment.
5. Subsidies to employers to provide on-the-job training to improve the skills of their workers.
6. Subsidies to universities and other institutions that develop new technologies.
7. Subsidies to business firms to adopt new technologies.
8. Subsidies to workers to enable them to adapt to new technologies.
9. And so on.

The above list may be too general because it covers all kinds of productivity problems. We can talk about increasing the potential productivity of the elderly, the disabled., or people who are not working up to their capabilities. We might prefer a problem like how to increase the productivity of the American automobile industry. The national productivity problem could be handled on an industry-by-industry basis, or with regard to different parts of the labor force, or with regard to specific firms. In those situations, we could have a list of alternatives and goals, and then come up with a package solution that may be better than anything the liberals or the conservatives were previously pushing. After we come up with that package, we call it an SOS and make it row 4 in a standard SOS table with row 1 the conservative position, row 2 the liberal, and row 3 the compromise. That SOS table then becomes a visual aid for advocacy purposes as well as decision-making purposes. It shows the SOS in its best possible light.

## G. Analysis and Advocacy

This bridges the usual gap between analysis and advocacy. Analysts are traditionally supposed to be neutral among alternatives. They just present how the alternatives relate to the goals and maybe which alternative is best in light of given goals. They leave it to the decision-maker to decide which is best depending on the relative weights of different goals and the decision maker's perceptions of the relations.

In an SOS situation, the analyst plays a different role. The analyst may be the person who comes up with the SOS, which is an act of creativity, not just being a technician. More important, the SOS by definition is not sensitive to whether we use liberal weights or conservative weights. By definition, it is better than the liberal alternative or the conservative alternative using either liberal or conservative goals and weights. In that kind of situation, the obligation of the analyst may be to try to get the SOS adopted, i.e., to become more of an advocate. The analyst still has an obligation not to engage in anything that might be interpreted as lawyer-type advocacy or business-advertising type advocacy. That means the analyst has an obligation to show the defects the SOS might have and how they can be overcome. The lawyer and the business advertiser consider themselves as having no obligation to point out good characteristics in their competitor's products or in the other side of the law case. If the analyst knows of a defect in the SOS (even just a possible defect and not a confirmed defect), the analyst should have an obligation to indicate it.

## H. Summarizing The Example

This example ties in with arriving at SOS's by virtue of covering the first approach, namely to expand the total resources available in order to do better than the liberals on their own goals and better than the conservatives on their own goals, simultaneously.

1. On taxes, the liberal and conservative goals are to lower taxes. If taxes cannot be lowered and have to be raised, liberals say taxes should be raised on the rich and not on the poor. The conservative position is the opposite. The SOS provides for lowering on both.

2. On spending, the liberal and conservative goals are to increase consumption, including government consumption. The liberals say that if consumption has to be cut back, then cut back on consuming defense items. For conservatives, it is the opposite. The SOS provides for increasing consumption of both defense items.

3. That is such an important SOS approach that there is a tendency to almost name the SOS idea after this approach by calling SOS's expanded-pie solutions. That is wrong, though, because there are other ways of arriving at SOS's besides expanding the total resources. The package deal and removing the problem (which are discussed later in this chapter) do not involve expanding the total resources. Neither does the combination approach. The third party benefactor in effect is expanding the total resources. [2]

## II. RAISING GOALS ABOVE WHAT IS CONSIDERED THE BEST

Speaking before the Hong Kong government, they said that they did not especially want to hear about solar energy versus nuclear energy, or trials versus pleas, or getting married, or any of those other less relevant examples. They wanted to know about an SOS to a problem involving Hong Kong that they considered to be a crucial problem that they were not able to work out.

The labor shortage was such a problem, which they were approaching from a very traditional perspective. On one hand was the alternative to import additional labor. All it required was to just stop arresting people who are seeking to cross the borders from every direction. These include the Vietnamese boat people, the people from the Chinese mainland, the Filipinos, and even some people from English speaking places (although not many) like Australia, Britain, or India. Most English speaking people are a little cautious about settling or staying in Hong Kong given that it will become a Chinese province in 1997.

It thus creates a dilemma that paralyzes decision-making if the choice is one of retaining the labor shortage and thereby missing opportunities to make Hong Kong even more prosperous than it is versus allowing labor in and thereby diluting the population of Hong Kong. This is partly a racist matter, but it is also a legitimate concern for a lot of expense involved in education and welfare, although the immigrants may be especially ambitious people who in the long run will pay more than their share of taxes. This may be especially true of the Vietnamese boat people, although coming by boat from Vietnam to Hong Kong is not much more difficult than crossing the border from Mexico to Texas. They are, however, giving up whatever they had in Vietnam.

The SOS that seemed to be a kind of blind spot by virtue of how the terms were defined is simply to redefine the labor force. They then have a labor surplus. Redefining the labor force means recognizing all the potential labor they have by virtue of elderly people who are capable of working who are not doing so, disabled people, mothers of preschool children, people with part-time or seasonal jobs, people who are looking for second jobs, and especially people whose jobs and productivity could be upgraded. The labor shortage problem also exists in Japan, Singapore, Korea, West Germany, and other high employment countries. Table 1-3 summarizes this example.[3]

## III. BIG BENEFITS FOR ONE SIDE, LOW COSTS FOR THE OTHER

### A. Litigation Situations

The approach to arriving at super-optimum solutions by having big benefits on one side and low costs on the other especially applies to resolving disputes between litigants in damage suits. For example, in the case of the Traveller's Insurance Company versus the Sanyo Electronics Company, the plaintiff demanded a minimum of $900,000 or else they would go to trial, especially since they had receipts to show they had already paid out $950,000 to their insurees for fire damage. The Sanyo Electronics Company offered to pay a maximum of $300,000 or else they would go to trial, because they considered payment of more than $300,000 as an admission of negligent wrongdoing whereas less than $300,000 could be written off as a nuisance payment to avoid litigation costs. The object for a court-appointed mediator in this case (operating from a super-optimum perspective) is to come up with a settlement that would be worth more than $900,000 to the Traveller's Insurance Company and simultaneously worth less than $300,000 to the Sanyo Electronics Company.

The solution was for the Sanyo Electronics Company to supply the agents of the insurance company with computers for use in their insurance work. Sanyo also agreed to provide large television sets for use as bonuses to the insurance agents to encourage them to sell more insurance. The Japanese insurance company which Sanyo employs also agreed to give the American insurance company about $300,000 worth of

TABLE 1-3. THE ASIAN LABOR SHORTAGE

| Alternatives | Criteria | | | | |
|---|---|---|---|---|---|
| | $C_1L_2$ Goal +GNP | $C_2L_1$ Goal - Disruption to Society | N Total Neutral Weights | Total $L_1$ & $C_2$ Weights (Nativism & Unionism) | Total $L_2$ & $C_1$ Weights (Open Door Policy) |
| $C_1$ Alternative | | | | | |
| Import Cheap Labor | 4 | 2 | 12 | 10 | 14* |
| $C_2$ Alternative | | | | | |
| Preserve National Purity | 2 | 4 | 12 | 14* | 10 |
| $L_1$ Alternative | | | | | |
| Preserve Union Wages | 2 | 4 | 12 | 14* | 10 |
| $L_2$ Alternative | | | | | |
| Provide Immigrant Opportunities | 4 | 2 | 12 | 10 | 14* |
| N Alternative | | | | | |
| Import some Labor | 3 | 3 | 12 | 12 | 12 |
| SOS Alternative | | | | | |
| + Labor Force + Productivity | 5 | 5 | 20 | 20** | 20** |

*NOTES:*

1. *Business conservatives welcome cheap labor to decrease their expenses and increase their profits. Cultural conservatives resist easy immigration as being disruptive to national purity.*

2. *Union liberals resist immigration as being disruptive to union wages. Intellectual liberals like to provide ambitious immigrants with opportunities to succeed.*

3. *By relieving the labor shortage, immigration increases the gross national product. There is, however, some disruption in absorbing the new immigrants.*

4. *The SOS Alternative involves increasing the labor force by upgrading the skills of the elderly, the disabled, and mothers of preschool children. Also making better use of people who work part-time or seasonally, or who could use a second or better job. Also increasing the productivity of present workers through new technologies and training.*

claims they had against the Americans but were unenthusiastic about trying to collect. Other elements were also included in the total settlement that had a value to the Traveller's Insurance Company of more than $1,000,000 but would cost Sanyo and its insurance company less than $200,000, mainly because all that Sanyo had to do was pull some computers and television sets out of its warehouses without having to manufacture anything new or buy anything new.

The illustrative example which follows involves a leading grower in the Peoria area (who employs approximately 700 farmworkers a year) being sued by the Migrant Legal Counsel which is a legal services agency that specializes in the legal problems of migratory farm workers. The workers as a large class action were suing to recover approximately $3,000,000 in wages that had been deducted to pay for loans, rents, and other expenses without proper legal authorization. The money had actually been loaned or advanced to the workers, but the procedures designed to prevent illegal exploitation had not been followed. The growers insisted they should pay nothing since they money they deducted was for loans actually made, regardless of the paperwork followed. The best expectations of the workers in terms of net gain would be rather low since whatever they collected they would have to repay, with the exception of maybe about $50,000 in compensation to some of the named plaintiffs who were fired or quit their jobs unless unlikely punitive damages could be obtained. The best expectations of the growers would be to spend $50,000 or more going to trial and win with no liability. Thus, the object for an SOS court-mediator would be to come up with a settlement that would be worth more than $50,000 to the farm workers and would simultaneously save more than $50,000 in litigation costs for the growers.

What follows is a description of the super-optimum solution in this specific case. The description is in two parts. The first part is mainly verbal. The second part is mainly computer-based. The essence of the solution is that the growers agree to deposit $100,000 to begin an employee credit union. Depositing $100,000 costs nothing to the growers since it is insured by the federal government and can be withdrawn after an agreed upon time period, possibly even with interest. The $100,000, however, serves as the basis for the beginning of an economic development fund which enables the workers through real estate leveraging to obtain a mortgage for building over $500,000 worth of housing for the workers as a big improvement over their current housing. The existence of the credit union also enables them to avoid having to get advances from the growers which generates a lot of friction as a result of alleged favoritism in giving and collecting the advances. There are other elements involved, too, such as new grievance procedures and reports regarding compliance with other rules governing the working conditions of migratory labor. The essence of the solution, though, is that both sides come out ahead of their original best expectations.

## B. THE SOS IN THE MIGRANT LABOR CASE

### 1. PRELIMINARY ELEMENTS
   1.   The establishment of a kind of bill of rights for the workers and an institutionalized grievance procedure with a grievance committee and provision for mediation and arbitration of grievances.

   2.   The submitting of an 9-part report by the lawyers for the growers as to exactly how the growers are now in compliance with the nine sets of violations listed on pages 7 and 8 of the complaint.

   3.   Compensation of the named plaintiffs for the special out-of-pocket expenses that they incurred as contrasted to the other 2,000 members of the class who were not listed by name in the complaint. There are seven named plaintiffs. Only one of the seven was present yesterday, namely Fidel Boyso. Three of the named defendants were present, namely Michael Rousonelos Sr., Michael Rousonelos Jr., and Gus Rousonelos, also known as Butch Rousonelos. It is definitely desirable right from the start to have the clients and not just the lawyers present. Otherwise, for this kind of solution the lawyers would logically say they have to go back and consult with their clients.

## 2. THE MAIN ELEMENT: THE ECONOMIC DEVELOPMENT CREDIT UNION

1.  It will be partly funded as a result of deposits made by the grower. The deposits need to be determined as to the amount, the length of time, and the interest. The amount I believe is about $100,000 for the first year with subsequent amounts to be determined. The length of time that the money will be kept on deposit needs to be fairly substantial, maybe as long as five years in order for the money to be available for loans. The interest rate would be the normal rate given under credit union provisions.

2.  A Board of Directors will be established. It will include mainly representatives of the workers. Maybe at least one representative of the growers. There will also be expertise supplied by professors of business administration or economics.

3.  The money should be especially loans for economic development projects, not consumer goods. Those projects will include housing for workers, education programs, and business investments that will benefit the community.

4.  Help is available in establishing the credit union from the Illinois Finance Agency. Help is also available for training workers.

5. The Illinois Credit Union League puts out a useful set of materials.

## 3. FEATURES THAT ARE ATTRACTIVE TO THE PLAINTIFF

1.  Being able to borrow money without begging for it or being discriminated against.

2.  Being able to pay back the money under reasonable repayment arrangements rather than in such large payments.

3.  The economic development projects will benefit the workers, such as housing, education, and businesses.

4.  The solution can apply to former workers who are eligible to borrow.

5.  It involves money from the defendant, possibly other farmers, and possibly grant money from the federal government, especially the Departments of Agriculture and Commerce.

6.  A benefit to the workers is that by the farm not going bankrupt, they have the jobs continuing to be available.

7.  The plaintiff's side also get psychological rewards from having originated the idea rather than having it imposed from the outside.

## 4. FEATURES ATTRACTIVE TO THE DEFENDANT

1.  A release from being sued, which runs the risk of substantial judgment concerning the deductions and possible penalties.

2.  A release from expensive litigation costs.

3.  Better relations with the workers.

4.  Being relieved of being in the lending business, of giving advances to forthcoming workers and present workers.

5. The possibility of the prestige that goes with inviting other farmers to participate in this credit union in order to have a lending institution that would relieve them of lending burdens.

6. Avoidance of what could be a revenge-oriented lawsuit or one designed to make an example of the grower.

7. Avoidance of possible bankruptcy.

8. Some psychological rewards from having improved upon the idea, especially with the funds on deposit, the other farms, and the federal grants.

9. Both sides may take considerable pleasure in the idea being adopted elsewhere in the country or even in other countries which have problems between farm workers and growers.

### C. The Computer Analysis

### 1. BASIC ALTERNATIVES AND CRITERIA
The alternatives are to either settle or go to trial for both sides.
The criteria include:

1. Setting up the grievance procedure.

2. Clarifying how the grower is now in compliance on the 9 alleged violations .

3. Some payment for the named members of the class.

4. The benefits and costs of the credit union.

### 2. THE PLAINTIFF'S PERSPECTIVE
If we look at the matrix on Table 15-1 from the plaintiff's perspective, we would have to think in terms of a 1-5 scale on most of the variables since they are too difficult to monitize.

1. On the grievance procedure, this is a mild plus to the plaintiff only from settling. It won't happen if we go to trial.

2. The information on compliance. That's also a mild plus.

3. Payment to the class representatives. Another mild plus.

4. The economic development credit union. This is at least a 5, meaning a big plus.

5. We could also throw in something for the settlement costs. If we figure the same $100 per hour, but then we're only talking about 20 hours rather than 100, then we're talking about 2k for settlement costs. That does not change the picture in any way to make it appear that the second place alternatives have a chance at first place.

6. If we go to trial, there is a possibility of collecting as much as $1.1 million. It might. be better to separate the deductions from the penalties. The deductions might be 600k, but they would then have to be paid back, which means virtually no gain. In terms of dollars, it's something greater than 0, but not much greater.

7. The penalties may be a 100k. Or maybe something between 100k and 500k. 500k is the maximum. It's not so likely that the maximum will be awarded. .

8. Their litigation costs, although there are also some settlement costs. The litigation costs figuring $100 per hour with 100 hours involved is $10,000.

9. If we look at the overall result, obviously the settlement is worth more than the expected value of going to trial, especially if the settlement includes placing took on deposit for economic development loans. We need not add across. The settlement scores are non-monetary. The trial scores are monetary. All we have to decide is whether the settlement scores are worth more than the trial scores. The answer seems to be clearly yes.

## 3. THE DEFENDANT'S PERSPECTIVE

From the defendant's perspective, on a simple level of analysis, we're talking about the same criteria. In fact, it might be helpful to put the defendant's perspective below the plaintiff's using the same columns.

The relation scores differ, even if the criteria and alternatives are the same.

1. The grievance procedure could be considered a plus for the grower. This is so in the sense that by resolving grievances in a more orderly manner, there will be better labor management relations leading to greater productivity.

2. Supplying the compliance information is not especially a benefit to the grower. It is a mild cost.

3. The payment to the named representatives is also a mild cost. There are only a few of them involved and the payment will not be very large.

4. The credit union can benefit the grower as well as the farm workers as indicated above where we listed the features that are beneficial to the rower. The only question is whether this is a mild benefit or a large benefit to the grower . As a compromise we can say 4.5.

5. The settlement costs may be a few thousand dollars.

6. Paying out the deductions and then collecting them back could result in some loss for the grower. Going to trial is likely to mean maybe a negative 150k. That means that it may be quite difficult to prove that the money was owed in about one fourth of the cases.

7. If it is realistic to think in terms of a 100k penalty on the plaintiff's perspective, it is probably realistic on the defendant's perspective too. It may be unrealistic to think that there would be no penalty at all for nine violations, some of which are serious.

8. Litigation costs may be about 15k. Lawyer costs are likely to be more for the grower than the plaintiff's side since the plaintiff is receiving free legal service supported by the Legal Aid Bureau of Chicago and the Legal Aid Corporation.

9. Looking at the defendant's perspective without trying to arrive at a total, one can see that settling is much more profitable. Going to trial gains nothing. It is only an attempt to cut the losses lower than what the settlement would be.

## 4. MODIFICATIONS AND CONCLUSIONS

1.   One thing about a 1-5 scale is that it doesn't provide for very much detail . It thus makes the benefits from the grievance procedure not very far from the benefits of the credit union, since one is score 4 and one is Score 5. We could give greater weight to the credit union on the grounds that it is a more important part of the settlement. We could give it at least a weight of 2 and the others a weight of 1 apiece. That brings out some of the difference better.

2.   It would be meaningful to develop at least these 2 data files, with the 8 criteria. We would use a 1-5 scale for all the non-monetary criteria and $1000 units for the monetary criteria.

3.   We could not do a quantitative threshold analysis very well unless we monetize everything or convert everything into 1-5 scale or maybe combine all the money items together and combine all the non-money items together.

4.   On the money items, it looks like going to trial is worth about 90k to the plaintiff but a negative 265k to the defendant. Settling, on the other hand, is worth a lot more than 90k to the plaintiff and is clearly worth a lot more than a -265k to the defendant.

5.   There is a gap in the totals column between the settlement total and the trial total for the plaintiff that looks too big to overcome by any reasonable changes in the amounts. That is especially true of the gap on the defendant's side.

6.   This reinforces the overall conclusion that for both sides settling under these terms is better than going to trial. There is some question as to whether settling is better than the original best expectations. We could add another column at the end called "SOS Totals."

7.   The best expectation of the plaintiff might be about 400k from going to trial. Is the credit union solution greater than 400k? 1 would say yes .

8.   The best expectation of the defendant might be to take a 15k loss on the litigation cost and avoid all liability. That seems unlikely. Is the credit union solution worth more than a loss of 15k? The answer is probably yes . Table 1-4 summarizes this example.

### D . SOME CONCLUSIONS

### 1. CHARACTERISTICS THAT MAKE THE CASE ESPECIALLY CHALLENGING

1.   A big element of racism by virtue of the growers being white Anglos and the workers almost 100 percent Hispanic.

2.   The company town idea, of the workers living in housing provided by the employer and buying from the company store. That reeks with the old 16-tons.

TABLE 1-4. SUPER-OPTIMIZING LITIGATION ANALYSIS
(Using Ramirez v. Rousonelos as an Illustrative Example)

| Alternatives | Criteria | | | | Relevant Totals |
|---|---|---|---|---|---|
| | Relevant Items of Value | | | | |
| | Credit Union, Housing, and Business Opportunities | Grievance Procedure | Payment to Named Plaintiffs | Compliance Information | |
| Plaintiff's SOS Settlement (Big Benefits) | 2,000 | > $0 | $50 | > $0 | > $1,000 |
| Plaintiff's Best Expectation = $1,000 | 0 | 0 | 0 | 0 | $1,000 |
| Likely Compromise Settlement = $500 | 0 | 0 | 0 | 0 | $500 |
| Defendant's Best Expectation = $0 | 0 | 0 | 0 | 0 | $0 |
| Defendant's SOS Settlement (Low Costs) | < $0 | < $0 | $50 | ~ $0 | <$0 |

NOTES:

1. The data in the above table comes from Chapter 15 on "Finding a Super-Optimum Solution in a Labor-Management Dispute," in S. Nagel and M. Mills, <u>Multi-Criteria Methods for Alternative Dispute Resolution: With Microcomputer Software Applications</u> (Quorum Books, 1990). All the above items are in $1,000's.

2. The plaintiff's wildest initial expectation is to be repaid approximately $1 million in wages as mentioned on page 160. That is a wild expectation since the money was deducted for goods, services, and advances that had been provided to the workers by the grower, but not in accordance with the proper paperwork procedures.

NOTES: *Table 1-4 continued*

3. *The defendant's wildest initial expectation is to have to pay nothing. That is a wild expectation since the defendant admittedly failed to comply with the proper deduction procedures with no good defense other than that the money was owed. The defendant would thus be likely to lose on the issue of whether they complied with the proper procedures. A penalty is likely to be assessed to deter such improperties on the part of the specific defendant and other potential defendants. The penalty is likely to be substantial in order to have deterrent value. There is also likely to be compensation to the named defendants for their efforts plus considerable litigation costs if the case goes to trial.*

4. *The object is thus to arrive at a super-optimum solution whereby the workers in a sense receive more than $1 million and the defendant pays less than nothing.*

5. *The key element in the super-optimum solution is the establishment of a credit union mainly consisting of $100,000 from the defendant to be deposited with interest for five years.*

6. *That $100,000 can quickly generate $2 million worth of housing by serving as a 10% down payment on a mortgage for existing or new housing units for the workers. The housing might be used as collateral for additional capital. It is also possible that a federal or state government agency will match the $100,000 as part of an economic development plan, thereby further increasing the lending opportunities.*

7. *The workers thereby obtain multiple family housing and a lending source for business opportunities that may be worth at least $2 million plus the benefits of an improved grievance procedures, payments to named plaintiffs, and compliance information. The total value is worth more than their wildest best expectation.*

8. *The growers thereby obtain the benefits of not having to provide housing for the workers. They also get interest on their savings and a subsequent return of the principal if requested. The grievance procedure can decrease friction. The compliance information can increase credibility. Payment to the named plaintiffs is a cost rather than a benefit, but it is more than offset by the benefits from the other relevant items of value. Therefore, the growers are making a net gain as a result of this SOS settlement which is the same as paying less than nothing.*

3. It also has a big divide and conquer kind of element with the old mansion slaves and fieldhand slaves pitted against each other. The Hispanics from Texas who are generally native-born Americans or close to it are given considerable favoritism over the Hispanics from Mexico.

4. Interesting conflict, especially on the side of the workers between their crusading lawyer and what they themselves are seeking. There is some of maybe the opposite kind of conflict on the other side, where the lawyers are very businesslike and the growers are more emotional. By bringing out the differences between the lawyers and the clients, we have four sides to the case. Or maybe we really have a lot more than four sides if we divide the Hispanics into Texans and Mexicans, and also divide the growers into young and old.

5. That is another interesting piece of conflict, that it is intergenerational where the son of the growers is college trained in modern business administration and has a very different attitude how things should be run from his father who has been trained in the equivalent of grower-farmworker streetfighting. Including his overseers who almost come to the point of saying that the way to resolve the problem is to kick a lot of ass as contrasted to the young son who talks in terms of setting up grievance procedures.

6. The computer-aided mediation adds an interesting element by virtue of how it helps to convert what otherwise would be much more emotional divisive argument into something which at least on the surface sounds like a matter of relatively simple calculations. That is especially illustrated in John Torrenez saying that it boils down to: (1) The lawyer for the farmworkers says it is an insult to the named plaintiffs to receive only 10 percent of the settlement if there is going to be a $500,000 settlement and they are only going to get about $50,000, when they constitute 100 percent of the named plaintiffs. (2) The lawyer for the growers says the named plaintiffs are getting way too much when one takes into consideration that they are only about 1 percent of all the plaintiffs. The calculations are a little more complicated than that, but it partly illustrates the desire of both sides to reduce the problem to some simple calculations rather than make it a more emotional problem.

7. The receptiveness to the super-optimizing is interesting in the sense of both sides treating it almost as a challenging game to try to come up with ideas that both sides will consider better than their original best expectations.

## 2. SEQUENCING PRINCIPLES

1. The importance of talking on the telephone in advance in order to get some basic understanding of each side's position before meeting in person. We probably also should have exchanged some papers, including the plaintiff's complaint and the defendant's response.

2. It is possible in one day to develop a super-optimum solution without having to have multiple meetings.

3. It makes sense to provide an introduction to super-optimum solution-finding in the beginning. The computer serves as a good visual aid. The electronics case is a good example.

4. It then makes sense for each side to briefly state its position with everybody present.

5. We then meet with the defendant. The defendant normally has to do the offering, and the plaintiff does the receiving. That is a more difficult position to be in. Thus, we should expect to spend more time with the defendant. The plaintiff, though, may be difficult to convince to accept the defendant's offer. There is nothing inherent in being the plaintiff or the defendant as to how difficult obtaining an agreement may be. It does make sense to start with the defendant though, as to what they are willing to offer the plaintiff in the way of a mutually beneficial solution.

6. We then meet with the plaintiff to see what they think could be offered that would be mutually beneficial.

7. We then took the plaintiff's ideas back to the defendant instead of meeting jointly.

8. The plaintiff's reactions were then presented to the defendant.

9. We then met jointly when we were sure that doing so would emphasize a handshaking atmosphere.

## 3. GENERAL PRINCIPLES

1. The arrangement in the Ramirez case was really more super-optimum than in the electronics case. The big feature in the electronics case was a seller or a manufacturer giving the plaintiff products which are valuable to the plaintiff but cost relatively little to the defendant.

2. The big feature in the Ramirez case was developing a set of institutions that could benefit both sides, such as the grievance procedures and economic development credit union. This comes more under the heading of a package arrangement than a solution that involves high benefits to one side at low cost to the other side.

3. It is important to get people in a super-optimum solution frame of mind by emphasizing that we are looking for mutually beneficial solutions and not compromises and not determinations that one side is in the right and another is in the wrong. Table 1-5 summarizes what is involved in resolving litigation disputes through super-optimum solutions.[4]

## IV. THIRD PARTY BENEFACTOR

### A. Housing For The Poor

On the problem of providing housing for the poor, Table 1-6 shows alternative policies and criteria. In light of the scores of the

TABLE 1-5. RESOLVING LITIGATION DISPUTES THROUGH SUPER-OPTIMUM SOLUTIONS

| Criteria | C GOAL | L GOAL | N GOAL | N GOAL | N TOTAL | L TOTAL | C TOTAL |
|---|---|---|---|---|---|---|---|
| | Benefits to the defendant | Benefits to the Plaintiff | Costs to the Defendant | Costs to the Plaintiff | (Neutral Weights) | (Liberal Weights) | (Conservative Weights) |
| Alternatives | | | | | | | |
| C Alternative Defendant Wins on Trial | 5 | 1 | 2 | 2 | 20 | 16 | 24* |
| L Alternative Plaintiff Wins on Trial | 1 | 5 | 2 | 2 | 20 | 24* | 16 |
| N Alternative Settle | 2.5 | 2.5 | 3 | 3 | 22 | 22 | 22 |
| SOS Alternative Insurance, Products, Credit Unions, etc. | 5 | 5 | 3 | 3 | 32 | 32** | 32** |

NOTES:

1. If the defendant wins on trial, this benefits the defendant, but hurts the plaintiff. The defendant may also be hurt by the costs of the litigation.

2. If the plaintiff wins on trial, this benefits the plaintiff, but hurts the defendant. The plaintiff may also be hurt by the cost of the litigation.

3. If there is a monetary settlement, the defendant does not gain as much as in a defendant victory, and the plaintiff does not gain as much as in a plaintiff victory. Neither side, however, loses as much as they would if the other side were to win.

NOTES: Table 1-6 continued

4.   An SOS solution involves the defendant giving the plaintiff insurance, manufactured products, or other items that the defendant makes.  Doing so may result in the plaintiff receiving things that are of more value to the plaintiff than the plaintiff's best expectations.  Doing so may also result in the defendant giving things that are of less value to the defendant than the defendant's best expectations.

TABLE 1-6.  AN SOS ANALYSIS OF HOUSING FOR THE POOR

| CRITERIA | C GOAL | L GOAL | N TOTAL | C TOTAL | L TOTAL |
|---|---|---|---|---|---|
| | Reduce Taxes and Aid Private Sector Housing | Decent Housing for the Poor | (Neutral Weights) | (Conservative Weights) | (Liberal Weights) |
| | C=3  L=1 | C=1  L=3 | | | |
| Alternatives | | | | | |
| C Alternative | | | | | |
| Marketplace | 4 | 2 | 12 | 14* | 10 |
| L Alternative | | | | | |
| Modified Public Housing | 2 | 4 | 12 | 10 | 14* |
| N Alternative | | | | | |
| In Between | 3 | 3 | 12 | 12 | 12 |
| SOS Alternative | | | | | |
| Rents Supplements and Skills Upgrading | >3.5 | >3.5 | >12 | >14** | >14** |

NOTES:

1.  The conservative approach to housing for the poor is to leave it up to the marketplace.  The liberal approach is to provide for public housing that is owned or subsidized by the government and rented to low-income people at rents below the market level.  The neutral position is to budget more for public housing than conservatives would, but less than liberals would.

*NOTES: Table 1-6 continued*

2.  Public housing when it was first developed in the 1930's meant large projects owned by the government.  As of the 1960's, liberals turned against such projects because they became unpleasant places in which to live given the congestion of so many poor people and juveniles in a small area.  The major modifications involved requiring future public housing to be low rise rather than high rise and also to give the tenants more control over the management process.

3.  Conservatives in the context of housing for the poor are interested in keeping tax expenditures down and in aiding private sector housing.  The liberal goal is decent housing for the poor. The marketplace may be able to provide some housing for the poor, but not above a minimum level of decency or quality.

4.  The SOS Alternative might be rent supplements or vouchers. They involve, for example, a low-income recipient paying $300 toward a $400 apartment and the government providing the $100 voucher to make up the difference.  The voucher can only be used for private sector housing. That system involves less tax expenditures than traditional public housing, and it does put money into the private sector marketplace.  It can also provide better quality housing than public housing.

5.  Along with rent supplements can go a program for upgrading the skills of recipients.  They can then increase their incomes and eventually no longer need the rent supplements.  The skills upgrading may be especially important for the homeless who may have virtually no incomes.

6.  The voucher system also has the extra benefit of facilitating economic class integration.  A requirement in using the voucher might be that one has to use them in neighborhoods that are above the concentrated poverty level.  Doing so facilitates school integration in terms of low-income children going to school with middle-class children.  It also stimulates ambition on the part of the parents more so than living in public housing.

policies on the goals, the condominium arrangement seems best for existing government-owned public housing. That policy is, however, resisted partly because the present public-housing management does not want to become the employee of the tenants.

In light of the scores of the policies on the goals, the rent supplements seem best for providing housing for the poor outside of government-owned public housing projects. That policy is, however, resisted partly because it means appropriating new federal funds. The program of home ownership for the poor might have been effectively administered if the intermediary were HUD employees who have no commission incentive to de-emphasize maintenance costs or to bribe property assessors as part of repeated foreclosure schemes with the federal government covering the mortgages.

One could add the policy of doing nothing to provide housing for the poor. Such a policy at first glance looks good with regard to the burden on the taxpayer. It could, however, result in unacceptable slum living conditions which could be an even greater burden on the taxpayer then helping to provide affordable housing.

Housing for the poor is an example in which the private sector has been reasonably effective, efficient, and equitable in comparison to public administration. In this context, public housing means government owned and operated housing projects for the poor. Private housing means rent subsidies to the private sector to enable the private sector to provide housing for low-income tenants.

On the matter of <u>effectiveness</u>, public housing has been a failure compared to rent supplement programs. In terms of quantity of housing made available, there has been little increased public housing in the United States since about 1970. In fact there have been some dramatic decreases, such as literally blowing up the Pruitt-lgoe Homes in St. Louis. They were considered bankrupt in the sense of consistently costing more to maintain than the monetary or non-monetary benefits could justify. On the other hand, the private sector is willing to make available almost unlimited housing to the poor, so long as poor people with rent supplements can pay the rent.

On the matter of <u>efficiency</u>, public housing projects have been extremely expensive per dwelling unit. They were originally designed to save money by being high rise, which decreases land costs and enables every floor to also be a ceiling with many common walls. The lack of more individualized dwelling units, however, has led to a lack of sense of ownership or even possession. That has led to vandalism and the failure to report it. Rent supplements, on the other hand, save money in such ways as (1) avoiding the initial building cost by using existing housing stock, (2) encouraging better care of the property, thereby lowering maintenance costs that might otherwise require higher rent supplements, and (3) increasing self-pride and ambition which lowers the costs of welfare and crime committing.

On the matter of <u>equity</u>, public housing has resulted in discrimination against poor whites and segregation of poor blacks. Whites have in effect been discriminated against as a result of public housing projects being located disproportionately in black neighborhoods where the projects have frequently become all black. Rent supplements, on the other hand, are as available to poor whites as they are to poor blacks. Also important is the fact that rend supplements can easily lead to racial and class integration, whereas big housing projects are not easily absorbed in white or middle class neighborhoods.

Public housing also does poorly on the political values of public participation, predictable rules, and procedural due process in view of how authoritarian and arbitrary public housing projects have traditionally been managed. This is in contrast to the greater dignity associated with rent supplements. The rent supplement program also serves as a liberal symbol of doing something important for the poor, while also being a conservative symbol of the meaningfulness or private-sector property.

It is relevant to note that although rent supplements are an example of good private administration of a societal function, that is not the case with the mortgage supplement program of the early 1970's. That program involved the federal government making funds available for poor people to buy homes through private real estate agents, rather than through HUD employees or other public administrators. The privately administered program became a scandal, worse than used car fraud of the Medicare-Medicaid frauds. Real estate agents failed to inform low income buyers of the maintenance costs of bad heating, plumbing, and electrical systems. Trying to meet those costs frequently interfered with meeting even the low mortgage payments. As a result, foreclosures were frequent, analogous to used car repossessions, but with the federal government making good on whatever was owed. The greed factor became so great that it was not enough to double or triple collect on the same house through foreclosures. Assessors were bribed to inflate the value of the houses to further increase what was collected. The program was soon abandoned even though it began with strong liberal and conservative support, and might have succeeded if it were administered by salaried government employees, rather than by private real estate agents operating on commissions.

### B. Food Prices In China

On the alternatives, high farm prices is the conservative alternative in this context, and low prices is the liberal alternative.

On the criteria, the <u>liberal</u> weights involve a 3 for urban desires, a 1 for rural desires, and a 2 for all the other goals. With the liberal weights, the SOS wins 76 to 48 for all the other alternatives. We then go back and put in the conservative weights. The <u>conservative</u> weights give a 2 to all the neutral goals just as liberal weights do, but they do a flip-flop on urban and rural desires. For the conservative in this context, rural desires get a weight of 3 rather than a 1, and urban desires get a 1 rather than a 3. The SOS is a winner even with the conservative weights, although now the high prices do better than they did before, but still not as well as the SOS. The <u>neutral</u> perspective is not to give everything a weight of 1, but rather to give everything a weight of 2. If the neutrals gave everything a weight of 1, they would be giving neutral goals less weight than either the liberals or the conservatives give them. Thus the neutral picture is that rural desires get a weight of 2, and so do urban desires. To the neutral, everything gets a weight of 2. The SOS wins with the neutral weights too.

A super-optimum solution is capable of being out in front and substantially over the conservative alternative of high prices for farmers' products using the conservative weights. It also wins over low prices for farmers' products using the liberal weights. And it wins over the compromise as a neutral alternative using the neutral weights. The SOS here involves the farmers getting better than high prices and the urbanites paying lower than low prices with the government providing a supplement like the minimum wage supplement.

Administrative feasibility must be satisfied. That involved the use of food stamps. They are given to urban food buyers. They cannot be easily counterfeited. The buyers give them to retailers, who in turn give them to wholesalers, who in turn give them to farmers, who turn them in for reimbursement. Criterion 8 talks about political feasibility  There should be a separate criterion for administrative feasibility.

Of special importance is that no farmer gets the supplement unless they agree to adopt more modern farming methods. Otherwise it is just a handout for subsidizing inefficient farming. By adopting more modern farming methods, productivity goes up. Food becomes available for export, foreign exchange then gets acquired for importing new technology. The new technology increases the GNP and everybody is better off, including the taxpayers who pay the supplement. They are better off because with the increased GNP the government could even reduce taxes if it wanted to do so. It could reduce taxes below a 20% level and still have more tax revenue if the GNP base has increased substantially. Urban workers could also be required to accept on-the-job training or other skills upgrading in return for the food stamps. Table 1-7 summarizes this example. [5]

TABLE 1-7. PRICING FOOD IN CHINA AND ELSEWHERE

| Criteria / Alternatives | C GOAL Rural Well Being | L GOAL Urban Well Being | N GOAL Adminis. Feasibility | N GOAL +Farming Methods | N GOAL +Export | N GOAL Import Technology | N GOAL +GNP | N GOAL Political Feasibility | N TOTALS (Neutral Weights) | L TOTAL (Liberal Weights) | C TOTAL (Conservative Weights) |
|---|---|---|---|---|---|---|---|---|---|---|---|
| C Alternative High Price | 5 | 1 | 3 | 4 | 4 | 4 | 4 | 1 | 52 (18) | 48 (14) | 56* (22) |
| L Alternative Low Price | 1 | 5 | 3 | 2 | 2 | 2 | 2 | 5 | 44 (18) | 48* (22) | 40 (14) |
| N Alternative Compromise | 3 | 3 | 3 | 3 | 3 | 3 | 3 | 3 | 48 (18) | 48 (18) | 48 (18) |
| SOS Alternative Price Supplement | 5.1 | 5.1 | 3 | 5 | 5 | 5 | 5 | 5 | 76.4 (26.4) | 76.4** (26.4) | 76.4** (26.4) |

NOTES: (TABLE 1.7)

1. The intermediate totals in parentheses are based on the first three goals. The bottom line totals are based on all the goals, including the indirect effects of the alternatives.

2. The SOS of a price supplement involves farmers receiving 101% of the price they are asking, but urban workers and other paying only 79% which is less than the 80% that they are willing and able to pay.

3 The difference of 22% is made up by food stamps given to the urban workers in return for agreeing to be in programs that upgrade their skills and productivity. The food stamps are used to pay for staple products (like rice or wheat) along with cash. Farmers can then redeem the stamps for cash, provided that they also agree to be in programs that increase their productivity.

4. Food stamps have administrative feasibility for ease in determining that workers and farmers are doing what they are supposed to do in return for the food stamps. They cannot be easily counterfeited. They serve as a check on how much the farmers have sold.

5. By increasing the productivity of farmers and workers, the secondary effects occur of improving farming methods, increasing exports, increasing the importing of new technologies, and increasing the GNP.

6. High prices are not politically feasible because of too much opposition from workers who consume, but do not produce food. The high prices though are acceptable if they can be met by way of price supplements, in the form of food stamps.

## V. COMBINING LIBERAL AND CONSERVATIVE ALTERNATIVES

Almost every university in the USA is an example of public and private mixed, at least every so-called private university is. About half of their funds come from alumni and student tuition and half from government grants. That is also about the same with so-called state universities that are now more dependent than they have been in the past on alumni and student tuition. The difference between public colleges and private colleges is lessening in the U.S. They are all a mixture of private funds (from students and alumni) and public funds (from either direct state tax dollars or lots of indirect federal aid to education). That especially includes grant money from government agencies for research, although the more research-oriented universities get more research grant money. Smaller colleges get fewer big grants, but the percentage of their total annual budget may consist of a sizable percentage of grant money, even though it does not amount to a lot of money compared to the University of Illinois.

This is an example of the kind of SOS that involves combining liberal and conservative alternatives where they are not mutually exclusive. The liberals want public schools and public universities supported by tax money and open to the general public. The conservatives want private snobbier schools that are more exclusive. What we have are public schools like the University of Illinois that will only admit the top 10% of their classes. This is snobbier than most second-rate ivy league schools, and certainly snobbier than Lake Forest College which is considered the snobbiest school in Illinois but will admit people of lower qualifications than the University of Illinois. Our state universities like Berkeley, Michigan, and Wisconsin are now the snobbiest places in the country, as compared to the small totally private liberal arts colleges that have relatively little intellectual prestige. On the other hand, those small liberal arts colleges that have lost their private charter (as indicated by the Grove City case) are highly dependent on federal funds. Thus, American higher education is achieving the goals of conservatives by providing for aristocratic schools that are the envy of the world while at the same time achieving the liberal goal of making them open to the public, as contrasted to open only to the children of snobby aristocrats or people with the right ethnic backgrounds. They also follow the liberal goal of making them oriented toward the public interest, partly because they receive so much government money for which they are supposed to do worthwhile things.

One can also say that American higher education is an SOS not just because it simultaneously satisfies liberal and conservative goals, but because it is viewed as superior to the higher education systems of any other country. One indication of that is the recent newspaper reports saying that close to 90% of the top Chinese Communist government leadership is now sending their children to American schools, even though the U.S. ideologically is at the opposite end of a continuum of which Communist China is at the other end. What it shows is that they think or recognize that American schools (regardless that they may turn their children against their Communist Party parents) are worth sending their children to so they can become better engineers, scientists, business people, or whatever. That is indeed a compliment to the system when its enemies want to go there, or especially when its enemies want their children to go there, even though they know doing so may turn their children against them.

This is a second example of where the liberal and conservative alternative can exist simultaneously. We previously had the example of the volunteer lawyers and the salaried lawyers of the Legal Services Program. The higher education area is an example where public money and private money co-exist so comfortably. One could say that the defense contracting is another example (but not one to be especially proud of) where the government pours in a lot of money and private stockholders take it home with them. The defense contracting industry is not an example of efficient economic organization. It is an example of a highly subsidized industry that might totally collapse if it had to sell only to the private market.

Under the higher education example, the alternatives are:

1. Private sector, or better put, private schools. That is the conservative solution. That is virtually the only system until recently in England and much of western Europe.

2. State-owned schools. That is the liberal solution. All the schools are state owned at the university level in China, Russia, and communist countries with minor exceptions. All the major universities in the U.S. between California and the east coast are also state-owned. There is no prominent major university with the exception of Northwestern and the University of Chicago between the Ivy League and Stanford. Once one gets west of Harvard, Yale, Princeton, or the University of Pennsylvania which is still in theory private, there is a desert of major private universities. On the west coast, Stanford is the only exception. There is no world-class university on the west coast other than Stanford that is private.

3. The compromise position would be to simply have some private schools and some state-owned schools. That was the case in the late 1800s and early 1900s when the U.S. did not have much of a university system.

4. The SOS (although still subject to improvement) is the kind of mix we have now which involves every major private school receiving lots of tax money. Harvard University is considered to be the leading private university in the U.S. Harvard gets probably more federal money than any other public school in the U.S. with the exception maybe of Michigan, Illinois, Berkeley, and a couple of others. The federal money goes where the quality professors are. It has nothing to do with whether the school is public or private. Likewise, the University of Illinois would collapse if it were not for private alumni contributions and student

tuition, including high student tuition that Abraham Lincoln would not have condoned when he set up the land grant college system. It is not oppressive, though, because students who cannot afford it can get financial aid. The SOS is thus public money to private schools and private money to public schools, providing a great mix of resources that makes the American higher education the envy of all countries. Also, there is a mix in the sense of democratic admissions that are not based on race, class, or nepotism, while at the same time lots of meritocracy elitism that would appeal to the most elitist British educator. The top students at Berkeley, for instance, probably score higher on entrance exams and other exams that the top students at Oxford and Cambridge do. The professors at Berkeley also score higher in contributing to the world's knowledge than the professors at Oxford and Cambridge do.

The goals are:

1. To have a highly educated population.
2. To have universities that produce new knowledge.
3. To be relatively inexpensive in terms of burden on the students and burden on the taxpayer.
4. The equity criteria of being available to everybody regardless of demographic background.

Those are two measures of effectiveness, one of efficiency, and one of equity. Table 1-8 summarizes this example. [6]

## VI. REMOVING OR DECREASING THE SOURCE OF THE CONFLICT

### A. POINTS FAVORING CAPITAL PUNISHMENT

1. It probably deters some murder, but not much given the other relevant factors such as the monetary or emotional benefits received at the time of committing a murder and the perception of the low probability of being executed

2. It sets a good example with regard to society's concern for deterring murder.

3. It represents total incapacitation of the defendant in the sense of not being able to recommit one's crime.

4. Rehabilitation does not seem to be very effective in the criminal justice system, although maybe more so with one-time murders than with chronic robbers, burglars, sex offenders, etc.

5. It saves the money of incarceration.

6. A majority of public opinion now seem to want it.

7. It may receive some support from conservative interests who welcome an emphasis on violent crimes to detract from business crimes.

8. As of now it is considered constitutional, provided that capital punishment laws are precisely written but allow for flexibility to consider specific circumstances.

## TABLE 1-8. COMBINING PUBLIC AND PRIVATE HIGHER EDUCATION

| Criteria<br><br>Alternatives | L GOAL<br>Highly Educated | L GOAL<br>Produce New Knowledge | C GOAL<br>-Tax Cost | L GOAL<br>Equity | N TOTAL<br>(Neutral Weights) | L TOTAL<br>(LIberal Weights) | C TOTAL<br>(Conserva-tive Weights) |
|---|---|---|---|---|---|---|---|
| C Alternative<br>Private Schools | 2 | 2 | 4 | 1 | 18 | 19 | 17* |
| L Alternative<br>State Owned Schools | 4 | 4 | 1 | 4 | 26 | 37* | 15 |
| N Alternative<br>Some Private & Some State | 3 | 3 | 2.5 | 3 | 23 | 29.5 | 16.5 |
| SOS Alternative<br>Public $ to Private/<br>Private $ to Public | 5 | 5 | 2 | 5 | 34 | 47** | 21** |

*NOTES:*

1. *The SOS Alternative of simultaneously combining public and private higher education is well-represented by the American higher education system.*

2. *Many major U.S. universities are <u>state</u> institutions. Major private universities also receive large amounts of government money in the form of grants, scholarships, and loans to students.*

3. *Many major U.S. universities are <u>private</u> institutions. Even the state universities are charging tuition increasingly. They also are increasing*

NOTES: *Table 1-8continued*

*their admission standards which makes them closer to elite private universities.   The state universities are also increasingly relying on corporate and alumni contributions to supplement taxes.*

*4.   Thus the private universities are heavily state-supported, and the state universities are heavily private-supported.   Both co-exist on both a high-level, and both co-exist at a lower level.   This is a good example of where   the   conservative   and   liberal   Alternatives   can   flourish simultaneously.*

### B. POINTS DISFAVORING CAPITAL PUNISHMENT

1.   It may encourage some murder by cheapening the value of life.
2.   It tends to be disproportionately inflicted upon minorities and the poor.
3.   It leads to due process violations with regard to convicting the innocent since there generally are no eye witnesses, or at least victim witnesses in murder cases.
4.   It wastes society's resources in obtaining executions.
5.   Public opinion is about evenly divided and fluctuates, with the majority opposed to capital punishment as of the 1960s and early 70s.
6.   It distracts from more widespread civil liberties violations like excessive use of pre-trial detention.
7.   Its constitutionality is questionable under the cruel and unusual punishment laws. It is cruel if it does not substantially deter. It is unusual if it is quite chancy as to whether it is going to be imposed, and it is a rare phenomenon.

### C. SOS - MURDER REDUCTION VIA:

1.   Gun control.
2.   Drug medicalization.
3.   Reducing violence socialization.
Table 1-9 summarizes this example.[6]

### D. OTHER EXAMPLES

1.   Resolving the abortion controversy through better birth control.
2.   Resolving the drug problem by taking away the profit through free medically prescribed drugs to addicts under a phase out plan.[7]

## VII. A PACKAGE OF ALTERNATIVES

### A. GENERAL

One of the first stages in criminal proceedings which seems to call for judicial reform is the stage at which a decision is made about an arrested suspect prior to his trial. The basic alternatives involve releasing or not releasing him prior to trial depending on (1) whether he can offer a sufficient money deposit to serve as a guarantee or incentive that he will return for trial, or (2) whether his characteristics are such that he is likely to return for his trial rather than risk being prosecuted as a trial jumper. The first alternative is referred to as the traditional bail bond system, and the second alternative as release on one's own recognizance or the ROR system. In past years, the bail system was by far the dominant method. This was so partly because of the belief that individuals were economically motivated and partly because the system favored middle-class people whose interests tended to dominate legal rule-making. The reform trend is increasingly toward a more objective and scientific ROR system for a number of reasons.

Studies by the Vera Institute in New York City have shown that by carefully screening arrested suspects into good risks and bad risks (largely on the basis of their roots in the community and the seriousness of their crimes), one can obtain a least as low a percentage of trial jumpers as one does with the traditional money-deposit system. Trial-day mail or phone reminders also help reduce trial jumping. These studies have further shown that, with the screening and notification system, a far higher percentage of arrested suspects can be released from jail pending their trial than under the money-deposit system. Such release means these good risks can (1) continue their jobs, (2) better prepare their cases to establish their innocence, (3) save the taxpayer money by not occupying jail space, and (4) be less bitter than if they spent time in j ail and were then acquitted. The money-deposit system so inherently discriminates against the poor that the United States Supreme Court may someday declare it to be in violation of the equal protection clause of the Constitution.

One objection to the ROR system is that it might result in releasing a number of arrested suspects who will commit crimes while awaiting trial. One response to this objection is that truly dangerous persons should be kept in jail pending a speedy trial regardless of how able they are to offer a large money deposit. Another response is to point out that pretrial crimes are more often due to long delays prior to trial than to poor screening or the lack of a bail bond requirement. The delay problem, however, is a separate area of judicial reform.

## TABLE 1-9. EVALUATING THE POLICY OF CAPITAL PUNISHMENT

| Criteria | B1 C GOAL -Crime & Murder | B2 L GOAL Separate Innocent Executions | C N GOAL -Tax Costs | EO L GOAL Discrim of Blacks & Poor | C GOAL Anti- Murder Symbol | N TOTAL (Neutral Weights) | L TOTAL (Liberal Weights) | C TOTAL (Conser- vative Weights) |
|---|---|---|---|---|---|---|---|---|
| **Alternatives** | | | | | | | | |
| C Alternative CP for All Murders | 3.1 | 1 | 2.5 | 2 | 5 | 27.2 | 22.1 | 32.3* |
| L Alternative No CP | 2.9 | 4 | 3.5 | 3.5 | 2 | 31.8 | 34.4* | 29.2 |
| N Alternative CP w/Special Murders & Procedures | 3 | 4 | 3 | 3 | 3 | 32 | 33 | 31 |
| SOS Alternative -Murder by Gun Control, Drug Medicalization Socialization. | 5 | 4.5 | 2 | 4 | 4 | 39 | 38.5** | 39.5** |

*NOTES:*

1. The first two goals are especially important. Conservatives emphasize the need to decrease crime and murder. Liberals emphasize the need to separate out the innocent and decrease executions.

2. There is only a small effect, if any, between allowing capital punishment and decreasing murder or other crimes. There is a bigger effect between not allowing capital punishment and avoiding executions, including innocent defendants.

3. Not allowing capital punishment saves the cost of expensive appeals and eliminates an especially undesirable form of discrimination.

NOTES: *Table 1-9 continued*

*Allowing capital punishment scores well an as anti-murder symbol, which helps explain conservative support for capital punishment.*

4. *Neutral positions on capital punishment allow for special murders such as the killing of police officers or mass murder. Neutral positions may also allow it under special procedures such as a jury recommendation, automatic appeal, or especially qualified jurors.*

5. *The SOS Alternative is to concentrate on greatly reducing murders through better gun control, drug treatment, and through childhood socialization which encourages a negative attitude toward violence.*

## B. PRETRIAL RELEASE OF ARRESTED DEFENDANTS: SPREADSHEETS

Table 1-10 analyzes how the criminal justice system might handle the problem of pretrial release of arrested defendants. The prevailing compromise policy is to hold people in jail prior to trial unless they can provide a money deposit to allow their release. The proposed conservative policy of the Reagan Administration was to hold more people in jail by explicitly adding the probability of crime-committing as a criterion for pretrial release. The SOS policy which has been increasingly adopted is to hold fewer people in jail while holding constant or improving the court-appearance rate by better screening, supervision, notification, prosecution, and delay reduction.

The goals in the pretrial release context include avoiding or minimizing undesirable occurrences such as (1) the embittering experience of being held in jail prior to trial without ever being convicted, (2) the arbitrary subjectivity which tends to be associated with who gets released and held, (3) jail riots due to the bitterness and overcrowding often associated with pretrial detention, (4) convictions of innocent defendants who agree to plead guilty in order to be released from pretrial detention with a sentence equal to the time already served, (5) the expense of having to expand overcrowded pretrial jails, (6) lost gross national product, (7) increases in welfare cases due to pretrial detention of family-income producers, (8) non-appearance in court of released defendants, and (9) crime-committing by released defendants.

Table 1-10 shows the relations between the policies and the goals using the same 1-5 scoring system as was used in other tables. The Reagan proposal scores low on the liberal and neutral goals, but high on the conservative goals. The liberal policy scores high on the liberal and neutral goals, but low on the conservative goals. The prevailing compromise policy scores in the middle on all the goals. The SOS package scores high on all the goals.

TABLE 1-10. EVALUATING ALTERNATIVE WAYS OF HANDLING PRETRIAL RELEASE

| Criteria | L GOAL | C GOAL | N GOAL | N TOTAL | L TOTAL | C TOTAL |
|---|---|---|---|---|---|---|
| | + Release Productivity | + Shows & Non Crime | -Taxes | (Neuural Weights) | (Liberal Weights) | (Conservative Weights) |
| Alternatives | | | | | | |
| C Alternative High Bond | 2 | 4 | 2.5 | 17 | 15 | 19* |
| L Alternative Low Bond or No Bond | 4 | 2 | 3.5 | 19 | 21* | 17 |
| N Alternative 10% Bond | 3 | 3 | 3 | 18 | 18 | 18 |
| SOS Alternative Screen, Report Notify, Prosecute,- Delay | 5 | 5 | 2 | 24 | 24** | 24** |

NOTES:

1. The conservative position is to set relatively high bonds in order to generate a high holding rate. Doing so increases the likelihood that arrested defendants will show up for trial and not commit another crime between arrest and trial.

2. The liberal position is to set relatively low bonds in order to generate a low holding rate. Doing so increases the likelihood that arrested defendants will be able to continue their jobs, avoid the bitterness of being held in jail prior to trial, and avoid the expensive incarceration costs.

3. The compromise position in many states like Illinois is to have relatively high bonds but require the defendant to provide only 10% of the total bond. This results in more defendants being released than the conservative alternative, but less defendents being released than the liberal alternative.

NOTES: *Table 1-10 continued*

4. *The SOS Alternative is designed to increase the release rate possibly even higher than what liberals advocate, but at the same time get the high rate of defendants showing up for trial without committing crimes in the meantime. This can be done by (1) systematically screening arrested defendants to hold those who are relatively high risks, (2) requiring released defendants to report to the courthouse every week or so, (3) notifying defendants a few days before a hearing by mail, phone, or in person, (4) prosecuting defendants who fail to show for their court dates, and (5) especially reducing delay between arrest and trial which otherwise leads to skipping out and to crime committing for those released and expensive incarceration costs for those held in jail pending trial.*

Under the differential weighting system, liberal goals a weight of 3 and conservative goals a weight of 1, as contrasted to conservatives giving liberal goals a weight of 1 and conservative goals a weight of 3. The SOS reform policy receives the highest overall score under all three weighting systems. Like the winning proposals in all these problems, it represents a way of achieving both the conservative and liberal goals simultaneously. The average defendant will appear even more in court without being arrested while released, which should please conservatives. They also result in holding less people in jail prior to trial which should please liberals.

The dollar cost of those reforms was not included as a goal, although it could easily be added. The dollar costs, however, are not so great to do a minimum amount of (1) screening to separate good and bad risks, (2) supervision by way of having released defendants report periodically to the courthouse prior to trial, (3) notification by postcard or other means immediately before the trial date, (4) selective prosecution of no-shows to make examples of them, and (5) reducing the amount of delay from arrest to trial so as to reduce the expense of holding defendants in jail and to reduce the probability of released defendants disappearing or committing crimes. With the costs being relatively low and the benefits being relatively high in terms of goals achieved, it is understandable that those SOS reform measures have become widely adopted, although perhaps not widely enough. [8]

## VIII. REDEFINING THE PROBLEM

Quite often a highly emotional controversy between liberals and conservatives may be capable of being resolved beyond the best expectations of each side through the approach of redefining the problem. They may be arguing over how to deal with a problem that is really relatively unimportant in terms of achieving their goals, as contrasted to a more important problem on which they might be likely to get mutually satisfying agreement. This involves seeing beyond a relatively superficial argument to the higher level goals which are endorsed by both liberals and conservatives although possibly not to the same relative degree.

### A . TRADITIONAL ALTERNATIVES AND GOALS

A concrete example is the controversy over the size of juries in criminal cases. Liberals argue in favor of preserving the traditional 12-person jury, as contrasted to allowing juries as small as only 6 people. Liberals view the larger jury as being important for protecting the innocent since it is more difficult for a prosecutor to convince 12 jurors unanimously of the defendant's guilt than it is to convince 6 jurors. Liberals may also argue that 12-person juries allow for more public participation, but that seems less important than decreasing convictions, although public participation may sound more acceptable.

Conservatives argue in favor of allowing 1-person juries. They view smaller juries as being important for convicting the guilty since it is easier for a prosecutor to convince 6 jurors unanimously of the defendant's guilt than it is to convince 12 jurors. Conservatives may also argue that 1-person juries reduce delay, but that seems less important than increasing convictions, although delay reduction may sound more acceptable.

Liberals in this context are thus especially sensitive to avoiding errors of convicting the innocent, although they also want to avoid errors of not convicting the guilty. Conservatives are especially sensitive to avoiding errors of not convicting the guilty, although they also want to avoid errors of convicting the innocent. So long as the problem is defined in terms of optimum jury size, there is an inherent trade-off between those two goals. Liberals see any reduction in jury size as sacrificing protection of the innocent, in favor of convicting the guilty. Conservatives see a retention of the 12-person jury as sacrificing the need to convict the guilty, in factor of a undue sensitivity to protecting the innocent who they tend to see as not being a significant percentage of the defendants who are tried.

## B. AN SOS SOLUTION

What may be needed in this policy controversy is to redefine the problem away from, "How many people should be present on a jury in criminal cases?" A more appropriate definition of the problem in light of what the liberals and conservatives are actually arguing over is "How can we simultaneously increase the probability of convicting guilty defendants and increase the probability of acquitting innocent defendants?" There is no inherent trade-off between those two goals. In fact, there may be no inherent trade-off between any two goals. By so restating the problem, one's attention is directed toward thinking about what procedural changes could achieve increases on both goals simultaneously, rather than thinking what is the ideal compromise, middling position, or equilibrium between 12-person and 6-person juries.

There are some procedural changes that could simultaneously increase goal achievement on both the liberal and conservative goals. They all involve increasing the general accuracy of juries and decreasing the general inaccuracy. One such procedural change would be allowing jurors to take notes. In most states, they are prohibited from doing so. It is unclear as to why that prohibition began. One plausible explanation is that when the jury system was started in about the 1500s in England, few people could read or write. It may have been felt that if those few jurors who could take notes were allowed to do so, then they would dominate jury decision-making. A 12-person jury could then in effect become a jury of one or two people who have been making a written record of what those jurors perceived as having occurred. As of 1990, virtually all jurors are capable of taking notes and should be allowed to do so. That would improve their accuracy in both convicting the guilty and acquitting the innocent.

Along related lines, an especially useful innovation would be to provide for automatic videotaping of jury trials and bench trials. This is a possible double super optimum solution. It is super-optimum in the sense that it increases the accuracy of convicting the guilty and acquitting the innocent simultaneously. Quite often in jury deliberations, there is disagreement among the jurors as to what was said by a certain witness, lawyer, or the judge. One juror who is especially domineering may say that the witness said the defendant was seen at the scene of the crime at 8:00 a.m. Other jurors may think it was 8:00 p.m. The disagreement can be quickly and accurately resolved with a videotape made by a Camcorder that can be played back on any TV set with a video playback capability. Otherwise the winning perception is the one held by whichever jurors may have the most aggressive personalities. That could result in either an error of acquitting a guilty person, or an error of convicting an innocent person.

The second sense in which the Camcorder videotaping is super-optimum is that it decreases costs and increases benefits simultaneously. It is substantially less expensive to videotape a jury trial than it is to pay a stenotypist to try to record verbatim what was said at the trial. The Camcorder can be operated by someone who can easily be taught what little is involved. The cost of each tape is nominal and can be re-used. The benefits are substantially increased because (1) one gets instant replay as contrasted to transcribing stenotyping months later, (2) one gets accurate replay as contrasted to the extensively ad-libbed record that is made by court reporters, (3) one can see facial expressions, (4) one can hear voice connotations, and (5) one can hear two or more people talking at the same time which tends toward gibberish of missing information in stenotyping notes.

In addition to note-taking and videotaping, there are a number of other ways of increasing general jury accuracy. They include allowing jurors to have access to a written copy of the judge's instructions. This helps improve the interpretation of the law by juries just as note-taking and videotaping improve their understanding of the facts. Most states do not provide for written judicial instructions. This also goes back to medieval times when relatively few people could read. It was felt that those few who could read the judge's instructions would dominate jury decision-making, just as those few who could write notes would also dominate. The contemporary reason for the inertia in allowing juries to have written instructions may relate to the fact that the instructions tend to favor safeguards for the innocent. Legal decision makers may be reluctant to do anything that will further increase acquittals and decrease convictions.

Other approaches to improving general juror accuracy that have been adopted in only a minority of states, if any, include:

1.   Allowing jurors to submit questions to the judge, the lawyers, or even the witnesses indirectly through the lawyers. This could clarify factual and legal ambiguities that lead to wrong decisions.

2.   Providing a training course for each juror that would last a full day before being eligible to decide cases. The course could clarify what is involved in conducting a trial, jury deliberating, judicial instructions, various kinds of evidence, and other matters. The course could allow jurors to ask questions during the course. The course could also have a test at the end to determine whether each juror has a minimum level of understanding of what is involved.

3.   Ability to read and write or other educational qualifications could improve the general accuracy of jurors. Such requirements, though, can be subject to abuse like southern literacy tests for voting. Even if the tests are objective, they could bias the composition of juries in favor of middle-class attitudes which favor the prosecution in criminal cases and the defendant insurance-companies in civil cases. Any measure designed to improve accuracy should not unthinkingly change the direction or bias of jury outcomes.

4.   Jury accuracy can be improved by having counsel on both sides. We now tend to guarantee counsel to indigent defendants in criminal

cases, but we do not adequately guarantee counsel to indigent litigants in civil cases where there is no contingency fee involved. The Legal Services Corporation is not sufficiently funded to guarantee counsel to indigent civil litigants, although the result is they do not litigate or go to trial, rather than go to trial without a lawyer.

## C. FACTORS INTERFERING WITH ADOPTION

One might ask why such procedures as taking notes and using videotaping have not been adopted already. The key answer with regard to videotaping is that it is a relatively new technology, although audio-taping has been around for sometime. The potential for taking meaningful jury notes has been around for at least a hundred years. An important answer may be the overemphasis on trade-off controversies in discussing jury decision-making such as jury size, the percentage needed to convict, the admissibility of various kinds of evidence, and other controversies in which going one way protects the innocent but facilitates convicting the guilty, and going the other way does the opposite.

Asking why note-taking has not been adopted, or why it may be a long time before videotaping will be adopted raises a separate set of SOS problems that have to do with getting SOS solutions adopted after they have been generated. A key problem is simply inertia, especially in the legal system where there is possibly an over-emphasis on preserving the past regardless of the present consequences. There is no system of evaluation that places so much emphasis on prior precedent, rather than present and future benefits and costs.

In any SOS adoption, there may also be problems of vested interests, property, and jobs. Changing procedural rules may often change substantive results contrary to powerful interest groups. For example, having a trial for liability separate from the trial for damages is likely to lead to a much higher percentage of victories for the defendant. The jury under such split trials cannot adjust the damages to take the plaintiff's contributory negligence into consideration. That kind of change in substantive results does not seem to be a factor in allowing note-taking or videotaping. Vested property can complicate the adoption of SOS solutions with regard to replacing public housing with rent supplements or moving unemployed coal miners to better jobs. That kind of consideration does not seem to be present here. Vested jobs can be a problem in mutually beneficial international tariff reductions. Videotaping would greatly reduce the need for court reporters, but they may not be a strong enough interest group to block videotaping, and they probably would not object to jurors taking notes. Table 1-11 summarizes this example.[9]

TABLE 1-11. 6-PERSON VERSUS 12-PERSON JURIES

| Criteria<br><br>Alternatives | C GOAL<br>Convict the Guilty | L GOAL<br>Acquit the Innocent | N TOTAL<br>(Neutral Weights) | L TOTAL<br>(Liberal Weights) | C TOTAL<br>(Conservative Weights) |
|---|---|---|---|---|---|
| C<br>Alternative<br>6-Person Juries | 4 | 2 | 12 | 10 | 14* |
| L<br>Alternative<br>12-Person Juries | 2 | 4 | 12 | 14* | 10 |
| N<br>Alternative<br>Between 6 & 12 or Unanimity | 3 | 3 | 12 | 12 | 12 |
| SOS<br>Alternative<br>Videotaping or Notetaking | 5 | 5 | 20 | 20** | 20** |

*NOTES:*

1. *Videotaping allows judges and juries to view during deliberations what was said at the trial. Doing so facilitates accurately resolving disputes over the evidence so as to increase the probability of convicting the truly guilty, and simultaneously increase the probability of acquitting the truly innocent.*

2. *Notetaking may also improve recall and the accuracy of decision-making. Likewise, allowing jurors to ask questions of the judge or the lawyers. Likewise, providing special training to jurors as to the meaning of relevant phrases and procedures.*

3. *Those matters are likely to do more for convicting the truly guilty than switching from 12 to 6 person juries. They are also likely to do more for acquitting the truly innocent than retaining the 12 person jury. This is an example of redefining the problem in terms of the goals, rather than the Alternatives.*

## D. THE IMPORTANCE OF PROBLEM DEFINITION
## AND SOS AWARENESS

Looking over the points that relate to the adoption of either note-taking or videotaping as a super-optimum solution to the problem of increasing both the conviction of the guilty and the acquitting of the innocent, one can draw at least two conclusions. First is that redefining the problem to emphasize simultaneous goal achievement can greatly facilitate the generating of super-optimum solutions. Perhaps as a general matter, one could even start with that approach in seeking to arrive at an SOS solution. It works even with alternatives that are inherently incapable of being combined such as liberals wanting juries that consist of 12 or more people, and conservatives wanting juries that consist of 6 or less people.

Second is the important point that the battle for achieving super-optimum solutions is not won by merely generating policy alternatives that satisfy the definition of an SOS solution. There may be problems of technology, inertia, vested interests, property, and jobs that need to be taken into consideration. The main reason for lack of adoption, however, may be a lack of awareness as to what there is to adopt. Thus, a key conclusion may be the importance of communicating basic ideas as to what is meant by a super-optimum solution, and how one or more super-optimum solutions may be possible in any policy controversy. That kind of communicating is the main purpose of this chapter and this book.

## IX. REDUCING COSTS AND INCREASING BENEFITS

Another useful perspective to have for generating SOS solutions is to think in terms of reducing costs and increasing benefits simultaneously. Like many of the methods for generating SOS solutions, this may run contrary to conventional thinking. The important considerations, however, are that (1) it pragmatically works as a method for developing SOS solutions, and that (2) SOS solutions where all major viewpoints come out ahead of their best expectations are socially desirable.

### A. COMPUTER-ASSISTED INSTRUCTION

Also like many of the methods for generating SOS solutions, this method is best understood with a concrete example followed by more generalized language. Table 1-12 shows the method applied to the problem of some aspects of elementary school education. As for the alternatives, the conservative emphasis in education policy is often on reducing costs including teachers' salaries, as manifested in their opposition to education tax increases, possibly without adequately

TABLE 1-12.   REDUCING COSTS AND INCREASING BENEFITS IN EDUCATION

| Criteria<br><br>Alternatives | C GOAL<br>-Taxes<br>(-Costs) | L GOAL<br>+Learning<br>(+Benefits) | N TOTAL<br>(Neutral<br>Weights) | L TOTAL<br>(LIberal<br>Weights) | C TOTAL<br>(Conservative<br>Weights) |
|---|---|---|---|---|---|
| C<br>Alternative<br>-Salaries<br>(-Learning) | 4 | 2 | 12 | 10 | 14* |
| L<br>Alternative<br>+Learning<br>(+Salaries) | 2 | 4 | 12 | 14* | 10 |
| N<br>Alternative<br>In Between on<br>Both<br>Dimensions | 3 | 3 | 12 | 12 | 12 |
| SOS<br>Alternative<br>Computer<br>Assisted<br>Instruction &<br>Videotaping | 5 | 5 | 20 | 20** | 20** |

*NOTES:*

1.  In the context of reducing costs and increasing benefits in education, the conservative approach tends to emphasize reducing costs. That may mean keeping salaries low, which could reduce the learning benefits by not attracting sufficiently well-qualified teachers.

2.   The liberal approach may over-emphasize increasing salaries in order to increase learning benefits. Doing so might cause an undue tax burden in which the incremental costs exceed the incremental benefits.

3.   The SOS approach seeks to find innovative teaching methods that simultaneously decrease the education costs while increasing the learning benefits. The use of computer-aided instruction may be a good example of such an approach.   Computers are less expensive

*NOTES: Table 1-12 continued*

*than teachers after the computers are bought. They may be an excellent supplement in terms of learning experience with appropriate software. Likewise videotaping can provide low cost supplementary instruction that may have incremental learning benefits greater than incremental costs.*

considering the reduced learning benefits. The liberal emphasis is often on increasing the learning experiences of students, possibly without adequately considering the cost in terms of increased salaries. The neutral or compromise position is somewhere between the low salaries for teachers that are associated with conservative taxpayers and the high salaries for teachers that are associated with liberal labor unions. That neutral position is also somewhere between the reduced learning experience that may be associated with low salaries and the increased learning experience that may be associated with high salaries in terms of quantity of salaried teachers as well as average salary per teacher.

As for the goals, conservatives place a relatively high value on the goal of reducing taxes or cutting costs. Liberals place a relatively high value on having enriched learning experiences, especially for inner-city children and others who are not so well-to-do. The conservative alternative of conservative salaries does well on the conservative goal, but generally not so well on learning quality and quantity. The liberal alternative of liberal salaries does relatively well on the liberal learning goal, but not so well on the conservative cost-saving goal. The neutral or compromise alternative logically falls between the other two alternatives in terms of its impact on both goals.

One SOS alternative in this context is to make more use of modern technology whereby one can lower the costs especially of the quantity of teachers needed, while simultaneously increasing many aspects of the learning experience. One technology for doing that is computer-assisted instruction. Children who love to play computer games are more likely to respond favorably to a game-playing orientation to learning reading, writing, arithmetic, social science, natural science, and other subjects. It is more of a fun experience than being lectured to, passively reading, or being home pretending to be sick. As of 1990, computer-assisted instruction now adds coordinated videotapes to the computer software by way of videodisks. This kind of technology is capable of combining the jobs of Pac-Man with Sesame Street by combining computer games with TV and movies in a useful interactive way. Pac-Man is not very useful, and Sesame Street is not very interactive.

Thus through modern educational technology one teacher could maybe supervise two or three classrooms working with computer-assisted instruction with or without a video component. That saves two teachers' salaries. It does mean some additional costs for the equipment, but the maintenance costs tend to be rather low for electronic as contrasted to mechanical devices. Software costs are less than book costs, especially if the software is developed by the teachers themselves and widely reproduced. The key consideration is that this kind of thinking can lead to an alternative that will easily win on the liberal totals by virtue of the increased benefits while holding costs down, and win on the conservative totals by virtue of the reduced costs while at least preserving the learning benefits.

## B. Other Examples

Many other examples could be given. One is shown in Table 1-13 regarding Federal Aviation Administration policy. There the conservative position emphasizes reducing costs to the airlines. The liberal position (relatively speaking) emphasizes higher safety. The neutral position compromises both monetary cost and safety. The SOS position might emphasize subsidies to develop technologies that could provide greater safety than we currently have at even lower cost. Such a technology might make more use of computerized flight control, including computerized-assisted flying (like computer-assisted instruction) from take-off to landing. Such assistance could be provided by flight control towers, as well as within planes. Doing so could save salary costs while providing increased benefits similar to the computer-assisted instruction.

Another example is given in Table 1-14. This example is about applying the general methodology to environmental policy, as contrasted to education or transportation policy. All three policy fields (as well as other policy fields) have in common the possibility of increasing benefits and reducing costs through new technologies or new systems for achieving desired goals. In environmental policy, the conservative alternatives tend to emphasize relying on the marketplace. Liberal alternatives tends to emphasize punishing business wrongdoers. Neutrals may also advocate punishment or regulation, especially where toxic pollution is involved, but often with many exceptions and procedural loopholes, thereby considerably lessening the punishment threat.

TABLE 1-13.  AN SOS ANALYSIS OF SOME ASPECTS OF FEDERAL
AVIATION ADMINISTRATION POLICY

| Criteria<br><br>Alternatives | N GOAL<br>-Taxpayer<br>L=2 C=2 | C GOAL<br>-Airline $<br>L=1 C=3 | L GOAL<br>Safety<br>L=4 C=2 | N TOTAL<br>(Neutral<br>Weights) | L TOTAL<br>(Liberal<br>Weights) | C TOTAL<br>(Conservative<br>Weights) |
|---|---|---|---|---|---|---|
| C<br>Alternative<br>Reduce Labor<br>& Equipment<br>Cost | 4 | 4 | 2 | 20 | 20 | 24* |
| L<br>Alternative<br>Pay High<br>Labor &<br>Equipment<br>Costs | 2 | 2 | 4 | 16 | 22* | 18 |
| N<br>Alternative<br>In Between | 3 | 3 | 3 | 18 | 21 | 21 |
| SOS<br>Alternative<br>1. Non-wage<br>Benefits<br>2. Subsidy<br>for High<br>Safety & Low<br>Cost Systems | 2 | 5 | 5 | 24 | 29** | 29* |

NOTES:

*1. This is an SOS analysis of the labor-management dispute between the Federal Aviation Administration and the Flight Controllers Union during the first term of the Reagan Administration.*

*2. The conservative Alternative was mainly to reduce the wage demands of the flight controllers by locking them out or replacing them if necessary. The liberal Alternative was to consider the wage demands of the flight controllers to be reasonable and to therefore pay them. The neutral position was somewhere between what the agency was offering and what the union was demanding.*

NOTES: *Table 1-13 continued*

3. *A key conservative goal was to keep down the costs to the airlines who would have to pay for some of the wage increase by way of increased airport fees. Conservatives were also concerned with keeping down the costs to the taxpayers. Liberals argued in favor of higher wages in order to compensate the workers for the stressful nature of the work. Liberals also advocated the buying of expensive equipment that would enable the workers to do their jobs with less stress and more safety.*

4. *An SOS Alternative might have various components. One might be to provide the workers with more benefits that do not involve increased wages such as shorter hours and more days off to relieve some of the stress of the work. A second component would be to subsidize new traffic control systems that would be safer and less stressful, but also less labor intensive thereby resulting in some layoffs. A third component might be a program to develop new skills for those flight controllers who might be laid off so they could obtain reasonably good jobs elsewhere.*

5. *The idea of new technologies that can increase benefits and reduce costs is an important type of SOS solution. Adopting it may, however, require special retraining for workers who are displaced by such new technologies. They are like workers displaced as a result of lowering tariffs or facilitating new entries into the labor force.*

TABLE 1-14.  DEALING WITH THE POLLUTION OF ARCHER DANIELS
MIDLAND

| Criteria<br><br>Alternatives | L GOAL<br>Reduce Pollution | C GOAL<br>Preserve Employment & Tax Base | N TOTAL<br>(Neutral Weights) | L TOTAL<br>(Liberal Weights) | C TOTAL<br>(Conservative Weights) |
|---|---|---|---|---|---|
| C<br>Alternative<br>Marketplace | 2 | 4 | 12 | 10 | 14* |
| L<br>Alternative<br>Punish Business Wrongdoers | 4 | 2 | 12 | 14* | 10 |
| N<br>Alternative<br>Exceptions | 3 | 3 | 12 | 12 | 12 |
| SOS<br>Alternative | 5 | 5 | 20 | 20** | 20** |

*NOTES:*

*The components of the SOS package might include:*

*1. Improve the manufacturing process to reduce pollution and simultaneously reduce expenses which makes the business more profitable.*

*2. Find commercial by-products for the undesirable waste.*

*3. Better communicate the non-toxic nature of the pollutions, but still reduce or eliminate their smell.*

One SOS alternative in the past has been to have well-placed subsidies to get manufacturing firms to adopt anti-pollution devices. Doing so could reduce pollution even better than the best expectation of liberals. Likewise doing so could be even more profitable to business than the best expectations of conservatives, especially if the subsidies more than cover the costs. That kind of "well-placed subsidy" may not be so beneficial to the taxpayer even with the reduced pollution if a better subsidy might exist. Such a subsidy could go to improving the manufacturing process so as to reduce pollution and simultaneously reduce manufacturing expenses, thereby making the business both cleaner and more profitable. That kind of pollution prevention technology is likely to be adopted by business forms without liberal threats, relatively inefficient subsidies, or the largely irrelevant marketplace. The new manufacturing process gets adopted because it is more efficient not because it is cleaner or more legal. That is generally the best kind of incentive to do what is socially desirable.

Still further examples could be given, especially if one broadly defines the concept of reducing costs and increasing benefits. There is overlap between this approach and some of the others, although it is better to have overlap in a check-list than to have gaps that would miss opportunities to achieve SOS solutions. One can consider the jury size problem to be related if one considers the goals to be increasing the benefits of convicting the guilty and decreasing the costs of convicting the innocent. An alternative way of phrasing the goals would be to (1) increase the benefits of acquitting the innocent and (2) decrease the costs of acquitting the guilty. The solution of videotaping the trials to aid the jurors' memory involves technology, but the SOS solution of note taking does not. Thus method of reducing costs and increasing benefits may involve improving the efficiency of procedures without necessitating technological innovation.

The last example is especially relevant to those who argue that SOS solutions are only possible with unrealistic increases in resources or unrealistic new technologies. The reality of many situations is that resources can often be increased and that new technologies can be developed. More important is the fact that many of these examples involve neither increased resources nor new technologies. Instead they involve thinking more imaginatively along unconventional but potentially productive lines, such as thinking about ways in which costs can be reduced and benefits can be increased simultaneously. Doing so can result in all major viewpoints coming out ahead of their best initial expectations.

### FOOTNOTES

1. For further details on the general nature of the nature of and need for super-optimum solutions, see Lawrence Susskind and Jeffrey Cruikshank, Breaking the Impasse: Consensual Approaches to Resolving Public Disputes (New York: Basic Books 1987); S. Nagel, Developing Nations and Super-Optimum Policy Analysis (Chicago: Nelson-Hall, 1991); Siabel Sawhill (ed.), Challenge to Leadership: Economic and Social Issues for the Next Decade (Washington, DC: Urban Institute, 1988); and S. Nagel, Higher Goals for America: Doing Better than the Best (Lanham, Md.: University Press of America, 1989).

2. On expanding the total resources, especially the gross national product, see Ira Magaziner and Robert Reich, Minding America's

Business: The Decline and Rise of the American Economy (New York: Harcourt, Brace, and Jovanovich, 1982); Amitai Etzioni, An Immodest Agenda: Rebuilding America Before the 21st Century (New York: McGraw Hill, 1983); Gar Alperovitz and Jeff Faux, Rebuilding America: A Blueprint for the New Economy (New York: Pantheon, 1984); Jerry Dermer (ed.), Competitiveness through Technology: What Business Needs from Government (Lexington, Mass.: Lexington-Heath, 1986); and Lawrence Lindsey, The Growth Experiment: How the New Tax Policy is Transforming the U.S. Economy (New York: Basic Books, 1990).

On increasing productivity in the public and private sectors, see Marc Holzer and S. Nagel (eds.), Productivity and Public Policy (Beverly Hills, Calif.: Sage, 1984); Rita Mae Kelly (ed.), Promoting Productivity in the Public Sector: Problems, Strategies, and Prospects (New York: St. Martin's, 1988); Marc Holzer and Arie Halachmi, Public Sector Productivity: A Resource Guide (New York: Garland, 1988); Michael LeBoeuf, The Productivity Challenge: How to Make it Work for America and You (New York: McGraw Hill, 1982; and Ryuzo Sato and Gilbert Suzawa, Research and Productivity: Endogenous Technical Change (Boston: Auburn House, 1983).

On increasing relevant innovation and creativity, see Don Kash, Perpetual Innovation: The New World of Competition (New York: Basic Books, 1989); Kristian Palda, Industrial Innovation: Its Place in the Public Policy Agenda (Toronto: The Fraser Institute, 1984); Veronica Mole and Dave Elliott, Enterprising Innovation: An Alternative Approach (London: Frances Pinter, 1987); John Agnew (ed.), Innovation Research and Public Policy (Syracuse, NY: Syracuse University, 1980); and Alex Osborn, Applied Imagination: Principles and Procedures of Creative Problem-Solving (New York: Scribner's, 1963).

3. On raising goals above what is considered the best, see Amital Etzioni, The Moral Dimension: Toward a New Economics (New York: The Free Press, 1988); Marcus Raskin, The Common Good: Its Politics, Policies, and Philosophy (New York, Routledge and Kegan Paul, 1986); Mary Clark, Arladne's Thread: The Search for New Modes of Thinking (New York: St. Martin's, 1989); and S. Nagel, Higher Goals for America: Doing Better than the Best (Lanham, Md.: University Press of America, 1989).

4. On big benefits for one side and low costs for the other as a method of arriving at super-optimum solutions, see the alternative dispute resolution literature that talks about each side giving on issues that are not so important to it and receiving on other issues that are important to it. See for example, William Ury, Jeanne Brett, and Stephen Goldberg, Getting Disputes Resolved: Designing Systems to Cut the Costs of Conflict (San Francisco: Jossey-Bass, 1988; Lawrence Susskind and Jeffrey Cruikshank, Breaking the Impasse: Consensual Approaches to Resolving Public Disputes (New York: Basic Books, 1987); S. Nagel and M. Mills, Multi-Criteria Methods for Alternative Dispute Resolution: with Microcomputer Software Applications (Westport, Conn.: Greenwood-

Quorum, 1990; and S. Nagel and M. Mills (eds.) <u>Systematic Analysis in Dispute Resolution</u> (Westport, Conn., Greenwood -Quorum, 1991).

On mediation as a special form of dispute resolution in contrast to win-lose procedures, see Kenneth Kressel and Dean Puritt (eds>), <u>Mediation Research: The Process and Effectiveness of Third-Party Intervention</u> (San Francisco: Jossey-Bass, 1989); Jay Folbert and Alison Taylor, <u>Mediation: A Comprehensive Guide to Resolving Conflicts Without Litigation</u> (San Francisco: Jossey-Bass, 1984); and Christopher Moore, <u>The Mediation Process: Practical Strategies for Resolving Conflict</u> (San Francisco: Jossey-Bass, 1986). Win-win solutions can be arrived at without third-party mediation if one or more of the negotiators successfully pursues a win-win or super-optimum solution, as described in Roger Fisher and William Ury, <u>Getting to Yes: Negotiating Agreement Without Giving In</u> (New York: Houghton-Mifflin, 1981); and Fred Jandt, <u>Win-Win Negotiating: Turning Conflict into Agreement</u> (New York: Wiley, 1985).

5.   On the third-party benefactor, especially in the context of the government intervening to reduce class conflict and ethnic conflict in housing and other urban problems, see Stuart Butler, <u>Enterprise Zones: Greenlining the Inner Cities</u> (New York: Universe Books, 1981); George Sternlieb and David Listokin (eds.), <u>New Tools for Economic Development: The Enterprise Zone, Development Bank, and RFC</u> (New Brunswick, N.J.: Rutgers University, 1981); Lester Salamon (ed.), <u>Beyond Privatization: The Tools of Government Action</u> (Washington, D.C.; Urban Institute, 1989); Lee Bawden and Felicity Skidmore (eds.), <u>Rethinking Employment Policy</u> (Washington, D.C.: Urban Institute, 1989); and Michael Ball, Michael Harloe, and Maartje Martens, <u>Housing and Social Change in Europe and the USA</u> (London: Routledge, 1988).

6.   On combining liberal and conservative alternatives, there is a literature dealing with the process of compromising and collaborating which is partly relevant. See Patrick Dobel, <u>Compromise and Political Action: Political Morality in Liberal and Democratic Life</u> (Savage, Md.: Rowman and Littlefield, 1990); and Barbara Gray, <u>Collaborating: Finding Common Ground for Multiparty Problems</u> (San Francisco: Jossey-Bass, 1989). More relevant literature, however, deals with how to combine non-mutually exclusive alternatives so that nothing is lost from either side and possibly a new higher synthesis is gained. That literature includes "Hegel: Dialectic and Nationalism" and "Marx and Dialectical Materialism," which are Chapters 30 and 33 respectively, in George Sabine, <u>A History of Political Theory</u> (New York: Holt, 1950). The idea of thesis, antithesis, and synthesis in Hegel and Marx leads to what one could consider to be a super-optimum solution, rather than a compromise. For further details on American higher education as providing a kind of super-optimum synthesis of the public and private sectors, see Samuel Gove and Thomas Stauffer (eds.), <u>Policy Controversies in Higher Education</u> (Westport, Conn.: Greenwood, 1986).

7. The literature on removing or decreasing the source of liberal-conservative conflicts includes the literature on dealing with dilemmas. See "The Dilemma" which is Chapter 13 in Lionel Ruby, Logic: An Introduction (Chicago, Ill.: Lippincott, 1950). The super-optimum solution is related to the idea of escaping through the horns of the dilemma by showing that there are other alternatives, such as an SOS alternative. Traditional reasoning is more associated with taking the dilemma by the horns whereby one shows that one horn or side is true and the other is false, or one is better than the other, analogous to a win-lose solution. For further details on the example of eliminating or reducing the capital punishment controversy by reducing the murder rate, see Robert Winslow, Crime in a Free Society (Encino, Calif.: Dickenson, 1977); Samuel Walker, Sense and Nonsense about Crime: A Policy Guide (Pacific Grove, Calif.: Brooks/Cole, 1989); and James Levine, Michael Musheno, Dennis Palumbo, Criminal Justice: A Public Policy Approach (New York: Harcourt, Brace and Jovanovich, 1980). The book by Walker has a kind of super-optimum perspective by showing defects in the conservative and liberal approaches to crime reduction and the need for a new synthesis of what each has to offer of a meaningful nature.

8. For general literature dealing with the approach of trying to develop a package of alternatives, one could look at the literature that attempts to philosophically defend eclecticism. See Harold Titus, Ethics for Today (New York: American Book Company, 1947). Literature on multi-criteria decision-making and spreadsheet software is also relevant to developing packages of alternatives and criteria. See Ching-Lai Hwang and Kwangsun Yoon, Multiple Attribute Decision Making: Methods and Applications (Berlin: Springer-Verlag, 1981); Nagel, Decision-Aiding Software: Skills, Obstacles and Applications (London: Macmillan, 1990); and Nagel (ed.), Applications of Decision-Aiding Software (London: Macmillan, 1991). For further details on the example of developing a package of alternatives for dealing with pretrial release, see Andy Hall, Pretrial Release Program Options (Washington, D.C.: National Institute of Justice, 1984); Wayne Thomas, Bail Reform in America (Berkeley, Calif.: University of California Press, 1976); Roy Flemming, Punishment Before Trial: An Organizational Perspective of Felony Bail Processes (New York: Longman, 1982).

9. For literature on the problem of jury size, see Hans Zeisel, "And Then There Were None: The Diminution of the Federal Jury," 38 *University of Chicago Law Review* 710 (1971), Lawrence Mills, "Six-Member and Twelve-Member Juries: An Empirical Study of Trial Results," 6 University of Michigan Journal of Law Reform 671 (1973), and S. Nagel and M. Neef, "Deductive Modeling to Determine an Optimum Jury Size and Fraction Required to Convict," *Washington University Law Quarterly* 1933 (1975).

For studies of the ways in which the general accuracy of juries can be improved with regard to simultaneously increasing the likelihood of convicting the guilty and acquitting the innocent, see Saul Kassin and Lawrence Wrightsman, *The American Jury on Trial: Psychological Perspectives* (Hemisphere Publishing Corporation, 1988), 199-168; and Steven Penrod, "Evaluating Techniques to Improve Juror Performance" (Unpublished paper presented at the American Judicature Society Conference on The American Jury and the Law, 1985).

There have been hundreds of studies of jury decision-making, but virtually none that are relevant to improving the public policies or legal rules that relate to the general accuracy of juries. See James Davis, Robert Bray, and Robert Holt, "The Empirical Study of Decision Processes in Juries: A Critical Review," in June Tapp and Felice Levine (eds.), *Law, Justice and the Individual in Society: Psychological and Legal Issues* (Holt, Rinehart and Winston, 1977). The typical outcome variable relates to whether the jury will decide in favor of the plaintiff or the defendant, not whether the jury will decide accurately. The typical input variable relates to the background or attitude characteristics of the jurors, not to the legal rules under which they operate such as prohibitions on note-taking or on having written instructions from the judge. It is easier to measure direction of jury decisions, rather than accuracy. It is also more relevant to the interests of psychologists and social scientists (as contrasted to lawyers) to talk about backgrounds and attitudes (rather than legal rules), although the legal rule of jury size fits psychology interests and can be more easily measured than the nature of legal precedents.

# CHAPTER 2

## CAUSAL ANALYSIS IN SOS
## ADOPTION AND IMPLEMENTATION

### I. THINKING ABOUT THE CONCEPT OF SOS PREDICTION

An SOS is a policy alternative in which both liberal and conservative come out ahead of their initial best expectations. It implies a normative analysis as to what alternative should be adopted. In dealing with SOS prediction, we are talking about what alternative will be adopted or why an alternative was adopted rather than what should be adopted.

They are closely related in the following senses:

1. In order to decide what should be adopted, we should show some awareness of what can be or will be under various circumstances. We should not recommend impossible alternatives.

2. If we want to explain why an alternative was adopted, it is best to do so in terms of what the participants, or decision-makers think should be adopted, or what they thought should have been adopted. That also means taking their goals into consideration in order to predict or explain.

3. Thus, prescription makes use of prediction in order to prescribe. Likewise, prediction makes use of prescription in order to predict.

An ordinary prediction differs from an SOS prediction in the following ways.

1. An SOS prediction may be concerned with predicting what SOS alternative will be adopted, and especially whether an SOS alternative will be adopted or whether the SOS alternative will be adopted.

2. It can also involve an attempt to explain why some situations lead to SOS alternatives and others do not.

## II.  CAUSAL ANALYSIS OF SOS ADOPTION

### A.  UP THE ANTE

One phenomenon that may tend to occur more with an SOS than with an ordinary solution is that after the solution has been suggested, each side feels the other side is getting such a good deal that each side tends to up the ante by increasing their demands.  That is an aspect of the psychology of super-optimum solutions.  Each side should really do just the opposite.  Each side should say, I am getting such a good deal that I should not be so demanding or else the whole thing might fall through.

An example is the labor dispute discussed in Chapter 6 on arriving at SOS solutions.  The attorney for the farm workers was bothered by the fact that the growers were getting off lightly, regardless how much the farm workers might be benefiting.  As a result, he came up with new demands that were not mentioned before.

We could name this the Mazmanian phenomenon in honor of Daniel Mazmanian's saying that he does not care how much Nagel is doing for the Policy Studies Organization, Nagel is benefiting too much himself. That is the phenomenon in dispute resolution where people are not so oriented toward maximizing their side.  The Mazmanian-type person is marching to a different drummer in which a key goal is keeping down the benefits of other people in the dispute resolution situation.  This is also the age-old phenomenon of cutting off one's body to spite one's head or some variation thereon whereby one suffers great costs in order to see to it that the other side does not get any benefits.  It is a mindset that tends to view dispute resolution as being a defeat if the other person comes out ahead.

That did not occur in the Sanyo case described in Chapter 1.  To the extent that the Sanyo case super-optimum solution was disrupted, it was not because the lawyers for the plaintiff wanted to see the Sanyo company hurt or did not want to see it benefit. The Sanyo case had virtually no emotion to it at all compared to the class, ideological, and personal conflict of the Ramirez case.  The lawyers for the plaintiff in the

Sanyo case did not like the SOS because they did not want to be paid off in computers, television sets, insurance claims, or annuities. They wanted cash. They therefore preferred the old-fashioned splitting the dollars difference. They would then take their one-third and go home. Therefore, a key implementation problem has to do with disputants in dispute resolution situations being represented by outsiders such as lawyers. Their interests may not be the same as the disputants. They may not be so interested in implementing an SOS that would benefit the disputants because the solution does not benefit them sufficiently over a traditional solution and may even be worse than a traditional solution.

## B. REPRESENTATIVES

Try to make sure that not only do the disputants come out ahead of their best expectations, but also their representatives. If their representatives do not come out so well, then they may present a bad roadblock toward implementing the SOS. In the Sanyo case, one thing that could have been done was to provide for cash side-payments. The Sanyo Company was not willing to do that. That would defeat the SOS if they had to pay a lot of cash to a plaintiff's lawyer, as contrasted to giving low-cost computers or television sets to the plaintiff.

Another solution is to make it explicit as part of the agreement that the plaintiff (Traveller's Insurance Company) will gladly pay a cash payment to the plaintiff's lawyer in view of the benefits that the plaintiff is getting. If the plaintiff is getting one million dollars worth of computers and television sets, they would not necessarily pay one-third of a million in cash to the lawyer, but at least one-third of half the $900,000 which was the plaintiff's original best expectation. The most the lawyers expected to get was probably $150,000, which would be one-third of $450,000 if the demand would only be cut in half if the defendant were offering zero. If the defendant were offering $300,000, then $1,200,000 is cut in half meaning a $600,000 settlement, and the plaintiff's lawyers get $200,000 or one-third of that The Traveler's Insurance Company would still come out ahead even if they gave their lawyer one-third of $900,000, or $300,000. They would still have $700,000 worth of computers, plus insurance claims worth maybe more than the $300,000. The important point is that explicit attention has to be paid to how the plaintiff's lawyer is going to be compensated and not just how the plaintiff is going to be compensated.

## C.  REGARDLESS HOW WELL THE OTHER SIDE DOES

A second key point is to somehow educate both sides into seeking to maximize their own benefits minus costs, regardless how well the other side does.  That should not be so hard to do even if one side considers it a benefit to make the other side suffer or deprive the other side of benefits. Surely even people with that point of view would value receiving benefits themselves directly, as being worth more than the indirect satisfaction of depriving the other side of benefits.

One can say that the lawyer in the Ramirez case may be messing things up more than the plaintiff clients.  The lawyer may be feeling more emotionally upset than the plaintiffs are.  That is partly an ego thing. Lawyers sometimes tend to have big egos, and maybe even more so with lawyers who represent migrant labor.  They may have a tendency to view themselves as the great white father coming to free the slaves and have all kinds of complexes about their importance. The labor lawyer in that case did indicate he was having problems with regard to ego and status matters that should have been considered more.  He was especially bothers by such things as the defendant's lawyer talking longer. Defendants do need to be brought around in a more time-consuming way than plaintiffs.  It is the defendants who have to give and the plaintiffs who receive.

## D.  SUSPICION THAT A TRAP IS INVOLVED

The Camp David Accord almost fell apart as a result of suspicion that a trap was involved.  The passage of time tends to cure that, although the agreement had to be reached before the passage of time could occur.

## E.  REMOVING VERSUS ADDING GOALS

An SOS may sometimes be more readily found or implemented by subtracting a goal rather than adding one.  That is true if one side is especially interested in Goal X in which the other side is negative or not interested.  If Goal X is dividing them, then removing it as a goal may facilitate a solution.  Normally, adding more goals provides each side with a package of things it can receive which it values, and the other side with a package of things it can receive which the first side does not consider as giving up very much.  The package solution is a most meaningful SOS approach, and it involves multi-criteria thinking.

If A rejects an SOS solution because B will also benefit, then that is a form of spitefulness.  If A fails to think toward an SOS solution because gain by B is perceived to mean a loss by A, then that may be unduly narrow thinking. It can result in missed opportunities to find ways in which both A and B can benefit. An example is the opposition of the American Society for Public Administration to marketing journals of its sections to libraries for fear that doing so will detract from the marketing of the Public Administration Review. It might, however, be quite possible that a marketing program could be developed in which PAR and the section journals could both come out ahead.

## F. VESTED JOBS AND PROPERTY AS AN OBSTACLE TO SOS ADOPTION

A big problem in replacing a traditional compromise with an SOS solution is there may already be vested jobs or property in the previous decision, they to be taken into consideration. An example is that both conservatives and liberals strongly endorse rent supplements over public housing projects. Conservatives do so partly because rent supplements represent a marketplace solution to housing for the poor. Liberals do so partly because rent supplements facilitate integration along economic and racial lines. The rent supplement program has, however, not replaced public housing.

A big part of the explanation is the vested jobs and property in the previous solution. Public housing was previously supported by liberals as a form of equitable socialism. It has been tolerated by conservatives as an approach to housing for the poor which would not involve integration at a time when integration was less acceptable. Neither of those original purposes have much explanatory value for the retention of public housing over a rent supplements program, but the existence of vested jobs and property does.

The key question is not what explains why the SOS solution has not been fully adopted, but rather what to do about that kind of interfering factor. The traditional compromise approach is a variation on grandfathering or a tolerated zoning use. Such a solution means that no new public housing projects are built but the old ones are allowed to die of old age. It also means that people holding jobs under the old system are allowed to retain them, but a minimum of replacement occurs when the former jobholders die, retire, or resign.

An SOS solution that relies more on well-place subsidies would phase out the property as quickly as possible, rather than wait for nature obsolescence. A fast phase-out though would not mean a wasteful dynamiting of the public housing projects as was done with the Pruitt-Igoe Homes in St. Louis. Instead, the projects could be made available along with appropriate subsidies for use a factories, warehouses, or other buildings as part of an inner-city Enterprise Zone project which is an

SOS in itself. The jobholders could also be provided with well-placed subsidies for retraining, buying small businesses, or other alternative activities that fit their skills.

This problem of what to do about vested jobs and property comes up in many SOS situations, such as tariff reduction which can be highly mutually beneficial internationally. Adequate provision needs to be made for people and property that have a vested interest in the previous, less beneficial activities.

## III. CAUSES OF SUCCESSFUL AND UNSUCCESSFUL SOS IMPLEMENTATION

### A. CLARIFYING SOS SUCCESS

The concept of super-optimum solutions has not been around as a formal concept for very long. It is possible that even in prehistoric times, two people may have argued over something and resolved their dispute in such a way that they both came out better than their initial best expectations. The idea as a formal concept probably did not get articulated until about the 1950's with the development of game theory in mathematics, operations research, and management science. The typical game or human interaction studied involved a relatively fixed pie in which the gains of one side were equal to the losses of the other side. Thus these were referred to as zero-sum games because the combined results for both sides added to zero. Game theorists mentioned non-zero-sum games, where both sides (or all sides) could come out ahead, as contrasted to a winner and a loser. However, they developed virtually no literature on the subject.

The idea of all sides coming out ahead (or at least not taking a loss) was actually formalized as a concept in the early 1900's by Vilfredo Pareto. That is the concept of the Pareto Optimum. For Pareto, it was a measurement concept. He never discussed causal factors for bringing it about, or for explaining variance as to why it sometimes exists and sometimes does not in human interaction. His concept is also a very weak one in the sense that one could devise a policy for a billion inhabitants of China in which nobody gains or loses except one person who gains one unit. That would be classified as a Pareto Optimum. Common sense though might say that surely one could do better than that, and such a result thus does not deserve to be called an optimum except in an arbitrary definitional sense, rather than in empirically observing how people use concepts like best, optimum, or even good.

In the 1970's alternative dispute resolution began to acquire popularity among lawyers, business people, union leaders, and others. It basically meant resolving disputes by alternatives other than going to court where one side wins and the other side loses. The original motivation for going to an alternative arbitrator or mediator (rather than a judge) was partly to avoid delay. Later, more emphasis was put on the purpose of achieving win-win solutions where everybody comes out ahead. Coming out ahead, though, tended to mean nothing more than coming out better than one's worst expectations.

Thus in a damages suit if the plaintiff demanded $100,000 and the defendant refused to offer more than $20,000, one might consider a $60,000 settlement as being a win-win settlement. The plaintiff could have received nothing as a result of losing on the liability issue, and the defendant could have wound up paying $100,000, rather than $60,000. Under more recent structured settlements, the plaintiff might receive $10,000 a year for every year over age 60 which would be worth more than $100,000 in the calculations of the plaintiff. The same arrangement could be worth possible less than $20,000 in the calculations of the defendant insurance company by way of its actuarial calculations and its depositing a reserve that draws compound interest to establish an endowment or annuity until the payments need to be made. that is more truly a super-optimum solution.

In the 1980's, super-optimizing took on a more meaningful form than the Pareto measurement concept, the non-zero-sum game, or the win-win dispute resolution. The new more meaningful form in the field of public policy was supply-side economics of the Reagan administration and economists like Arthur Laffer, along with industrial policy of such opposition candidates as Gary Hart and economists like Robert Reich. The emphasis in both perspectives is on the idea of the expanded pie or gross national product where all major viewpoints can come out ahead of their best expectations largely through well-placed subsidies and tax breaks.

A good example relates to dealing with the national deficit. Traditional conservatives argue in favor of reducing domestic spending and increasing taxes on consumers like the value-added tax. The traditional liberals argue for reducing defense spending and increasing taxes on the rich like the progressive income tax. both the SOS conservatives associated with supply-side economics and the SOS liberals associated with industrial policy tend to argue that the best way to reduce the deficit may be to increase spending, but spending that will stimulate increased productivity and thus increase the GNP which is the tax base. One can then obtain more tax income to reduce the deficit even with a constant or lowered tax rate. Both sides also argue that the deficit might be better dealt with by reducing some kinds of taxes where doing so is a tax break designed to stimulate increased productivity in a manner similar to a well-placed spending subsidy.

## B. SOME EXPERIENCES OF THE REAGAN ADMINISTRATION

Thus going into the 1980's under the Reagan administration, the United States served as a partial laboratory to try these new super-optimizing ideas of supply-side Reaganomics to see how well they would work in enabling all major segments of the population to come out ahead of their best expectations. Even those who have favorable attitudes toward the Reagan administration will generally concede that Reaganomics did not do as well as expected. It certainly did not increase the GNP beyond inflation enough to reduce the deficit. In fact, the deficit during the eight years of the Reagan administration tripled in the sense that the per capita deficit as of 1988 was three times what it was as of 1980. That also means that as of about 1984, President Reagan had succeeded in incurring more of an accumulated national debt than all the previous presidents put together by causing the national debt to double even on a per capita basis.

What went wrong with the idea that well-placed subsidies and tax breaks could stimulate productivity and the GNP enough so that we could have more spending, lower taxes, less deficit, and a higher standard of living simultaneously? As a matter of hindsight, there seem to be three key causal factors which can serve as a learning experience for improving future SOS policy-making and implementation. The first factor is that well-placed subsidies and tax breaks require that strings be attached in the sense of a quid pro quo in return for the subsidy or tax break that will be likely to result in increased national productivity. The 30% across-the-board tax cut was the opposite of that. It had no strings attached or quid pro quo. The reasoning was that somehow the invisible hand of laissez-faire capitalism would guide the money saved from not having to pay taxes into improving the technology of U.S. steel making, automobile manufacturing, and other industries.

Instead, the money saved went disproportionately into three relatively unproductive uses. One was real estate, largely for speculative purposes. Buying real estate for the purpose of building a new modernized factory can add to national productivity. Buying real estate for the purpose of waiting for a highway to go through or urban sprawl to come by does nothing for national productivity. The second unproductive use was luxury goods. It is interesting to note that as of 1980, the only long distance area codes in the United States were on land. After the 30% tax cut, the quantity of yachts with telephones became so great off the

Atlantic coast and the Pacific coast that two new area codes had to be established just for all the yachts using their cellular telephones. The third relatively unproductive purpose was high executive salaries for American corporate executives bearing little relation to the extent to which they had improved the market share of their companies. General Motors is a good example where the annual salary of the chief executive rose multiple times while their market share drastically decreased in favor of Toyota and other Japanese manufacturers whose salaries are a fraction of the CEO salary at General Motors.

Tax cuts that might have made a lot more sense could have included not a 30% tax cut to US Steel, but a 60% tax cut or even 100% tax cut, meaning no obligation to pay any income taxes for the time period covered. The key aspect is not the size of the tax cut but rather the requirement that US Steel in return for the tax cut introduce more oxygenated steel making which is more competitive than traditional blast furnaces. Getting US Steel to do so may have required substantially more than a 30% tax cut, but with that kind of string attached. It might have required a 200% tax cut whereby US Steel would figure out what taxes it owed and then the U.S. government would pay that amount to US Steel rather than vice versa. That would in effect be a subsidy, though, rather than a tax cut. US Steel does have a great deal of trouble getting needed capital for adopting new technologies ever since it has been put into competition with Japanese, German, and Scandinavian steel and had to respond competitively.

The second big causal factor that interfered with the successful implementation of supply-side economics in the Reagan administration was that where strings were attached, the amount of money needed to get the strings accepted was too small. A good example was the Enterprise Zones idea. Its basic feature was offering inducements to private enterprise to locate or relocate in the inner city in order to provide productive employment opportunities for people who might otherwise be  ·  unemployed and a drain on the taxpayer and the deficit. The idea was partly borrowed from the British Labor Party and the Carter administration to the credit of the Reagan administration in being receptive to new ideas. The size of the subsidies, however, were too small to offer much of an inducement. Insult was added to cheapness by attempting to offer business firms partial exemptions form economic regulations governing minimum wages, maximum hours, child labor, equal employment, environmental protection, workplace safety, and whatever other regulations could be relaxed, but congress would not go along with that. The amount of money for the 30% tax cut was huge, but no strings attached. The Enterprise zones had lots of strings attached as to what the business firms were to do in employing people, but the amount of money was to paltry.

The third causal factor needed for successful implementation is to have people who are skilled in knowing the technical aspects of a well-placed subsidy or tax break versus money down the drain. A good example of the lack of concern for that causal element is in the grants of the Department of Housing and Urban Development in the 1980's. Those grants had big money behind them and lots of strings attached. The grants had potential for contracting for meaningful scattered-site housing and urban development for the poor and lower middle-class people in ways that could stimulate their ambition toward being more productive as contrasted to old-fashioned concentrated public housing. The people who administered the grants, though, frequently had no training in housing or urban development. They did, however, know how to distinguish a Republican campaign contributor form applicants who had not met that criterion. As a result, some of the HUD programs were filled with corruption for which the criminal prosecutions and missed opportunities have still not been completed.

In order to provide for well-placed subsidies, it is helpful to have people who are not only trained in the substance of what they are administering such as housing and urban development, but also more generalized training in systematic public policy evaluation. The training does not have to be part of a formal degree program. It could be training offered within the Department of Housing and Urban Development or the Office of Personnel Management. It should, however, be more than a half-day or a weekend. It should probably involved at lease the equivalent of a semester of solid reading, discussion, and lectures by practitioners and academics who have some recognized expertise in the substantive area and the general evaluative procedures.

The supply-side policies of the 1980's were clearly not as successful as they could have been. Maybe they were not successful at all if the goal was to reduce the deficit. Nevertheless, President Reagan deserves considerable credit for having been the first president (and not likely to the be the last) to have super-optimizing philosophy that emphasizes expanding the GNP-pie as a way of enabling the rich and poor to both come out ahead rather than think in terms of trade-offs. That SOS orientation can also apply to blacks and whites, females and males, north and south, and other categories of people who are traditionally thought of as being in conflict over a relatively fixed pie. President Reagan did succeed in arriving at a super-optimum solution in foreign policy by bringing about the arms control agreements. They made both the United States and the Soviet Union better off than their best expectations, although the full benefits of the peace dividends have not yet been received. President Reagan seems to have been a more imaginative thinker on these SOS-related ideas than either the Republican or Democratic candidate who ran for the presidency to replace him.

## C. SOME EXPERIENCES FROM GREAT SOCIETY LEGISLATION

In addition to strings attached, big money, and competent personnel, there are other causal factors that have already been observed in the short time that the American government has been experimenting with SOS-related policies. The above examples mainly involve Republicans. A good example involving Democrats as the key policy-makers is the air pollution legislation of 1972, which is closely associated with Senator Edmund Muskie, a would-be Democratic candidate for president. As with President Reagan, Senator Muskie deserves credit for innovative SOS thinking but one should still recognize possible errors that interfered with effective implementation. More specifically, we are referring to the provisions in the air pollution legislation designed to stimulate the development of the electric automobile.

The electric automobile if it were effective would be a super-optimum solution to many problems simultaneously, including pollution, energy, and the sagging automobile industry. An electric automobile does not have an internal combustion engine. It runs on a big battery, or a small battery with big storage power. It therefore does not spew cancer-causing exhaust fumes. It does not run on gasoline, and thus it is not dependent on Arab countries or the oil companies. The price of an effective electric automobile would probably be substantially less than an internal combustion automobile. That would be good for consumers and the volume of automobile sales, possibly with an even better profit ratio.

The big problem with present electric cars is that they either require a long extension cord like the electric cars in the Dodgem rides in amusement parks or they require inconvenient recharging every few miles. The object is to develop a battery that will store enough electricity so that a car can go about 450 miles without recharging. That is the distance that internal combustion cars can generally go without needing more gasoline, figuring 30 miles to the gallon and a 15 gallon tank. Batteries can now be created that will move a motor vehicle 450 miles without recharging, but one needs to attach a truck to the back of one's car to carry the huge battery, which is not a very efficient way to travel. It just so happens that although the electricity field has seen amazing developments over the last 150 years such as electric lights, radio-TV phonographs, movie projectors, refrigerators, telephones, computers, etc., there has been virtually no great breakthroughs in the storage battery since Mr. Volta invented the voltaic cell in the early 1800's. We now have dry batteries instead of his wet battery, but they do not store a lot more energy.

If we could get a real breakthrough in being able to store energy, we could not only solve the problem of air pollution due to automobiles, we could maybe solve all our energy problems. That is so because the biggest obstacle to using large-scale solar energy is our inability to store solar energy for rainy days. It has been proposed to build a large microwave in the sky above the cloud layer, and then never have to worry about rainy or cloudy days. The microwave would tilt slightly every second toward a different place on earth and send a laser beam of solar energy through the clouds to Dusseldorf, Tokyo, Chicago, etc. Unfortunately with current technology, the microwave platform would have to be about a mile square. We are having a great deal of trouble getting platforms in the sky that are ten feet square, let alone 5,280 feet square. The cost is horrendous. We would not need any microwave in the sky if we had big storage batteries on earth. All we would need is a lot of saucer contraptions and solar-cell devices to pick up the sun when it is shining and store its energy for the cloudy days.

In 1972, the air pollution legislation sought to stimulate the development of a powerful battery that would be small enough to fit into cars and inexpensive enough to be affordable by the average person. The traditional way to stimulate such a development has been to promise the inventor a monopolistic patent. The idea of monopolistic patents as incentives was one of the innovative contributions of the founding fathers of the United States since they incorporated the idea into Article 1 of the Constitution. For about 100 years, the monopolistic patent did serve the purpose of stimulating technological innovation. As of the 20th century, though, there have probably been more cases where innovative inventors have been discouraged by the patent system. What now often happens is an imaginative thinker develops a truly new and useful idea. He or she then seeks to patent or market it, and is sued by a big corporation that has a related patent. The imaginative inventor can not hold out for ten years and a million dollars worth of litigation to establish his or her idea as being original and different.

Senator Muskie (as a precursor of the well-placed subsidy) specified in his 1972 air pollution legislation that the stimulant to inventing this highly useful storage battery would be a statutorily specified guarantee that the inventor would be able to count on the federal government replacing its fleet of motor vehicles with the new battery-driven electric cars and trucks. That is a subsidy that may amount to billions of dollars with just the federal government as a customer, but much more than that since with the federal prize, one could then service the world market for trillions of dollars.

This is a well-placed subsidy in the sense that (for one thing) it has strings attached. It specifies that the battery must enable a car to go about 450 miles, be small, and be inexpensive. It has big money as a reward. It is also being administered by the National Academy of Sciences. They are competent people when it comes to examining battery inventions, or at least they know where to find the right physicists and engineers. It even has super-optimum characteristics. Conservatives generally want to retain the patent system. Liberals want it abolished or greatly modified. The conservative approach may stimulate some inventiveness, even though the inventor may have a false notion of what is involved in getting and marketing a patentable product. The liberal approach may stimulate desirable competition among firms in an industry that might otherwise be controlled by a patent-holder. The well-placed subsidy can stimulate inventiveness while at the same time not providing a stultifying monopoly.

In spite of those good characteristics of this kind of subsidy, no one has come forward to collect the prize. What is wrong? One could say that maybe it is technologically too difficult. One could also say that maybe this is not such a well-placed subsidy after. The defect here is that the subsidy is only obtained after one has succeeded in developing the technological innovation. No provision was made for setting up a system of grants to enable physicists, engineers, and other would-be inventors of various relevant aspects to obtain funding to develop components and stages that would eventually lead to the final desired product. What is needed is a program somewhat like the National Science Foundation or the National Institutes of Health. They both provide grants for pure research and some applied research. Their grants are not big enough to develop an atomic bomb or to put a man on the moon, but big enough to move research incrementally in the right direction.

What may be lacking in delegating this kind of funding to the National Science Foundation is a need for encouraging unconventional thinking. A big problem with the NSF that makes its subsidies often not so well-placed is that virtually all its subsidies must pass the test of peer review or review by other experts in one's field. That is clearly an improvement on review by patronage personnel emphasizing partisan loyalty. The people who participate as reviewers in peer review, however, may be overly sensitive to applicants who propose to do something that will make the conventional experts look wrong or unimaginative. In other words, what may be needed is review of grant applications by technical experts in the Department of Energy who are not academics with sensitive egos, and who will be able to welcome unconventional but possibly promising grant applications.

## D. SUCCESSFUL SOS EXPERIENCES

The above examples from the 30% tax cut, Enterprise Zones, HUD grants, and subsidies for electric cars were all defective in some important way. Perhaps no well-placed subsidy or tax break can be perfect. We need to learn form past experiences as to how future subsidies and tax breaks can be made better. We also need to avoid the paralysis that might come from over-emphasizing past mistakes. It may be better to try to achieve an imaginative well-placed subsidy or tax break and only get halfway to one's goal than to resort to (1) conservative do-nothing approaches, (2) liberal over-regulation approaches, or (3) half-hearted compromises.

We should also note that there have been a number of liberal and conservative policies adopted within the last 20 years that could qualify as successful super-optimum solutions. One example is the rent-supplement policy for dealing with low-income housing. The traditional conservative approach is to leave low-income housing to the marketplace where such housing is understandably non-existent since private enterprise cannot afford to provide decent housing to poor people without government help. The traditional liberal approach is government-owned public housing which has concentrated poor people into jungle-like dormitories to the detriment of the tenants, HUD as a landlord, and the taxpayers. The super-optimum solution has been to provide a rent supplement to low-income people so they can rent decent housing in the private market. Under such a system, the tenants have decent housing and an increased sense of self-worth which may result in more productive ambition. The landlords have tenants who can afford to pay a reasonable rent. The taxpayer is better off because the government does not have to build or maintain the housing. The tenants may also be saving taxpayers money by being more productive wage earners, and thereby contributing multiplier and compounding effects to the gross national product. The system also results in integrated neighborhoods and better role models and peer groups for the children. That is partly a liberal SOS policy from the Great Society and the Carter administration but carried on by the Reagan administration in recognition of its value and its emphasis on the private sector.

An example of a successful SOS-type policy from the Reagan administration (besides the arms control example already mentioned) is the marketable pollution right. It was implemented by the EPA under Reagan, although mentioned before then. It mainly applies to water or air pollution. It could involve each business firm on a given river segment receiving so many units of pollution rights. The quantity of rights given depends on formulas which take into consideration the size of the firm, the nature of its products, and how well it is doing in keeping down pollution. A firm that is doing a relatively bad job in generating 500 pollution units may only receive 300 pollution rights. It then has to either reduce its pollution or buy further rights from other business firms that have a surplus. Those other business firms may demand high payment for rights in their surplus, especially if they are competing business firms. That system may cause the polluter to reduce its pollution more than would occur under traditional government regulation, and more than would occur if society relies on the generally irrelevant marketplace to reduce pollution. The system is super-optimum by pleasing conservatives with its reliance on the private market in the buying and selling of pollution rights, and by pleasing liberals with its ability to be adopted (unlike pollution taxes) and to be reasonably effective in pollution reduction (unlike regulation which is subject to easier evasions and delays).

From these examples, one might be able to conclude that successfully implemented super-optimum solutions tend to have the following characteristics:

1. Strings attached if subsidies or tax breaks are involved, with monitoring that is capable of determining whether the strings or specifications are being properly met.

2. Sufficient money to get the job done, regardless whether we are talking about a subsidy, a tax break, or some other kind of government appropriation.

3. Competent and objective personnel to administer the policy.

4. Proper timing and sequencing of the stages involved in achieving the goals.

5. Support from both conservatives and liberals.

6. Failure of previous do-nothing and over-regulation policies.

7. Imaginative thinking in developing the SOS solution in the first place and in working to get it adopted and implemented.

8. Reading about other policy situations where SOS-type solutions were attempted or should have been attempted in order to learn form past mistakes as to the causes of successful SOS policy implementation.

# PART TWO:

# THE ECONOMIC PROCESS
# OF SOS SOLUTIONS

# CHAPTER 3

## INCENTIVES, GROWTH, AND PRODUCTIVITY

### I. INTRODUCTION

This chapter on incentives, growth, and productivity deals with important cross-cutting matters. The idea of increased societal productivity is so important for all the policy problems that it is worth a chapter of its own. Growth of resources may be the answer to trade-offs, scarce resources, and deprivation of all kinds. Just as the answer to being poor is to get rich or at least get more money, likewise the answer to how to deal with so many expensive problems is also to get more money to deal with them. Getting more money does not mean running printing presses, it means producing goods that have value that can be sold for money.

One might then ask how one increases societal productivity. A key answer is well-placed subsidies and tax breaks. One then says how do you know a well-placed one from an ill-placed one. The answer to that question is that one systematically thinks about the goals, the alternatives, the relations between alternatives and goals, and one observes overall scores and sensitivity analysis, as contrasted to a more ideological approach or a more sloppy approach. Saying well-placed subsidies and tax breaks is the same thing as saying providing incentives to be more productive.

## II. AN INCENTIVES PERSPECTIVE

### A. ENCOURAGING SOCIALLY DESIRED BEHAVIOR IN GENERAL

All policy problems can be viewed as problems that involve encouraging socially desired behavior. A good checklist for generating ideas on how public policy can encourage socially desired behavior is to think in terms of:
1. Increasing the benefits of doing right.
2. Decreasing the costs of doing right.
3. Increasing the costs of doing wrong.
4. Decreasing the benefits of doing wrong.
5. Increasing the probability that the benefits and costs will occur.

Each specific problem involves different doers, benefits, and costs. For example, an incentives approach to the problems of unemployment and inflation might involve the following five-pronged approach in accordance with the above framework:

1. Tax incentives to business firms and labor unions for keeping prices and wages down. Also monetary incentives to employers to hire the unemployed and monetary incentives to the unemployed to accept training and jobs.

2. Decreasing the costs of finding jobs and workers through better information systems.

3. Increasing the costs of violating price-wage guidelines and work incentives by withdrawing benefits and (in rare cases) by fines and other negative penalties.

4. Confiscating the benefits of price-wage violations by special taxes on the gains.

5. More accurate information on prices, wages, and unemployment in order to allocate the benefits and costs more effectively.

As a second example of this kind of perspective, we might look at crime reduction. The following five-pronged approach would be especially appropriate there:

1. The main benefit of complying with the law should be that doing so gives one access to opportunities that are cut off to law violators. That means legitimate career opportunities must be provided to those who would otherwise turn to crime.

2. One cost of doing right may be a loss of prestige among youthful gang members who consider criminal behavior an indicator of

toughness. There is a need for working to redirect such peer group values so that toughness can be displayed in more constructive ways.

3.  The costs of doing wrong can include negative incentives of long prison sentences, but it may be more meaningful to emphasize the withdrawal of career opportunities which would otherwise be present.

4.  Provisions should be made for facilitating the confiscating of the property gains of criminal wrongdoing, and decreasing the vulnerability of the targets of crime to lessen the benefits obtained.

5.  The probability of arrest and conviction can be increased partly through more professionalism among law enforcement personnel.

One could apply that kind of analysis to all policy problems. One might consider such an approach to be an optimum set of procedures for optimizing societal goals. One can, however, do better than the optimum with regard to procedure as well as substance. Doing better in this context means not having situations occur where people need to be stimulated to do the right thing or deterred from doing the wrong thing. There are two ways to arrange for such situations to never occur, either by making them physically or mentally impossible.

An example of making wrongdoing physically impossible is not allowing cars to be sold that can go faster than a certain speed limit, such as 55 miles per hour except in short spurts. Then there is much less need to have a system of punishments for doing wrong or a system designed to determine who the wrongdoers are. Another example would be prohibiting the manufacture of certain kinds of aerosol cans that do great harm to the ozone in the environment. Still another example would be prohibiting the existence of nuclear breeder reactors to supply energy in view of their likelihood of leading to the production of bomb-grade plutonium.

An example of making certain kinds of wrongdoing mentally impossible or close to it is murder, robbery, burglary, and other street crimes among most middle-class people. When affronted in a store, on a bus, or elsewhere, the average person never thinks of the possibility of pulling a gun or going home and getting one in order to kill the person who has insulted him. It is an unthinkable thought. Likewise, when driving late at night and observing a convenience store or a gas station that is open with no customers around, the average person never thinks of robbing the place. It is a though t as unthinkable as flapping one's arms to fly to an appointment when one is late. The reason murder and robbery are unthinkable is not that they are physically impossible or because of a fear of the penalties, but because for most people their socialization has been such that those thoughts are not within the realm of one's normal thinking.

A <u>society operating at the optimum or above it</u> on various policy problems can thus be defined as a society which distributes benefits and costs in such a way as to encourage socially desired behavior with regard to unemployment, inflation, crime, and other social problems, but which also does as much as possible to make undesirable behavior impossible and/or unthinkable.

## B.  SOME ASPECTS OF WELL-PLACED SUBSIDIES

A question was raised as to where the money is going to come form to pay the well-placed subsidies.

1.  The usual liberal answer is to take it from defense spending.

2.  The usual conservative answer is to take it from the domestic spending.

3.  The SOS answer is that the subsidy money comes from the subsidy money in the sense that the early subsidies tend to stimulate increased productivity.  This generates increased gross national product, which in turn generates increased tax revenues.  This in turn generates a lot more subsidies than were available in the first round, and so on in each subsequent round.  It is better than a perpetual motion machine where the output is constant.  Here the output keeps increasing.

A question was also raised as to whether well-placed subsidies are the answer to all the public policy problems.

1.  One answer is that all public policy problems could benefit form well-placed subsidies.

2.  Well-placed subsidies alone, however, are not enough for dealing with any of the policy problems.

Examples of other kinds of legislation besides subsidy legislation that were given include:

1.  If one wants to improve inner city schools, throwing money at them in the form of compensatory education will not do it because the main drawback to inner city schools is the lack of peer group stimulation toward going on to college.  That requires legislation directed toward economic class integration which may mean the use of rent supplements which do cost money.  But that is a different kind of spending than spending for education.

2.  On the matter of voter registration and turnout, the key need is legislation which registers people by virtue of the census of on-site registration.  That costs no subsidy money.  Allowing people to vote in any polling place costs no subsidy money.

3.  The main example that we gave was the Johnson administration's idea of spending $15 billion to eliminate the poverty gap as the solution to the poverty problem.

4. In the context of technological innovation, the need for changing the patent system and the product liability system to facilitate technological innovation and diffusion. This is contrasted with just throwing money at would-be innovators or would-be adopters.

Every aspect of the poverty problem involves something other than moving every poor person with a family of four from a below $10,000 a year income up to $10,000.

1. On voting rights for the poor, what was said above applies.

2. On educational opportunities, what was said above also applies.

3. On the matter of criminal justice, moving up to the line between poverty and non-poverty is not going to necessarily make a big dent in the extent to which people who are at that line are involved in criminal behavior. It may actually increase their criminal behavior by giving rising expectations. It also is not going to make any significant dent on their ability to hire counsel. A person with a $10,000 income is still going to be dependent on the public defender.

4. Housing opportunities are not going to substantially change. Although they could change, because being at the $10,000 figure rather than the $5,000 figure may put one above a threshold where a rent supplement become more meaningful than living in public housing.

5. Employment opportunities are not going to increase without a program for upgrading skills, though that costs money. But it is different than simply giving a person who has a $5,000 income a negative income tax to bring the person up to $10,000. There is no guarantee that the extra money is going to be spent for any upgrading of skills that will increase employment opportunities.

6. Consumer problems are likely to be just as bad or worse in terms of abusive creditors using abusive collection methods, or in terms of stores in the poorer neighborhoods having poorer quality products that will not sell in middle class neighborhoods.

## C. INCENTIVES FOR ENCOURAGING SOCIALLY DESIRED BEHAVIOR

The environmental incentives table recognizes that if public policy wants to encourage socially desired behavior, then one approach to doing so is to make the benefits minus costs of doing right greater than the benefits minus costs of doing wrong. That logically leads to four categories of incentives which are shown in the table. They relate to (1) ways of increasing the benefits of right doing in the pollution reduction field, (2) ways of reducing the costs of right doing, (3) ways of increasing the costs of wrongdoing, (4) ways of reducing the benefits of wrongdoing, and (5) ways of increasing the probability that the appropriate benefits and costs will actually occur.

A second broad approach to encouraging socially desired behavior is to concentrate on building physical and mental blocks against doing wrong, so that potential wrongdoers are not so likely to ever need to think about whether the benefits minus costs of right doing outweigh the benefits minus costs of wrongdoing. The table does not show any specific examples. One example of a physical block with regard to the pollution (which occurs from people throwing away containers that are not biodegradable) is to simply not have nay such containers made. Then public policy does not have to punish people for throwing away the nonexistent containers or reward them for turning them in. Creating biodegradable containers (which largely means paper containers) for products like beer may require a research subsidy to develop the right kind of carton.

An example of a mental block would be to create habits of throwing things in wastebaskets on the part of little children to the point where it becomes totally unthinkable when they are adults that they would push an old refrigerator or a car into a river, rather than have it brought to a junkyard. They bring it to the junkyard not because they are worried about being fined or regarded, but because the behavior of putting such non-biodegradable metal into blocking a river is unthinkable for a civilized human being.

## D. NECESSITY-INVENTION

Saying that necessity-invention will take care of it is not enough. The time span may be way too long. Necessity-invention will eventually work, but a lot of harm done if the process is not accelerated. Necessity-invention may result in only a minimally satisfactory invention. It does not guarantee anything highly imaginative or highly useful or highly SOS. It simply guarantees meeting a minimum threshold. It simply means finding an oil substitute. The oil substitute may be very expensive, very inefficient, but a substitute.

In order to stimulate faster and better necessity-invention, the well-placed subsidies are needed. In the case of battery development, Japan is working on the problem with well-placed subsidies. To my knowledge there is nothing in the way of any kind of big program in the United States, nothing approaching a man on the moon, or the Manhattan Project, or a cure for cancer. The need for an electric substitute for oil, though, may be as great as those. Some may be much greater than finding a way to get a man on the moon.

## III.  A GROWTH PERSPECTIVE

In discussing the general means for achieving the super-optimum goals, one must recognize that those means are going to cost large amounts of money for appropriate subsidies, tax breaks, and some forms of regulation.  A super-optimum perspective tends to be optimistic in setting goals and in believing that the means can be found for achieving them.  This is not, however, a naive optimism, but rather one that is based on what is realistically possible, especially if one proceeds with a positive orientation.

A growth perspective implies that the funding to support the achievement of the super-optimum goals will come mainly from growth of the economy rather than from a redistribution of wealth.  In fact, a redistribution from the rich to the poor may interfere with economic growth by unduly reducing incentives to save, invest, and even work as hard or as well as one otherwise would, regardless whether one is rich or poor.  Likewise, a redistribution from the poor to the rich through regressive taxes and investment incentives could also similarly interfere with economic growth and public morale.

A growth perspective tends to be endorsed by both conservatives (who favor supply-side economics and Reaganomics) and by liberals (who favor industrial policy and economic planning).  They even tend to agree that the main means to economic growth are tax breaks and subsidies, although they may disagree as to exactly what form they should take.  President Reagan originally put considerable faith in the idea of a 30% across-the-board tax cut to stimulate the economy.  The economy was not very well stimulated partly because of conflicting tight-money policies to reduce inflation, but also because tax cuts with no strings attached may tend to wind up disproportionately in real estate, luxury goods, and higher executive salaries.  Presidential candidate Gary Hart indicted a willingness to provide tax breaks to business much higher than 30% provided that the tax breaks are only given if the money is used for modernizing industrial practices, giving on-the-job training, or other productivity-improving activities.

Some of the costs could be covered by improving the U.S. defense capability at a lower cost by concentrating more on weapons systems which are more effective and efficient.  That may mean more emphasis on Trident submarines and low-flying cruise missiles, and less emphasis on easily destroyed B-1 bombers, aircraft carriers, and MX missile silos.  It may also mean more realistic defensive systems, such as a radar and laser-firing system for destroying enemy nuclear submarines, rather than a star wars system for supposedly destroying all incoming enemy missiles.  Making defense expenditures more effective and efficient and thereby reducing them makes more sense. This is in contrast to increasing questionable defense expenditures by taking from on-the-job training programs and subsidies for technological innovation. It is no coincidence that the United States and the Soviet Union have been ranking lowest among the industrial nations on productivity growth as of about 1980, and highest among the industrial nations on defense expenditures.

On the matter of bipartisan growth, both conservatives and liberals also tend to endorse the idea of more systematic governmental decision-making in order to achieve economic growth. Conservatives consider such decision-making to be a form of bringing good business practice to government. Liberals consider it to be a form of economic planning. systematic governmental decision-making manifests itself in using contemporary methods of benefit-cost analysis to (1) choose among discrete alternatives, (2) choose under conditions of risk, (3) choose where doing too much or too little is undesirable, and (4) to allocate scarce resources in light of given goals and relations.

## IV. INCENTIVES RELATED TO GROWTH

### A. OUTLINE

1. The key is incentives money
2. Where does the incentives money go?
   a. Increasing the productivity of capital equipment
   b. Increasing the productivity of labor and talent
   c. Increasing the productivity of natural resources
3. What are the effects of increased productivity?
   a. On improving economic growth, taxes, and the budget deficit
   b. On improving foreign trade and the trade deficit
4. Where does the incentives money come from?
   a. The increased tax base without increased tax rates
   b. Decreased defense expenditures within increased defense capability
5. The spillover effects into other public policy problems
   a. Economic problems
   b. Social problems
   c. Science policy problems
   d. Political problems
6. Some conclusions

## B.  U.S. IS STILL THE RICHEST COUNTRY IN THE WORLD IN TERMS OF TOTAL ASSETS

Herb Stein is writing on deficits and surpluses in the 1989 bulletins of the American Enterprise Institute.  A big point that he is making is that in 1982, the U.S. was the leading creditor in the world.  by 1987, the U.S. was the leading debtor in the world.  It sounds as if the richest person in the world became the poorest person in the world.  That is a big part of the Reagan legacy.  The U.S. is not the poorest country in the world.  Poverty is measured by assets, not by debt.  The U.S. is still the richest country in the world in terms of total assets, although maybe no longer in the top five if assets are divided by population.  No longer in the top ten if annual income is divided by population.  But still the richest in terms of the sum total of all the value of all the land and factories and building, although Japan is moving up fast.

## C.  DEBT REALLY HURTS

Where the debt really hurts is in two ways:
1.   The domestic debt means the money the federal government owes, as contrasted to the money the nation owes.  The interest has become so high that it now is approaching about one-third of all federal expenditures, or somewhere between 20% and 30%.  That means paying money by the federal government to banks and people who own federal bonds is maybe 100 times what the federal government is paying to people on welfare, and many times more than what the federal government is paying out to support schools, health, and transportation facilities.  What is happening is that the federal government's ability to spend and to use federal expenditures for incentive sand to control the business cycle has become greatly hampered by being so much in debt.
2.   Maybe worse than that on the domestic side is that in order to make payments, the federal government has to constantly borrow more money.  In the long run, that drives interest rates up, thereby making it difficult for American business to borrow money at low interest rates and hampering the growth of the economy.  The nation as a whole owes much money to foreign countries as a result of a consumption binge by the federal government and the general public in the 1980s.  We can pay back the money in three ways.  One is by selling them a lot of goods and getting yen, marks, and other foreign money.  Another is by borrowing from them so we can pay them what we owe them.  A third is by selling American business or real estate, i.e., American assets.  Giving them American investments is not so bad.  Selling them a lot of goods would be fine if we had something worthwhile that other people wanted to buy.

Borrowing from them has the same disadvantages, only worse, as borrowing internally. When we borrow internally at least we are paying the interest into the economy, as contrasted to sending it overseas.

## D. BUDGET DEFICIT AND THE INTERNATIONAL TRADE DEFICIT LOOK LIKE GOOD THINGS

The Reagan administration tried to make both the internal debt and the external debt (i.e., the federal budget deficit and the international trade deficit) look like good things, rather than bad things. They were partly right.

The fact that we can buy a lot more than we sell shows we have good credit, a lot of assets, and that we are a rich country. The drawback, though, is that one cannot go on like that forever or maybe more than a generation. We are in effect selling off the family jewels in order to pay for current consumption, including selling Midwest farmland and investment in American corporations. Eventually carried to its logical extreme, Americans will all be tenants of Japanese and West German landlords and employees of Japanese and West German factories. The Japanese landlords may be nicer than the American landlords, but it is better to be an owner than a tenant. What eventually could happen (especially if there is a change in the friendly attitudes of Germany and Japan) is that the United States could become the equivalent of a low level developing country. Americans would then be virtually serfs designed to produce raw materials for the countries that own them. Those countries acquired ownership not by conquering the U.S. but through good old capitalistic means of buying it.

The Reagan administration's argument about why the domestic debt is really a good thing is contrary to what Republicans have always previously said. It is great if you can spend more than you can take in. It cannot go on forever, and it is already doing harm at the present time in terms of perverting federal expenditures. From a national productivity perspective with regard to using tax breaks and subsidies for incentives, one could say it greatly decreased the flexibility there. The Reagan administration, though, would argue that if in pre-Reagan times the national budget were $1 trillion and only 10% was interest on the national debt and now it is $2 trillion and 30% with interest on the national debt, part of the increased national debt is offset by the increased GNP. Also, one could argue that if $1 trillion is 1,000 billion and we now have 2,000 billion, then before we were spending 100 billion for interest and now we are spending 300 billion, the important thing is that we now have $1,700 billion left over, whereas before we only had $900 billion left over. It is like the half empty and half-filled bottle.

There is too much emphasis on the fact that the interest has tripled and that the GNP has only doubled. What there should be more emphasis on is that the money left over is an extra $800 billion.

## E. IRONIES IN THIS DEBATE

One of the ironies in this debate is that Reaganites could use the same argument against the liberals that liberals use in arguing for high progressive income taxes. The liberals say that a person who is paying in a 60% bracket (which would be higher than the brackets that actually exist) should not complain if that person is making $1 million per year. The person should emphasize that he had $400,000 per year left to throw around. I.e., emphasize the positive, not the $600,000 paid to the government for taxes. Likewise, the Reaganites can emphasize the extra money that we now have in spite of the increased debt and the increased interest.

Another irony is that the increased GNP has come about as a result of Reagan doing what liberals have frequently advocated ought to be done in he past, namely stimulate the economy with extra spending even if it means deficit spending. The reason we have a higher GNP now and relatively higher prosperity is because federal spending has way exceeded federal income. What all this illustrates is that the world is full of trade-offs, or at least often is. And in the past it was more trade-off oriented than it maybe should have been. Reaganites can argue that you cannot have it both ways, that you cannot have all this extra money available for incentives, i.e., subsidies, and all this economy stimulation as a result of increased federal spending if you are also going to have a balanced budge. The balanced budget would mean that the federal government would take in by way of taxes whatever extra spending it would be doing. Or the federal government would have to cut back on spending even more than is has in the domestic area.

The fallacy in all that is that there is no necessary that there be a trade-off. Trade-off thinking is the same as zero-sum thinking. There is no reason why the GNP cannot increase with considerable economic growth and lots of prosperity without tremendous debt, interest and selling of the U.S. to foreigners. Means for achieving all those goals simultaneously emphasize well placed incentives.

## F. USING INCENTIVES TO INCREASE PRODUCTIVITY

Use incentives to greatly increase American productivity. That would be in conformity with Reaganomics, supply-side economics, and industrial policy, but use incentives with strings attached instead of across-the-board tax cuts. Strings would include retooling the steel industry and the auto industry, providing on the job training to increase productivity of workers, incentive subsidies to hire the aged, the unemployed, the underemployed, mothers of preschool children, the handicapped, and all the people who are producing virtually nothing whose potential productivity has a very high marginal rate of return when you start at the zero level. A relatively small investment can produce a substantial return. All those devices can simultaneously increase the GNP and increase the tax revenues without raising tax rates because the tax base would be increased. Those same devices could result in lowering prices through greater productivity and making American products more competitive. The same devices could also stimulate improved quality, thereby further increasing American competitiveness.

## G. THE UPWARD SPIRAL

The object as is shown in Table 4-2 is to develop methods that will result in increasing the GNP. An increase in the GNP will result in an increase in taxes without increasing tax rates. An increase in tax rates could have an adverse effect on the economy, although it would depend on what taxes are increased. Without getting into the possibility of having a tax increase that is not adverse to the economy, one can just talk in terms of increasing the tax base. If tax intake goes up, then the budget deficit goes down. The devices designed to increase the GNP feed through increased productivity which in turn increases the GNP. Increased productivity means getting more product for a smaller cost. Doing so increases foreign trade, which decreases the trade deficit. Economic growth or increased GNP enables us to have multiple cakes and be able to eat them all. This is without a trade-off where we have to give up one good thing in order to get another good thing.

## H. WHY HAS IT NOT BEEN DONE ALREADY?

One might ask why this has not been done already.

1. Prior to 1980, a trade-off attitude prevailed that in order to get inflation down employment had to go up, and vice versa. Or in order to get prosperity up, which is a good thing, the deficit had to rise, which is a bad thing.

2. In 1980, the Reagan administration came to office recognizing that it was possible to break out of that trade-off thinking through a system of economic incentives. However, they largely blew the opportunity by throwing away funds available for incentives on a 30%

across the board tax cut with no strings attached. Nobody had to retake, retrain, provide training, get a job, employ somebody, or do anything. It was 30% less taxes that went into buying real estate, luxury goods, and higher corporate salaries, with nothing to show in terms of increased productivity. It was blind faith that somehow the invisible hand of the Adam Smith marketplace would direct the money into retooling the steel industry.

3. The Democrats are moving more toward systematic industrial policy. They are developing a program of incentives with strings attached that could work.

## I. THINGS TO WATCH OUT FOR

Some of the things that the Democrats have to watch out for, though, that could wreck the strings-attached incentive program are:

1. An ignorance to the international economics that could cause an increase in tariffs and quotas on foreign goods on the theory that this would help the trade deficit by keeping out foreign products. It would probably have exactly the opposite effect. It would decrease the real GNP by lowering the American standard of living. It would decrease the ability and willingness of foreign countries to buy American goods more that offsetting whatever would have been kept out.

2. There could be an undesirable tendency to raise taxes that could have an offsetting effect. The traditional Democratic program (as espoused by Jesse Jackson) is to raise taxes on the rich. In theory, that may sound fine. In practice, if it means taxing money that otherwise would go toward retooling the steel industry, then it would be defeating not only for steel workers, but for the total economy. This does not mean that rich people cannot be taxed because they invest their money in investments that are productive to the economy. That is more the traditional Republican idea, which is substantially untrue. They disproportionately invest their money in luxury goods and real estate. They do invest some of their money in stocks and bonds that do help the economy. The more important point, though, is that the government could come up with the money that the steel industry needs more easily than private investors can. This is especially so since the steel industry needs so much money, and it is such a bad investment for private investors because it is not likely to pay off for a while. What this means is that if Jesse Jackson is going to talk about extra taxes on the rich, he has got to come up with an alternative source of investment money, which he is not talking about. It is like the Republicans who talk about abolishing welfare and offering nothing as an alternative source of income for people who are unemployed. The logical alternative source is

employment. Thus one cannot talk about abolishing welfare unless one talks about a massive program for employment opportunities including school training, on-the-job training, day care programs, incentives money to take advantage of those opportunities, and incentives money to create those opportunities.

3.  What this amounts to is that one cannot talk about strings attached incentives out of the context of the seamless web of the total public policy picture and the total economy. One cannot pull the plug on welfare or on taxes on the rich without taking into consideration what some of the side effects are going to be and doing something in advance abut those undesirable side effects.

## J.  OBTAINING INCENTIVES MONEY FROM REDUCED DEFENSE SPENDING

One could possibly obtain a lot more money for the incentives by way of reduced defense expenditures without reducing defense capability. That may require another arrow in the picture because it is not completely clear where the incentives money comes form. One source is reducing defense expenditures by presidential decision, but at the same time holding constant or even increasing defense capability. The other big source of incentives money comes by way of the increased GNP which results in increased taxes due to the bigger tax base without an increase in rates, which feeds back on the incentives money by providing more of it. It is important in this scheme to show that although taxes go up, the tax rates stay constant. Likewise although defense expenditures go down, defense capability can stay constant. The fact that tax rates stay constant is also a presidential decision, and one that is easier to make than to hold constant defense capability. Defense capability can be held constant by getting rid of weapons systems that seem relatively meaningless including the B-1 bomber, the MX missile, and star wars. Instead concentrate on weapons systems that make more sense, like Trident submarines, conventional capability, and reducing the need for such high defense capability by developing even more effective arms control agreements.

## K.  SEPARATE SEGMENTS

This analysis needs to be broken down into separate segments covering such matters as:
1.  Where does the incentives money go to.
> 1A. On the go-to side we could subdivide into effects on the foreign  trade deficit.

1B. Effects on the domestic budget deficit.

1C. Effects on the GNP.

1D. Effects on Taxes.

1E. Effects on productivity.

2. On where does the incentives money come from, that can be subdivided into:

2A. Reduce defense expenditures without reduced defense capability.

2B. Increase GNP as part of the supply-side economics effect.

Each of those can be further subdivided. For example, number 2A on defense expenditures can be subdivided into (1) weapons systems to cut back. Such as B-1 bombers, MX missiles, and star wars, as well as miscellaneous non-working systems like certain tanks and rifles, although they involve relative small amounts of money; and (2) Trident submarines, conventional warfare, and arms control on the positive side.

## L. SUBUNITS ON RELATING INCENTIVES AND PRODUCTIVITY

With regard to the relation between incentives and productivity, we have a whole set of subunits, including:

1. The retooling of industries that are using relatively obsolete capital.

2. The employing of people who are relatively unproductive or underproductive. That has two sides to it. One side is the incentives needed to get the employers to do the employing. The other side is the incentives to get the potential employees to move, to get into training programs, to accept the jobs offered, and to show up for work.

3. If productivity is a function of capital, labor, and natural resources, we should say something about natural resources although we do not have to have symmetry or equality on all three dimensions. There does not seem to be anything that seriously wrong with our natural resources, as contrasted to our capital and labor. Natural resources mainly means land, minerals, and energy resources. We have great land. It could be taken better care of with better conservation and irrigation, but that is not a serious problem in American productivity. We have no great shortage on minerals of any important kind.

It is the energy part of the land-mineral-energy sub-breakdown of natural resources on which we are not doing so well. The American energy picture is close to miserable. In central Illinois, a good deal of potential economic development is not possible because the wasteful Clinton nuclear-energy plant now makes energy costs too high for business firms that would otherwise locate in the area. This is happening in many places in the U.S. The costs of energy are becoming too high to locate in various areas that otherwise would be good places. There is also the sin of omission relating to the failure to take advantage of energy sources that could be inexpensively developed, including modern nuclear energy and modern solar energy. Perhaps Washington will eventually push for a totally new nuclear energy program that is capable of low cost and highly safe energy. Doing so would involve modern techniques that the private energy industry in the U.S. has refused to adopt. The reasons are partly their inertia in getting into costly and unsafe techniques, and then lacking incentives to get out of them since they have monopolistic customer relations. Electricity may be the most incompetent, inefficient major industry in the U.S. Unfortunately it is quite basic since all industry depends on energy to run factories, regardless what the factories are making.

## M. NEW DEVELOPMENTS AND SUMMARY

Recent world developments affect the defense capability factor. The idea of meaningful arms control is now more a possibility than it has been. The seriousness of the trade and budget deficits has, however, become greater. The idea of increasing productivity by putting relatively unproductive people to work previously referred to people in the labor force who were unemployed. The idea has now expanded to include the aged, the handicapped, preschool mothers, the underemployed, and the unsatisfactorily employed. They were either generally not counted as being in the labor force, or were wrongly counted as being employed. For our purposes a person is not employed or at least is not fully employed if they are not working in accordance with their productive abilities.

Incentives and productivity are the means and national well-being is the end. There is a reciprocal relation in the sense that incentives stimulate productivity, which stimulates national well-being, which in turn stimulates incentives money. There is a backward moving arrow in Table 4-2 from increased GNP to increased taxes to incentives money. That is a key arrow in Reaganomics. The key arrow that the Democrats have to contribute is in the nature of the incentives with an emphasis on strings attached, big money, and professional administration. This is bipartisan thinking that Reagan could endorse, although it would mean admitting the 30% cut was wrong in not having strings-attached incentives. The Democrats could endorse the general ideas, although it would mean they were wrong in attacking the Reaganomics position that there is no need for legislating increased taxes. One might also note relative to both positions that although lowering the trade deficit and lowering the budget deficit are goals, the really important goal is economic growth. Those two deficits are just side effects. It is fine that they get reduced, but what we are primarily concerned with is national prosperity at an increasing rate and widespread across regions, rural and urban areas, rich and poor, black and white, male and female, and other societal groups.

## V.  SOME COMPARISONS BETWEEN JAPANESE AND AMERICAN PRODUCTIVITY

The typical Japanese firm wants to be the most important firm in the industry even if it is losing money. The typical American firm is happy with being 20th in the industry if it is making profits.

The big indictor should be which of those two basic orientations is better for society and the global market. The Japanese approach is much better if becoming first in the industry is achieved by making high quality products at low prices, even if the firm almost goes bankrupt doing so. The world benefits even if the firm loses. The American firm that is making big profits and providing the work with low quality merchandise at high prices is obviously less socially desirable.

Japanese firms are sometimes killing themselves not out of altruism, but out of a desire to be on top. But not to be on top by using cheap-shot advertising with sexy girls on American cars which just appeals to people's worst instincts in getting them to buy products.

Both the American firms and the Japanese firms are operating to promote their own self-interests. The difference is that the Japanese concept of self-interest is to be acclaimed as the leader in the field. The American concept is just to make a lot of money even if the products are disliked, as long as you can sell them for more than they cost to make. American products are not necessarily disliked, but they are sometimes laughed at like gas guzzlers in developing countries.

Even on R & D, American firms do not deserve so much credit. Most American R & D is developed in American universities, not American business firms. The U.S. deserves a lot of credit for inventiveness, including the winning of Nobel prizes, but that is not GM. That is the University of Illinois and other universities. Japan does poorly on that score in both its business firms and its universities. They are not cash contributors to the world when it comes to inventiveness. They are especially implementers, rather than inventors.

Each business firm in the world trying to maximize income minus expenses is by no means good for the world, rather than maximizing market share. This does more to refute Adam Smith and traditional capitalism than anything Karl Marx had to say. Marx was operating largely out of theory, rather than out of the experience that had not yet arrived in the world.

The Japanese business firms are doing well in that they are moving toward 100% of the market share in may basic industries of the world. They will probably never reach the point of 100%, but that is what they are striving for. Yet they or their companies are not getting rich, in terms of income over expenses and assets over liabilities. The reasons are:

1. They charge low prices that hurt how much profit they can make on a Toyota or Sony TV set because they want to sell a lot of Toyotas. They want as high a percent of the market as possible.

2. They provide all kinds of benefits to the consumer that are expensive to the manufacturer buy that help sell their products and thereby increase their market share.

3. They thus almost deviate substantially from what is taught in American business schools. They are lowering their revenue by lowering their prices. They are increasing their expenses by offering various features that no regulatory agency is requiring them to offer.

4. Yet they are greatly disrupting the business of U.S. Steel, GM, and other giants of American industry. Japan is benefiting because it means lots of income for Japanese workers and lots of income in the form of taxes for Japanese governments. The Japanese CEO's are not exactly impoverished, but they do not live as luxuriously as the people who run GM and U.S. Steel who are doing a poorer job.

Competition is fine for the quality of life of the world and a nation that competes well like Japan does. That, however, is not advertising-competition. It is also not cheating competition where a business firm sees how much it can cheat its customers or cheat its workers. It is competition to see who can produce the most sought-after product because of its low price and its quality content. That may be crazy behavior, but Japan as a nation is laughing hysterically all the way to the bank.

## VI. HOW INCREASED PRODUCTIVITY TENDS TO LEAD TO INCREASED PRODUCTIVITY

That is a new kind of indirect effect that is part of an upward spiral idea as contrasted to a vicious circle or downward spiral idea. The previous aspects include:

Multiplier effect whereby increased productivity means increased income to whoever is being more productive. That person's increased income means increased spending, which means increased income for others, and so on down a multiplier line. The multiplier effect is an example of increased productivity producing further increased productivity, because the income earned becomes someone else's income by way of spending. Some of that may go into savings which is available for investment purposes and thereby means increased productivity. Even the portion that goes into consumption may stimulate increased productivity by firms that are seeking to capture that consumption money.

The <u>compounding effect</u> whereby increased productivity means increased income to whoever is being more productive. That means the person who is paying more in taxes is given a constant or even slightly decreasing tax rate. If that tax money gets into well-placed subsidies to produce more productivity, then in that sense the increased productivity is being compounded. Society is getting interest on its interest, or growth on its growth.

The <u>intergenerational effect</u> whereby the increased productivity of an adult serves as an inspirational role model for a child or grandchild, thereby increasing the child's productivity.

The fourth aspect of the upward spiral is <u>increased productivity may manifest itself in new products that consumers want to have such as cars, televisions, tape players, video players, etc.</u> The existence of those products causes people to be more productive so they can earn more income in order to buy them. In the absence of those products, people have less incentive to work harder since those products which they desire do not exist.

## VII. COUNCIL ON INTERNATIONAL COMPETITIVENESS

### A. WHAT IS WRONG WITH THE AMERICAN ECONOMY: VIRTUALLY ALL THE DECISION-MAKERS IN THE ECONOMY ARE GEARED TOWARD FIGHTING OVER ZERO-SUM MATTERS LIKE WAGES

Management wants low wages, workers want high wages, the government takes a hand-off position until a compromise is reached. Two years later maybe the company is out of business because it has shortsightedly failed to keep up with international competition. That is a super lose-lose situation where management gave in to some extent on low wages, workers gave in to some extent on high wages, and management goes bankrupt and workers are out of a job because they were to shortsighted to see what the real needs of both sides are. That is the essence of the Japanese success story, namely the government (or more specifically the ministry of International Trade and Investment) providing the foresightedness that neither management nor labor can admittedly provide so well.  Workers want higher wages now, not the possibility of bigger income later.  Management wants to cut expenses now, not the possibility of higher profits later.  This is a super-malimum solutions in which everybody suffers including management, labor, and especially society.

It is partly a matter of semantics.  If one talks about the government, that creates a negative intervention of some kind of regulatory agency.  If one talks about MITI, that may create some kind of images of Japanese intervention, at least with regard to ideas.  Americans find it hard to believe that somebody else, even Japan, may have developed a better way of running an economy.  There is a need for an American phrase like Ministry of International Trade and Investment.  We already have it, although it is in the process of being of utterly questionable value, namely the Council on Competitiveness.  Under the chairmanship of Mr. Quayle, its function has been almost 100% in all these kind of disputes to argue in favor of lower wages, longer hours without overtime, unsafe workplaces, cutting on environmental standards, cutting on union involvement, and cutting on everything.

## B. POSITION OF THE COUNCIL ON COMPETITIVENESS

The Council's position is that our international competitiveness is increased by cutting expenses and thereby enabling business firms to be able to lower their prices.  Big fallacies in that include:

1.  Cutting expenses just results in fatter profits, not in lower prices.

2.  The cutting of labor costs is a disincentive to automate. anything that is a disincentive to automate is a real evil with regard to increasing international competitiveness.

3.  The whole philosophy of cutting expenses and raising prices is what has gotten the U.S. into trouble internationally in losing customers to the Japanese philosophy of increasing market share by providing more expensive quality and lowering prices.

4.  Always taking the management side against society and against the workers destroys the credibility of the Council on Competitiveness. It does not have the image of being above partisan battles, like the MITI has.

5.  Having it headed up by someone like Mr. Quayle does not help its credibility either.

## C.  HOW THAT INSTITUTION COULD BE CHANGED

1.   It <u>needs some money, and lots of it</u>, in order to be able to do well-placed subsidies, to introduce new technologies, and upgrade skills.

2.   It needs to be headed and have on its <u>decision-making body people who are associated with business, labor, the academic world,</u> and maybe especially the think tanks including Brookings, AEI, and the American Heritage people.  The American Heritage people can be trusted more than Mr. Quayle can to understand what is going on.

3.   They need <u>lots of staff that are well trained</u>.  It has to be done on a firm-by-firm basis and not just pontificating mainly against the EPA, the EEOC, the FTC, and all the other federal agencies to get them to cut back on their activities.  they need both a macro level and a micro level.  The micro level requires people who will visit every company in the United States.  Not one person doing it all, but every business firm listed in business directories that hires more than 10 people, or for a starter more than 100 people, divided by industries since each industry has different problems.  The staff needs to be highly knowledgeable about each industry, although much better staff people who can be someone who knows nothing at all about the printing industry other than lay knowledge but who is capable of learning fast and has a flexible mind and can understand the basic idea that with proper computerization printers can provide better quality at lower prices.  The concentration should be on industries that have exportable products.  Printing is not such a good example.  We do not sell much printing overseas even if we are doing good quality at a low price, and overseas printers do not sell to the United States.  PSO has never been approached by a Japanese printer or any non-American printer.  The making of printing presses, though, is an exportable industry.  That is too narrow, though.  The making of printing presses is not that different form the making of other industrial machinery.  The staff people may especially need some on-the-job training themselves with regard to what is involved in modern robotics.  The principles are just as applicable to bottling milk as to making printing presses.  The object is to lay out an automation plan that increases quality control, decreases unit costs, increases volume, decreases working expense, and increases profits.  In the realm of law firm automation it has reached the point where no law firm can operate without automation and expect to be profitable for very long.  People who are experts on law firm automation may not be experts on the automation of packaging milk.  One maybe needs to think in terms of automating services versus automating manufacturing, but not necessarily.  There is a lot more to be said for a generalist mind with better than lay awareness of what is involved than someone who is a

specialist in printing presses, or milk, or any subject matter. In fact, the milk specialist may have spent so much time learning the traditional ways of milk, manufacturing that they think that is the way God makes milk. They are less likely to be flexible than someone who does not have a vested interest in years of learning the traditional way of doing things.

What we are talking about here with regard to this institution are the four or five principles of <u>successful implementation</u>, namely big money, strings attached good staff, and creative thinking. The strings-attached has not been explicitly mentioned. Unlike a regulatory agency, this agency needs no power whatsoever to issue injunctions or to take people to court. It has the power to withhold well-placed subsidies or better yet, to give them to firms that are competing with the firm that does not want to change. That can bring about change much better than any threats. a good example is integrating southern schools which never occurred under threats, but occurred very rapidly after 1964 when federal aid to education money was greatly expanded and only available to schools that would integrate. It then became worthwhile to integrate. We are talking about making it worthwhile to automate. The word automate, though, has some negative connotations since it implies the absence of the human element. Talking about computerizing crates an image of somebody working at a computer. People's understandings of computers do tend to include a human element. People cannot picture a computer keyboard typing by itself. One of the ironies is that computers do a lot of work by themselves. If the keys do not move, then the disk drive or the hard disk is in effect moving and is causing printout to occur. The lay person still thinks there is a human element there, that some human being put the floppy disk into the machine or some human being is responsible for whatever is on the floppy disk or the hard disk. That is important to getting acceptance. Not because it provides jobs for some people to put floppy disks into disk drives, but because it gives people greater confidence in the output to know there is some human supervision involved. Even the work robotics does not imply some science fiction robot walking around. Most people have a notion that robotics simply means the assembly line moves as a result of some human being turning it on and watching over it to make sure it does not jam. But there is nobody around that looks like a robot.

## D. ASKING HOW COME JAPAN IS DOING SO WELL IN TERMS OF ECONOMIC GROWTH AND THE UNITED STATES IS NOT DOING SO WELL

The answer definitely does seem to be the idea of <u>having an MITI which does well-placed subsidies, tax breaks designed to upgrade skills and introduce new technologies,</u> as contrasted to other *nonsense reasons* that are sometimes given, such as:

1. <u>American workers are lazy.</u> Japanese workers are hard-working. The truth of the matter is that American workers work physically much harder because they do not have computerization which means you can sit at a console rather than pound an anvil all day.

2. <u>Japanese people save their money and Americans spend their money.</u> that may be true, but irrelevant. The big money for new technologies comes from taxes, not savings accounts in Japan.

3. <u>Japanese entrepreneurs are oriented toward marketshare rather than income minus expenses. That is true.</u> But a key reason why they have that orientation is that it is the <u>kind of orientation the MITI rewards</u>. The MITI is not interested in maximizing profits for any individual business firm. It wants Japan to move toward having 100% of the market in every major industry, and it wants each firm to think along those lines. but at the same time, the MITI subsidizes multiple firms n the same industry in order to encourage competition.

4. <u>Japanese business firms are competitive.</u> American firms in the past and in the domestic market, but especially in the past, have been monopolistic as individual firms or as groups of firms. This has hurt their incentive to innovate. That is true. But again, it is the government that largely determines whether there will be competition or monopoly in Japan. The MITI could choose to fund only one automobile company or one electronics company. It deliberately encourages competition that might otherwise not exist.

5. The U.S. is held back by <u>immigrants</u>. The truth of the matter is that Japan is held back by not getting fresh ideas and fresh ambition. As a result, they have to do more borrowing from other countries than the United States does. Immigrants to the U.S. tend to be especially ambitious people who are the main source of America's strength in the past. But that factor is not enough to automatically result in the adoption of new technologies and upgrading of skills.

6. The U.S. is held back by Japanese competition which somehow stifles our advancing. We need high tariffs to keep out Japanese goods. Just the opposite seems obviously the case if one thinks about it. <u>One of the main things that has stimulated some innovation on the part of American industry is Japanese competition</u>. High tariffs would result in

domestic market monopolies and a restoration of the relatively lazy do-nothing attitude. Not totally do-nothing. General Motors was very good on emphasizing style changes rather than price reductions or quality improvement. They are also very good on lots of sexy advertising. That does not sell cars internationally.

Conservatives like to blame American labor, liberals like to blame American management. Point number 1 is a kind of conservative blaming position. So is number 5, and so is number 6. Number 3, which puts down American entrepreneurs, and number 4, is a kind of blaming position. Number 2 is a somewhat neutral blaming position, although it could be phrased in liberal terms. It could be phrased in conservative terms by saying the reason Americans do not save more is because they are not given big enough tax incentives to do so, like capital gains, tax, meaning no capital gains taxes. Talk about the need for more savings usually degenerates into why we have to not tax rich people because they are such good saving people and they will not do saving if they are taxed. The reality is that the sum total of all the non-rich savings accounts add up to much more than all the rich savings accounts. The more important point though is that technology is not funded out of savings accounts, at least not in Japan. It is funded out of taxes. In the United States it is funded out of diverting profits into new technologies. This means it is largely not being done because that is asking too much of business firms to divert profits into new technologies rather than into higher salaries for both management and workers. The super-optimum position is not especially interested in blaming either labor or management, partly because blaming does not do much good but also because both labor and management are not as relevant as the role of public policy. The key thing is not to attach public policy either, but of pushing a positive approach.

### E. THE PHRASE SUPER-OPTIMIZING

With regard to phrases, the phrase "super-optimizing" does seem to grab people. Everybody that hears the phrase and learns what it stands for likes the idea. Only one person in the couple of years that it has been used has expressed any negative reaction, namely Yehezkel Dror who thinks it sounds too grandiose, presumptuous or pompous. It is grandiose. It does get at the idea of better than the best. But once it is defined and explained, it is not that far out. In fact, once it is defined and explained, a typical reaction is that it is not so wild. And very meaningful. It is pompous for someone to come along and say, I have better ideas than George Bush or Tom Harkin, or somebody like that. That is not what SOS says. What SOS says is George Bush has wonderful ideas, Tom Harkin has wonderful ideas. They appear to conflict with each other. Let us see if there is some way in which we can simultaneously achieve both of their laudable goals. Perhaps there are ways even more effective than their current advocacy.

Let us get away from talking so much about how the ideas conflict and the need to compromise in the middle, and simply try to think about how both sets of ideas, mainly meaning both sets of goals, can be simultaneously achieved. That is not so pompous. In fact, it is even capable of being accused of being a handmaiden to the politicians in that it is their goals that are taken as givens. What is different form the usual handmaiden idea is that it is the goals of both liberals and conservatives, or Democrats and Republicans, that are simultaneously taken as givens. It is not being a handmaiden to one side. That is the position of the gun-for-hire, the traditional lawyer, the advocate. We are talking about being an SOS analyst, not a policy analyst.

A policy analyst normally takes the policies as givens too, and simply decides among the given policy alternatives which is best or what the advantages and disadvantages of each are. An SOS analyst tries to come up with some new alternatives by taking the goals as givens. Also taken as givens are some constraint conditions, but not too many as part of SOS analysis means thinking about ways of getting around constraints, especially conflicting constraints. Even the goals might be questioned, where one can say that some of the goals that are mentioned are not the total picture but are just the goals that sound good to the general public. Let us get out on a table what is really wanted, and try to develop an SOS that will achieve even those otherwise embarrassing goals.

What we are talking about fits in with discussing the idea of well-placed subsidies with strings attached in order to get new technologies adopted and skills upgraded. The same ideas could apply to any kind of skill. It could apply to farming, for example. It does not have to involve an employer-employee relation. The county agents who work for USDA in some ways are like the staff people we are talking about. They have played an important role in informing farmers about new herbicides, pesticides, new technology, and new forms of hybrid seeds. The county agents collectively are a kind of MITI for agriculture without any money. They do not give farmers any money to buy tractors, they just tell farmers about the newest thing in tractors. The USDA does hand out plenty of money to farmers, though, but in the worst kind of dole that makes welfare handouts look productive. Agricultural subsidies reward nonproductivity. They deliberately reward taking land out of production, meaning they reward doing nothing, producing zero bushels per acre. That is the ultimate low point with regard to encouraging productivity.

Table 3-1 provides an SOS analysis of alternative positions on tariffs, including tariffs between the United States and Japan.

TABLE 3-1. EVALUATING ALTERNATIVE POSITIONS ON TARIFFS

| Criteria | C GOAL<br><br>High Business | L GOAL<br><br>High Wages | N GOAL<br><br>Low Prices | N GOAL<br><br>Low Taxes | N TOTAL<br><br>(Nuetral Weights) | L TOTAL<br><br>(Liberal Weights) | C TOTAL<br><br>(Conservative Weights) |
|---|---|---|---|---|---|---|---|
| **Alternatives** | | | | | | | |
| C Alternative<br><br>Pro Business Conservatives High Tariffs | 4 | 4 | 2 | 2 | 24 | 24 | 24 |
| C Alternative<br><br>Free World Market Conservatives Low Tariffs | 2 | 2 | 4 | 4 | 24 | 24 | 24 |
| L Alternative<br><br>Pro-Union Liberals High Tariffs | 4 | 4 | 2 | 2 | 24 | 24 | 24 |
| L Alternative<br><br>International ist Liberals Low Tariffs | 2 | 2 | 4 | 4 | 24 | 24 | 24 |
| N Alternative<br><br>Middling Tariffs | 3 | 3 | 3 | 3 | 24 | 24 | 24 |
| S Alternative<br><br>Well-placed Subsidies & Tax Breaks | 5 | 5 | 5 | 5 | 40 | 40 | 40 |

*NOTES:*

*1. On the issue of tariffs, conservatives who believe in free competitive markets both internationally and domestically tend to favor low tariffs.*

NOTES: Table 3-1

Likewise, so do liberals who have an internationalist orientation and who recognize the mutual benefits from buying overseas goods that have low prices, high quality, and the ability to stimulate competitive activity on the part of American firms.

2. On the other hand, conservatives who support monopolistic American businesses with their unreasonable profits are in favor of high tariffs. Likewise, pro-union liberals who do not want foreign competition are also in favor of high tariffs.

3. Traditionally American conservatives have supported high tariffs, and American liberals have supported low tariffs. The new SOS position is to support low or no tariffs, especially to stimulate worldwide competition to the long-run benefit of more efficient production and more prosperous consumption.

4. The object is to develop plans for well-placed subsidies and tax breaks that will enable the United States to compete effectively for world market shares without the interference and mutual downgrading of high tariffs. That especially means encouraging the adoption and diffusion of new technologies, and the upgrading of worker skills to be able to put the new technologies to good use. The result, at least in the long run, is likely to be high business profits, high workers' wages, low consumer prices, high consumer quality, and lower tax rates in view of the increased GNP as a tax base.

# CHAPTER 4

## COMPETITION IN THE PUBLIC
## AND PRIVATE SECTORS

### I. COMPETITION IN THE PRIVATE SECTOR

### A. COMPETITION AND COOPERATION SIMULTANEOUSLY

#### 1. IN THE WORKPLACE

Some people make the wrong dichotomy between competition and cooperation as if they are in conflict with each other. Some Japanese assembly plants emphasize cooperation and competition simultaneously. Competition occurs partly by teams working against each other, but each person on the team is expected to cooperate almost to the point of giving one's life for the team. The teams are both highly competitive and cooperative with each other. They are fighting to see which team will do the best, but at the same time seeking to advance the well-being of the assembly plant. Also, within each team there is competition between the individual team members, with those falling behind subjected to severe rebuke. There are thus two levels of competition among team members on the same team and among teams. There are also two levels of cooperation by people working together within each team to make their team win and the teams working together to boost the overall productivity of the assembly plant. Both kinds of activity are desirable. They can and should operate simultaneously.

## 2. THE ACADEMIC WORLD OF NOBEL PRIZES

In the academic world, many of the Nobel prizes (maybe 90 percent of those won within the past ten years) have been won by people who are part of teams. They are not working alone. They have a number of assistants and colleagues and associates, although one person may be the acknowledged leader who gets the prize but who cannot do it by himself or herself. The competition between those teams trying to crack the genetic code was ferocious, as indicated by the double helix discovery. It is not so ferocious as trying to assassinate each other. It is ferocious with the separate teams working around the clock in order to find the solution before the other team does. There is actually cooperation among those academic teams, although it is not explicit. They are all working toward a common goal of cracking the genetic code, finding a cure for cancer, or whatever it is. Whatever one team discovers gets known by other teams, given the propensity of academics to publish what they learn, as contrasted to private companies. Academics not only publish, but also present at conferences even before publication can occur.

## 3. EXAMPLES

Specific examples could be used form each place as:
1. Competition and cooperation within the workplace.
2. Competition and cooperation between business firms.
3. Competition and cooperation in the academic world.
4. Competition and cooperation at the international level.

## 4. PRIVATE-PUBLIC ORIENTATION

This does tie in a bit with the private-public orientation, not because private is competition and public is cooperative. It ties in since the solution to the private-public problem is to do both public and private. Likewise the solution to the competitive-cooperation problem is to do both competition and cooperation. That is not having much in common though. There are numerous dilemmas in which the solution is to do both.

### B. COMPETITION CONTRASTED WITH MONOPOLY, RATHER THAN WITH COOPERATION

## 1. POST OFFICE AS A GOVERNMENT MONOPOLY

There is a need to talk about encouraging competition even among government owned entities. That could include thinking about breaking up the post office so people could have a choice as to what post office they are going to send their mail out of. As of now, they only have choice with regard to Express mail. Such mail is very important to people who send it and does amount to a lot of dollars, especially on a per letter basis, but it is a relatively trivial aspect of the total quantity of mail carried. One could have competition more easily between private post offices and the government post office.

One big problem is artificial rules on both sides. The government post office has its hands tied by rules that are totally arbitrary, such as being prohibited form using FAX mail. Private carriers have their hands tied as well by such rules as saying they cannot put private mail into mail boxes. That is highly arbitrary. The person who has a mail box in his hallway or in front of his house should be able to allow people other than the post office to put things in it. The post office argues that it is protecting the private mailbox owner from having a lot of junk thrown in his mailbox. Maybe it should be up to the private mailbox owner to decide whether he wants junk put in it by the local pizza store or whoever is distributing circulars. The circular distributors would find it easier to put their circulars in the mailbox at the curb than have to put them in the doors. Likewise with the private mail distributor. The rule should be that so long as the distributor is not creating a nuisance by way of littering, they should be able to put things in mailboxes that are not locked unless the owner objects.

## 2. TYPICAL PRIVATE MONOPOLIES ARE ELECTRICITY AND TELEPHONING

We need not get into every kind of monopoly and what should be done about them individually. The typical monopolies are electricity and telephoning. The answers to what should be done about them are fairly simple. There is no reason why MCI and other such companies could not service local telephone as well as long distance telephone. The answer, though, is that they are basically just WATS resellers. They have no equipment of their own. There are no WATS discounts to be bought locally. The telephone company allows people in Champaign to make all the phone calls they want within the Champaign area at a flat fee. There is no discount available for making a trillion calls versus ten calls. Thus there would be no advantage from buying local telephone service from a middleman like MCI since the middleman gets no break by organizing a lot of people together. The local telephoning competition would have to come form real telephone companies, not just resellers.

There are enough other real telephone companies in the world besides Illinois Bell or the other Bells to provide competition if telephoning like television and radio could be handled without wires.

Long distance telephoning is handled without wires. Therefore it seems technically possible for a person to be able to phone down the lock by way of a satellite, although that might be highly inefficient. If the call can go through an overhead wire or underground wire for 3 cents, it might cost 30 cents for the variable cost alone forgetting for the moment about the fixed cost, to bounce the call off a satellite system.

The bouncing of electricity rather than telephoning, though, could be highly profitable. It would not take much for a firm in St. Louis to be able to compete with Illinois Power Company charging lower rates, especially if the St. Louis firm does not have the burden of having to pay off an outrageously expensive and wasteful Clinton Power Plant. This is a public policy problem in that the Illinois Public Utilities Commission will not allow the St. Louis firm to compete in this Illinois area. Illinois Power will complain that it has invested a lot of dollars in the Clinton Power Plant, and that it is entitled to have a monopoly so it can pay off what it has invested.

The answer to that might be that unless there is a binding legal contract guaranteeing a monopoly, then the legislature is free to change its mind in passing a new statute that authorizes out of state electric companies, or even upstate or downstate electrical companies to come into the Champaign-Urbana area. In fact, the legislature could even subsidize them to do so in order to provide desirable competition. If Illinois Power goes bankrupt, the consumers will probably be better off because its facilities will be bought up by a more efficient company. It would be hard to ever find another company less efficient.

### 3. COMPETITION IN PLACE OF GOVERNMENT AND PRIVATE MONOPOLIES

From the point of the consumer, the consumer is better off if the consumer has two electrical companies to buy from whether they are both government owned, both privately owned, or one government owned and one privately owned. So long as the companies know that they could lose their consumers to their competition, they provide much better service at lower costs than if they feel they have a captive set of consumers who have no place to go.

## C. ENCOURAGING COMPETITION AND COOPERATION IN THE WORKPLACE, MARKETPLACE, ACADEMIA, AND THE WORLD

### 1. WORKPLACE

With regard to the workplace, the article entitled "Management by Stress" is relevant. It is discussed in the previous section entitled "Competition and Cooperation Simultaneously in the Workplace." There is also a lot of relevant literature in public administration textbooks dealing with personnel, management, and also private sector personnel management textbooks.

## 2. MARKETPLACE

With regard to the marketplace, there are chapters in the economic regulation textbooks. They are nearly all obsolete though. They still talk about natural monopolies, and they talk about regulation for encouraging socially desired behavior, rather than well-placed subsidies and tax breaks. Some of the more modern literature, though, that deals with industrial policy and supply-side economics may be worth including. See the above discussion of monopoly and competition in mail service, electricity, and telephoning.

## 3. ACADEMIC COMPETITION

On academic competition little has been written. There are books, though, that deal with intellectual innovation. They are in with the productivity and creativity books. They may contain some good ideas on how to stimulate inventions and discoveries. The phenomenon tends to be almost totally haphazard. Public policy does a lot more with regard to worker productivity and business firm productivity than it does with regard to stimulating the winning of Nobel Prizes. The prevailing attitude seems to be that it is a mysterious process that public policy cannot do anything about, that it just sort of happens. Public policy could definitely provide subsidies for academics to do more innovative things than is currently the case.

The NSF, for example, may almost have more of a stultifying influence on innovation than a stimulating influence. One of its key principles is peer review, which means that new ideas are much less likely to be supported than ideas that people on peer review committees already have. They tend to endorse ideas like they themselves support. That means they tend to support people who are like themselves, as contrasted to people with new ideas who may be like a threat. There is a real need for requiring affirmative action in NSF programs whereby approximately 20% of the funding in each unit should go for stimulating new ideas. In the political science unit, for example, there ought to be 20% of the budget for a program called "Innovative Ideas in Political Science." The applications would be required to show that there is nothing they could cite that would be very relevant to what they are proposing to do. They would be required to show that none of the previous literature is especially relevant, although it may have some connection. It may be better to encourage crackpot ideas than to fund nothing but redundant mainstream material that adds nothing new.

That, however, sounds like it is getting away from the competition versus cooperation idea.  It sounds like it is just a concern for public policy designed to stimulate innovation.  The competition comes in offering prizes for certain kinds of new ideas on a highly competitive basis.  An example would be the federal government's offering to buy or totally replace its automotive fleet with electric cars for anybody who can develop an electric car that meets certain specifications.  This has caused some competition among innovative car developers. None of them so far has been able to meet the specifications, partly because of the need for more research funds rather than emphasizing a prize for a developed product.

It is harder to have competition like that in political science.  The analogy would be like having a contest to see who could develop the best set of ideas for improving the efficiency of the Office of Personnel Management regarding its hiring guidelines, or improving the Office of Management and Budget regarding its budgeting guidelines.  Political scientists would object to a contest like that as being too practical , and not sufficiently theoretical.

One thing that needs to be made clear is that we are not talking about competition to see who can do the most useless things, but competition to see who can do the most useful things.  Competition is of no value of it is people competing for some new kind of correlation coefficient that meets some kind of abstract math criteria.  That is the statistical equivalent of squaring the circle, trisecting an angle without a protractor, or getting decimal roots of four-digit numbers in one's head without using a calculator.  Those are all problems that pure mathematicians have been trying to solve for centuries that would serve no useful purpose if they ever solved them.  That kind of competition should not be encouraged, although it should not be discouraged in the sense of prohibiting anybody form doing it.  Trying to find a perpetual motion machine may be impossible, but if it is ever done it would be highly useful.  Trying to trisect an angle without a protractor may also be impossible, but even if it is someday done, it would be useless.  Even third or fourth grade children know how to sue a protractor to trisect an angle, and they do it with great accuracy.  One could divide an angle into any number of parts with a protractor.  Why play games pretending protractors do not exist, or pretending that calculators do not exist in order to play games seeing what kind of impressive calculations one can make in one's head.

## 4.  INTERNATIONAL REALM

In the international realm, the best material dealing with competition is in the international economics textbooks or in the international trade chapter in more elementary economic textbooks.

The best material dealing with cooperation is in the international organizations textbooks or in the international organizations chapter in more elementary international relations textbooks.

## D.  OTHER AND GENERAL ASPECTS

### 1.  MATERIAL DEALING WITH COMPETITION AND COOPERATION IN THE ABSTRACT

There is a lot of textbook material on all of these realms, the workplace, the marketplace, the international realm, and to a less extent the academic and innovative realm.  There is also material dealing with competition and cooperation in the abstract in the social psychology literature.  There are chapters, or at least a chapter on  the subject in Kimble Young's sociology textbook.

### 2.  INNOVATIVE IDEAS ABOUT COMPETITION

The key question is what is there that can be said on the subject that goes beyond the textbook literature.  Some of the innovative ideas include:

1.  The idea of competition within so-called natural monopolies in the private sector.

2.  The idea of competition where a government-owned operation is involved.

3.  The idea of competition among workers to the point of what may to outsiders look like extreme stress, as is described in the stress by management article.  The kind of competition that is sometimes looked upon with favor among workers is piecework, which is not necessarily competition since a worker can be paid on a piecework basis who is the only worker working for the firm.  It does not require any kind of competitive interaction.  It is just a different kind of incentive system as contrasted to being paid by the hour.  What is interesting is the idea of workers being more productive in spite of the fact that at least to outsiders it looks like they are under extreme stress even to the point of looking like they would be likely to have a nervous breakdown when in reality the stress is comparable to that of playing on a football team or basketball team, and it becomes almost a fun game.

4.  The idea of extreme competition among academics as being socially desirable.  Normally competition is thought of as being desirable primarily among business firms and is frowned upon in the academic world.

5.  The idea of extreme competition among countries being good, as long as it is not violent.  Violent competition is not desirable whether it is among countries, businesses, workers, or academics.

6. The idea of combining extreme cooperation with extreme competition has some innovative aspects to it whereby workers can be extremely competitive within a team to see who can do the best job but at the same time they recognize that they have to work together in order for their team to win over the competing teams.

A good example is a relay race with four people on each relay team. Each tries to outrun other members of the team. They do not do so in a destructive way whereby they put thumbtacks in each other's shoes. They do so in a positive competitive way where each member of the relay team wants desperately to do better than everybody else on the relay team, but at the same time recognizing that the big honors or additional honors are form having the team win over other teams. That means cheering the other members of one's own team, although partly to provide stiff competition for one's self. That is in recognition that none will be better running against good players than having the competition be weak.

A good example is also in ping pong, or table tennis, where good players refuse to play with people that they can beat by more than a certain number of points. It hurts their game, it wastes their time. They only want to play against people who have a reasonably good chance of beating them because they recognize that improves their own playing. They may even welcome players who will beat them in order to improve their game. It is that kind of competitive attitude that needs to be encouraged. The table tennis analogy could be extended by talking in terms of playing doubles. A good table tennis player in a doubles match wants to excel as an individual while at the same time wants his team to win. It is a good combination of competition between two people on the same side along with cooperation. Each player wants to be a separate hero while at the same time having the sum of the two heroes add up to being an unbeatable team.

Any team that does not have people striving to be individual heroes and only thinking in terms of sacrificing for the good of the team will not do as well as a team that combines both a highly competitive internal spirit and enough cooperation to enable the sum of the parts to outdo the sum of the parts on the opposing teams. There has been no sports hero in any field of sports such as baseball, basketball, or football who ever won much recognition by being great on assisting others. The all-time most valuable player awards (and those are team awards not individual awards) go to leading pitchers, hitters, quarterbacks, and basketball scorers. They do not go to the person who feeds off to the leading basketball scorer or to the person who is great on lateral passes to the runners in football.

## 3. LIBERALS AND CONSERVATIVES TO STILL FIGHT

This material ties in with SOS analysis in trying to bring out the fact that even though an SOS solution enables liberals and conservatives to come out ahead of their best expectations, that does not mean that they submerge their identities in some kind of cooperative effort which loses their individual contributions. Many would say free speech is the most important public policy, because that is where public policy ideas get generated. Its essence is to encourage individuality, and not to encourage people to become part of some kind of cooperative effort where public policy ideas get generated. Its essence is to encourage individuality, and not to encourage people to become part of some kind of cooperative effort where one does not deviate from the mainstream. We want super-optimum solutions where everybody comes out ahead, but everybody still preserves their separate competitive existence. We want liberals and conservatives to still fight, not in the sense of doing anything violent toward each other, but in the sense of competing to see who can come up with the best solutions for social problems and public policy problems. SOS analysis is a bringing together to resolve disputes on a high level of super satisfaction, but not a bringing together to wipe out individuality and competition. We want simultaneously to have vigorous competition partly because it leads to super-optimum solutions.

Someone might say that after achieving the super-optimum solution, then the vigorous competition is no longer needed. The answer to that is that there are always new problems to be resolved because it is impossible to achieve a state of being where there are no scarce resources, where everybody says that they have all they want in terms of health, job opportunities, housing, environmental protection, compliance with the law, and everything else regarding public policy problems.

We know well from previous experience that the more people get the more their appetites frequently get whetted for wanting more. People who have virtually noting in pre-literate societies frequently have very little ambition to improve, partly because they are so much in a rut they find it difficult to conceive that anything could make life better. People who are on the rise, though, get rising expectations and the satisfying of their previous goals causes them to raise their expectations and their future goals. Thus, society can always benefit from competition as to how those goals can be best satisfied at any given point in time with super-optimum solutions.

## II.  COMPETITION IN THE PUBLIC SECTOR

## A.  CONSOLIDATION VERSUS COMPETITION AMONG AGENCIES

A good example would be in the environmental field where policy analysis people in the early 70's pushed for the establishment of an environmental protection agency at the federal level and in all 50 states, arguing that having environmental responsibilities dispersed in so many separate agencies made for a lack of coordination.  Now having them all concentrated in a single agency though makes for a lack of competition.  We could have an SOS in that context by giving the EPA all kinds of coordinating and generalized planning authority without taking away any of the responsibilities from the other agencies.  It does not have to be a trade-off.  The other agencies can even increase their responsibility.  The Department of Agriculture, for example, could increase its responsibility for seeing to it that environmentally harmful pesticides are not used more so than they did prior to 1970 while at the same time having EPA also looking into the subject.  Or the degradation of forests through clear cutting and other anti-conservation devices can be strengthened in the forest service which is in Interior or Agriculture.  At the same time, the EPA can also be concerned with protecting the forest environment, including cross-national coordination that might relate to the harm that acid rain, global warming, or ozone depletion does to forests in other countries.  The key point is that competition is meaningful between government agencies just as it is meaningful between political parties and intelligent ideas and business firms, industries, and nations, and little children playing hopscotch.  It is applicable to stimulating doing a better job regardless what the job is.  Even if it is contrary to traditional administration and organization ideas about pyramidal structures and centralization of authority.

The environmental field has been used to talk about branches of government, levels of government and incentives.  It can also be used to talk about the consolidation of agencies versus competition among agencies.  We should add an SOS table on that important cross-cutting subject.  It happens to apply to the environmental field more clearly than elsewhere because the environmental field is relatively new.  Every other problem already had a government agency dealing with it prior to 1970.  The environmental field acquired its key governmental agency in about 1970.  So did the energy field.  There was no Department of Energy prior to the 1970's.  There was not even a subunit on energy in some other department or some unit on environment in some other department unlike the Department of Education which was formerly part of HEW.  And before that there was an Office of Education before HEW was established. Thus the environment and energy fields presented recent opportunities to decide the question of consolidation versus competition. The feeling was almost unanimously in favor of consolidation. In fact, the concept of competition was not even mentioned as a consideration. It was just considered an obvious conclusion that one did not have ten different agencies all operating in the same area with duplication and conflict and gaps. The trade-off thinking led to taking power away from those agencies and giving it to the EPA. SOS thinking would have resulted in strengthening their power while simultaneously creating an Environmental Protection Agency.

If we think in terms of a liberal approach toward the consolidation versus competition issue, or consolidation versus non-consolidation in the environmental field, the liberal approach was definitely pro-EPA on grounds this would more effectively deal with pollution problems. The conservative approach was not so pro, but not so clearly anti-EPA either, but more in that direction. With some conservatives being explicitly anti-EPA like Herman Kahn and Julian Simon. The neutral approach would be a weak EPA. Reagan can be considered anti-EPA. He appointed Mrs. Buford to head the agency, who immediately asked to have the budget cut to almost nothing, which is the equivalent of dissolving the agency. The super-optimum solution on the question of consolidation versus non-consolidation is to both consolidate and strengthen the components. That would not necessarily please conservatives since they really not only wanted a weak EPA, they also wanted weak components too. The farmers did not want the power of the Department of Agriculture to clamp down on bad pesticides to be increased. For them, arguing in favor of the Department of Agriculture retaining pesticide control versus the EPA getting it was viewed in light of the fact that they could control the United States of America more than they could control EPA. If USDA though was going to be given a congressional mandate to crack down on harmful pesticides, the farmers might prefer a weak EPA in that area than a strong USDA.

There are four possibilities. Weak both, strong both, strong EPA with weak USDA, or weak EPA and strong USDA. The liberals were in favor of the third, the conservatives really wanted the first but argued in favor of the fourth in order to keep the EPA weak. The liberals really should have argued in favor of the second but wrongly perceived that somehow a strong USDA would get in the way of a strong EPA rather than supplement a strong EPA.

If one goal is to protect the environment, then clearly that is better done by having both a strong EPA and a strong USDA on the matter of environmental protection. One though has to recognize that protecting business interests is also a goal in this context and strong on both does not do that. The conservative position does not really have a goal of protecting USDA or the Interior or any other government agency that was involved with environmental matters. Which actually includes almost all of them. Clearly, the State Department is very much involved in anything that is international and not just involving Canada or Mexico. The United States is capable of wrecking the environment of every country in the world by shipping them harmful pesticides or harmful other products. That particularly gets into the jurisdiction of the Commerce Department with regard to international trade agreements and can relate to American automobiles not complying with the exhaust requirements of other countries--either explicit requirements or the public interest of other countries.

This is not an SOS situation where both environmental interests and business interests come out ahead of their best expectations. It is only where the pro-consolidation and the pro-decentralization both come out ahead of their best expectations. Centralization though and decentralization are often just camouflage for some other economic interests. Business may greatly favor decentralization of the states when it comes to environmental protection since the states are easier to manipulate by business boosters. They do not favor decentralization of the states though when it comes to regulating interstate transportation, especially trucking where different and possibly conflicting state rules can make the trucking of goods needlessly expensive as contrasted to a uniform national system.

This is a subject that is actually more worth discussing in the competition part of the SOS Methods Book than in the environmental part, although the EPA can be used as an illustrative example. What it mainly contributes is a broadening of the usefulness of the concept of competition to include competition among government agencies which carried to its logical extreme might involve competing police departments, fire departments, public schools.

1. The public school idea and the fire and police idea are already almost old hat. All three have to compete with various forms of private protection. The public schools compete with private schools. The public schools compete with each other in the sense that people are somewhat free to move from Chicago to another school district outside of Chicago if the Chicago schools are not coming up to a minimum level. They can also change police departments and fire departments by moving to another location too. That is a form of geographical competition. It does not work so well with cable TV or electric power companies, because they are almost 100% uniformly inefficient, arrogant, whereas some police forces are much better than others and some public school systems are better than others, and so are some fire departments. It is interesting to

note in recent news that the city of Chicago is seriously contemplating throwing out Commonwealth Edison as intolerable and inviting bids from all electric companies anywhere in the world to supply electricity to the city of Chicago. That should be actively encouraged by free market conservatives as well as anti-big business liberals. It could establish a wonderful new precedent that could lead to the same kind of breakup of monopoly and replace it with competition as occurred in long-distance telephoning, or a good deal of airline passenger activity.

2.  Within the same city one can do some choosing between public and private schools and also private police protection. There is not that much market for private fire protection. Fire departments seem to be almost the opposite of electricity companies in that they tend to be almost uniformly above an acceptable level of competence, with the electric companies being almost uniformly below an acceptable level of competence, and the police departments and schools varying with some above and some below and some in the middle.

3.  It does not seem so likely that within the same city one would have two Chicago police departments. The closest thing is that within the city of Chicago there are state police, city police, and federal police. All three levels of government compete in some areas, especially in the more major crimes. The FBI is not going to arrest somebody for overtime parking, but all three levels of police might be interested in a kidnapping case or a terrorism case or a case involving anti-trust violations. Any anti-trust case that cuts across numerous states, as most are likely to do, involves competition among the states for which they can most effectively stop the abuse of consumers that may be occurring. A former Illinois Attorney General before he went to prison for income tax evasion won many votes by suing General Motors or other big businesses for various kinds of consumer fraud that was occurring in states other than Illinois just as much as in Illinois.

## B.  COMPETITION AMONG PUBLIC SCHOOLS POLICE DEPARTMENTS, AND POLITICAL PARTIES

Public school education can be made more competitive in the following ways:

1.  More competition among teachers with salary rewards for quality work or for working in neighborhoods where teachers are reluctant to work.

2.  More competition among students for academic honors and less competition for sports honors.

3.  More competition among school districts by publicizing how well school districts are doing on SAT scores, college entrance percentages,

and other variables, including publicity over time so that they are in effect competing with their past.

4. Rent supplements and anti-snob zoning laws in order to facilitate people voting with their feet by moving to better school districts more easily.

5. Conservatives talk about vouchers that would enable public school children to go to private schools. That is not an example of competition to improve quality. It is frequently motivated by and results in pure racism and economic class bias.

6. A voucher system could be meaningful to enable public school children to pay transportation costs and school lunch costs to attend a public school in the middle class neighborhoods of their district, or even outside their district. That is an example of a use of vouchers to promote integration rather than to promote private school racism or private school religious fundamentalism or parochial Catholic schools under the guise of competition to promote quality.

7. We could also talk about competition at the higher education level, which gets into regional and international competition. One of the best ways the government can promote competition among universities or among business firms is to publicize how well each producer is doing on various objective criteria so as to embarrass many universities in the United States that lay people think are good universities such as expensive private universities, the military academies, religious schools. Those universities are not likely to do very well on Nobel Prize winners, or even the percentage or quantity of people who go on to become doctors or lawyers or professors, especially if one thinks in terms of benefit/cost ratios. The state universities would look much better than the lay public thinks given the low tuitions and the high results in terms of various quality indicators.

Competition with regard to police protection:

1. The first thing that comes to mind is hiring private police. That is all right for rich business firms. A ghetto dweller is not going to hire a private police company to protect his family from being burglarized and mugged.

2. As mentioned above, publicizing quality indicators for different police departments across the country or different police stations within a given city stimulates better output including quality indicators over time so that one competes with oneself the way a jogger tries to improve.

3. The rent supplement idea enables people who live in neighborhoods with bad police protection to move elsewhere more easily just as it enables people to move who live in neighborhoods with bad schools. Most of what is said above about competition among schools can also apply to police protection and other government services.

4. More competition among police officers for internal police department rewards such as salary increases, promotions, and honors.

5. In dealing with competition at the governmental service level, some of the methods that apply in the private sector may not be so applicable, but thinking about them might stimulate some applicable ideas such as contracting out to domestic or international business firms. This is not the same as a business firm hiring a private detective agency. What it means is that the city of Chicago would have the responsibility for providing good police protection throughout the city, but instead of doing it through Chicago employees it might hire a professional agency if the agency or business firm can meet the specifications with regard to personnel and equipment. There would then by competition among such business firms to get the contracts. All contracts would be subject to renewal every year or so in order to make it clear that the contracts do not last forever regardless of a drop in the quality of service. It is quite possible that such a contracting out could lead to a more sensitive police operation in the inner city than is currently provided by an arrogant police force that in effect does have a contract forever.

One-party non-competition.

1. This is a totally different area in which to encourage competition. Here it definitely does not make sense to say we will contract out to business firms to set up political parties.

2. The device that is sometimes advocated for getting more competition among parties is proportional representation rather than single-member districts where only a major or dominant political party can win. Proportional representation provides too much diffusion and gives too much power to small swing parties in forming a ruling condition.

3. Free speech is very important in developing opposition which develops opposition political parties. That means no restrictions on political communication with regard to content.

4. There may have to be restrictions on spending so as to prevent one party from spending itself into a monopolistic position. The best way to deal with that is through government financing of elections which pays the costs of both the incumbent party and the opposition, as well as other major parties if there are any.

5. The government can provide facilities for political parties that are capable of getting at least ten percent or so of the vote. The facilities can include a speaking hall, radio time, TV time. The object is to subsidize the low-income parties that are not minor splinter parties but are major viewpoints as indicated by the percentage of votes they are capable of getting but would not be very competitive without a subsidy,

which the dominant party does not need. This would not run contrary to majority rule. The minority party would still have to convince voters that it is the better or best party in order to get elected.

6. Redistricting so as to give opposition parties a fair chance of getting represented in the legislature. That is the proportionate representation that goes with geography, not with saying that a party that gets one percent of the votes is entitled to one percent of the legislators.

7. Anything that increases registration and turnout is likely to increase political action and a diversity of major viewpoints. If only a relatively small portion of the population is registered and votes, that segment of the population in effect has a monopoly on running the government even though within that segment there may be more than one party.

## III.  THE PUBLIC AND THE PRIVATE SECTORS

The East German economy has been a relative failure compared to the West German economy since World War II. This has been used as a factor to show the superiority of capitalism over socialism. Some contrary evidence is the fact that the Swedish socialistic economy has flourished since World War II in spite of relatively few people and resources. The Spanish capitalistic economy has been a much greater failure than the East German socialistic economy since World War II. One can get much greater predictability out of knowing whether a society has a competitive economy and political system (versus a monopolistic one) than out of knowing whether it is a capitalistic private-ownership economy (or a socialistic government ownership economy).

Both East Germany and Spain have been failures in terms of providing high standards of living for their people. They both have one-party monopolistic political systems, although one was communist and the other was fascist. They both have monopolistic economic systems which try to deep out foreign goods through high tariffs, with government-favored business firms, although one had government-owned firms the other had privately-owned firms

Both West Germany and Sweden have been successes in terms of providing high standards of living for their people. They both have competitive political systems, with strong two-party competition, whereby the out-part is constantly trying to offer better ideas than the in-party. They both encourage competition among business firms and allow foreign competition. Thus comparing East Germany and West Germany does point to ways in which public policy can improve the quality of life, but it is a public policy that encourages competition over monopoly, not necessarily one that encourages capitalism over socialism.

Table 4-1 shows that political and economic competition relate to a high degree of prosperity. Both kinds of competition have been present in prosperous West Germany and Sweden. Until relatively recently, both kinds of competition have been absent in relatively impoverished East Germany and Spain. Table 4-2 analyzes competition as an SOS economic solution. In that table, the conservative alternative is the unregulated marketplace, which may lead to privatized monopolies. The liberal alternative is public ownership, which leads to government monopolies. The mixed economy with both kinds of monopolies is a form of compromise. The SOS alternative is stimulating competition through well-placed seed money to facilitate the establishment of competing business firms.

TABLE 4-1. POLITICAL AND ECONOMIC COMPETITION
AS KEY CAUSES OF PROSPERITY

|  |  | COMPETITION (Casual Variable) (In Politics and Economics) | |
|---|---|---|---|
|  |  | No | Yes |
| PROSPERITY OR HIGH STANDARD OF LIVING (Effect Variable) | Yes |  | West Germany (Capitalism) Sweden (Socialism) |
|  | No | East Germany (Socialism) Spain Pre-1980 (Capitalism) |  |

NOTES:

1. The table only includes industrial nations. A separate table could be made for developing nations.

2. Among industrialized nations, those that provide for competition in politics and economics have more prosperity than those who do not provide for competition in both activities. Industrialized nations that

NOTES: 4-1 continued

Table *provide for competition in only one of the two activities are likely to have middling prosperity, although competition in politics may be more important to prosperity than competition in economics.*

3.  *The table is mainly designed to relate political and economic competition as key causes in prosperity. One could also interpret the table as tending to show that countries that have economic competition are more likely to have political competition and vice versa.*

4.  *One could also interpret the table as tending to show that industrialized nations are more likely to have a higher standard of living than non-industrialized nations regardless of political and economic competition. Another conclusion which the table generates is that whether a country has capitalistic private ownership or socialistic government ownership is virtually irrelevant to prosperity in comparison to political-economic competition and industrialization.*

TABLE 4-2.  COMPETITION AS AN SOS ECONOMIC SOLUTION

| Criteria | C GOAL | L GOAL | N TOTAL | C TOTAL | L TOTAL |
|---|---|---|---|---|---|
| | Business Profits | Low Prices | (Neutral Weights) | (Conservative Weights) | (Liberal Weights) |
| Alternatives | | | | | |
| C Alternative Marketplace (Monopoly) | 4 | 2 | 12 | 14* | 10 |
| L Alternative Govt. Ownership or Tight Regulation | 2 | 4 | 12 | 10 | 14* |
| N Alternative Some of Both (Mixed Economy) | 3 | 3 | 12 | 12 | 12 |
| SOS Alternative Stimulate Competition Through Well-Placed Subsidies | ≥3.5 | ≧3.5 | >14 | >14** | >14** |

*NOTES:*

1. *The conservative Alternative of an unregulated marketplace may lead to only one or a few firms dominating most industries. That arrangement may be profitable in the short run, although contrary to low prices.*

2. *The liberal Alternative of government ownership or tight regulation tends to mean a government monopoly or stifled private enterprise. That means reduced business profits, although it might mean artificially low prices to satisfy consumers as voters.*

3. *The mixed economy scores in the middle on both business profits and low prices.*

4. *The SOS Alternative may draw upon the stimulus to innovation and efficiency of private profit making. The SOS Alternative may encourage competition through well-placed seed money. Doing so results in lower prices through a competitive marketplace, rather than through a monopolistic one or through artificial price constraints.*

# PART THREE:

# THE SOCIAL PSYCHOLOGY OF SOS SOLUTIONS

# CHAPTER 5

## THE POSITIVE PSYCHOLOGY OF
## SUPER-OPTIMUM SOLUTIONS

Thidschapter is concerned with such psychological aspects of super-optimum solutions as:

1. Methods for generating alternative policies or decisions, including SOS policies and decisions.
2. Combining pessimism and optimism in super-optimizing analysis.
3. Relations between high societal goals and societal happiness.
4. Risk taking.
5. Socialization and public policy.
6. Balancing positive and negative discretion.

### I. METHODS FOR GENERATING ALTERNATIVE
### POLICIES AND DECISIONS

The purpose of this section is to describe a variety of methods for generating ideas concerning public policies, administrative decision, or other ideas, across all substantive fields. These ideas are relevant to reaching conclusions as to what alternative, combination of alternatives, or allocation of scarce resources should be adopted in order to achieve given goals in light of the relations between the alternatives and the goals.

Other literature has been developed dealing with generating goals and relations. Generating goals is largely a normative or value-oriented matter. Generating relations between goals and alternatives is largely an empirical or observation-based matter. Generating alternatives is more a matter of creativity. Like all forms of creativity, however, generating alternatives can be stimulated by appropriate interaction, incentives, working conditions, and other factors.[1]

The list of factors is organized in terms of pushing factors, facilitators, and pulling factors. That three-part organization comes from Frederick Jackson Turner's analysis of the causes of people moving west in the 1800's. The pushing factors included undesirable aspects of the east, such as crowding, lack of jobs, and debts. Facilitating factors included wagon trails, railroads, river systems, and other means of transportation. Pulling factors included attractions in the west, such as free land and business opportunities.

The material emphasizes general ideas about generating ideas. The generation of ideas may be the most important skill to be developed by public administrators, social science scholars, or anybody.

## A. PUSHING FACTORS

### 1. OTHER PEOPLE
Talk with someone else about generating alternatives. Trying to explain alternative ways of achieving something with an audience listening stimulates more ideas than either talking or thinking to one's self. Put one's head together with someone else who is trying to come up with ideas. The interaction of two or more people trying to generate ideas tends to work better than one person alone.

Have contact with stimulating colleagues via correspondence, conventions, informal campus relations, or other on-the-job relations. Work with graduate students and undergraduates to develop dissertations, seminar papers, and term papers. Work with different people to provide a variety of interaction.

Arrange to be asked questions by people with a variety of orientations, including sincere inquiry, skepticism, cynicism, and even a touch of malice. Try to operate in an interdisciplinary environment for a greater variety of perspectives. Apply one's creative ideas to see what happens in practice.

## 2. COMMITMENTS

Accept a commitment to write an article, a book chapter, or a conference paper on how to deal with a policy problem. That is likely to generate new alternatives. Teach in those field in which one wants to generate policy alternatives. Take on obligations to co-author articles, chapters, or papers.

Take on obligations to do consulting work which involves generating alternatives. Prepare grant proposals. Arrange for competitive situations as a stimulus to developing new ideas.

## B. FACILITATORS

### 1. LITERATURE

Consult the literature in the field. There may be lots of alternatives already suggested. There are some software checklists that might be worth trying such as "Trigger" published by Thoughtware and the "Idea Generator" published by Experience in Software, Inc., 2039 Shattuck Avenue, Suite 401, Berkeley, CA, 94701. Keep up with the newest ideas in various policy fields. Read provocative literature.

Know the general literature in the fields in which one is interested. Read some of the literature on creativity including the list of references attached to this article. Have theoretical frameworks that can serve as checklists and prods for developing alternatives.

Be familiar with the methods of knowing, including how to inductively generalize, how to deduce conclusions, how to determine what authorities hold, and how to do sensitivity analysis. Think about ways of generating ideas like this list, or adding to this list.

### 2. WORKING STYLE

Talk out loud about the possible alternatives. Dictating is better than thinking in generating ideas. Delegate work to others in order to have more time to think. Have a pencil and paper handy at all times or dictating equipment to write or dictate ideas that come to one's mind before they are lost.

Schedule time periods for creative development and implementation of ideas. The more time periods the better. Occasionally travel in order to provide a variety of environments. Have good assistance on matters that relate to office management, data processing, library work, secretarial help, computer programming, etc.

Take a break and then come back to a problem, especially after a night's sleep which may bring forth new ideas. Clarify to one's self the general areas in which one wants to be creative. Think positively about one's capability to developing alternatives and answers.

## 3.  MULTI-CRITERIA DECISION MAKING

Try listing some alternatives, even if one only has in mind one or two alternatives to begin with.  Merely trying to generate a list tends to result in more items being listed than one originally had in mind or thought one had in mind.

After generating some alternatives, then generate some criteria for evaluating them.  That will lead to more alternatives.  After generating alternatives and criteria, then generate some relations between the alternatives and criteria.  That will lead to more alternatives.

After generating alternatives, criteria, and relations, then generate some initial conclusions.  That may lead to more alternatives.  After generating alternatives, criteria, relations, and initial conclusions, then do various forms of sensitivity analysis designed to determine what it would take to bring a second or other place alternative up to first place. That may generate still more alternatives.

If there is a situation where there are two conflicting sides, each one favoring a different alternative, look to see what kind of alternative could maybe satisfy the goals of both sides.  If there is a situation where there are conflicting sides, each favoring a different alternative, look to the possibility of a compromise alternative that will partially satisfy each side if it is not possible to find an alternative that will fully satisfy both sides.

When observing how the alternatives score on the criteria, ask how each alternative can be improved.  Try to convert the alternatives, criteria, relations, tentative conclusions, and sensitivity analysis into a publishable table with notes.  That may generate new alternatives.

### C.  PULLING FACTORS:  REWARDS

Be motivated to want to generate alternatives.  Arrange to be in situations where one is rewarded for generating alternatives.  Explicitly think about the benefits one receives from generating alternatives, such as recognition, grants, publishing opportunities, graduate students, and consulting opportunities.

Non-intellectual rewards can also be arranged for.  That might include money, power, love, food, sleep, and pure recreation.  Operate in a permissive environment that encourages experimentation and new ideas.  The earlier one can get into such an environment the better, preferably starting at birth.

Some people use heredity as an excuse for not being brighter or more creative.  In both areas, there is a substantial range in which each person can operate.  If one is more determined, then one can operate closer to the top (rather than the bottom) of one's inherited range.  Creativity is probably less a matter of heredity than intelligence is. It is more susceptible to the kind of pushing, facilitating, and pulling factors mentioned above. Thus one can more easily arrange to be a more creative person than one can arrange to be a brighter person by seeking more favorable occurrences of those factors. Doing so can be regarding in itself, as well as producing the kinds of rewards mentioned above. The broader rewards accrue not only to the individual, but also to the many potential beneficiaries of individual creativity. It is an ability well worth stimulating by both society and by one's self.

## D.  BALANCING FACT-LEARNING WITH STIMULATING CREATIVITY AND REASONING POWERS

Both fact-learning and creativity are important in education. People do need to know some basic facts like the law of gravity, $2 + 2 = 4$, Columbus discovered American in about 1492, etc.

### 1.  PEOPLE NEED TO KNOW SOME FACTS

To say that people need to know some facts does not mean that it should be the main purpose, or even a major purpose of education. It should be a minor purpose in a good educational system. Maybe the division should be 20% fact learning and 80% learning how to reason and be creative. Teach people a fact, and they will be able to answer one question on a trivia quiz. Teach a person how to reason, and he may be able to win a Nobel Prize some day and contribute a lot more to the world even if the does not win a Nobel Prize. Make that about 10% fact learning and 90% reasoning and creativity.

In spite of what should be, the empirical reality is just the opposite. Most education is about 90% fact learning and 10% reasoning. The reason is that the people who teach find it a lot easier to communicate facts than to teach reason, and especially how to be creative. It is partly a vicious circle because that is the training they receive. That is the training they pass on. The cycle needs to be broken. In the childhood socialization model, we need to provide for a big module for encouraging creativity and reasoning.

### 2.  CREATIVITY IS MUCH MORE IMPORTANT

Between reasoning and creativity, creativity is much more important. And much harder to teach. At the elementary school level, one can teach simple logic. It is sometimes done in arithmetic classes. It is attempted in geometry classes but quite divorced from anything worth reasoning about. The most meaningful logic course deals with controversial subject matter that relates to social institutions, not parallel lines. If students learn that 2 + 2 = 4 and 3 + 1 = 4, then it is logical that 2 + 2 would equal 3 + 1. That is not the kind of logic, though, that is especially important for reasoning in the real world. The most important kind of logic is reasoning by analogy where one says X causes Y, Z is like X with regard to what is relevant, therefore Z probably also causes Y. Or, Z is not like X with regard to what is relevant, therefore Z probably does not cause Y. There is no notion of arithmetic equality in that kind of reasoning. Almost nothing is equal or identical in the real world. Things are just probable. What logic needs to emphasize is the logic of similarities and analogies, and the logic of probabilities.

Elementary school children can understand simple analogies. That is not part of their usual learning. They can also understand simple probabilities, but that is not part of it. The first time they may encounter analogies is on the ACT. It is almost as if analogies have been held back from them so that they can be subjected to a Miller's analogy test. The first time they may encounter probabilistic reasoning is in a college finite math course, or in a high school math course where the probabilities are nonsense because they are not empirical probabilities but mathematical probabilities, like the probability of getting two heads in two tosses of a coin. That is not the kind of probability that anyone ever faces in real life, but it is the sort of thing emphasized in discussing probabilities in a textbook. In real life, people are constantly thinking of implicit empirical probabilities, like the probability of getting hit by a car when walking across a street when the car is a certain distance away and could accelerate while the person is crossing. People maintain that the car will maintain whatever speed the car is moving at.

## 3. TEACHING CREATIVITY: NO RIGHT ANSWERS

Teaching creativity may mean presenting students with problems for which there are no right answers. That is almost unheard of. That is what we do in SOS analysis. There are no right answers in the following senses:

1. Any answer that one comes up with is subject to improvement.

2. Any answer is subject to what-if analysis whereby the answer changes if one changes the goals, alternatives available, or relations.

3. The best problems are those that sound impossible and where the instructor and the students brainstorm tentative answers.

4. The answers clearly depend on the weights that re assigned to the goals and what the goals are. Those are value judgments. They have some objective reality when we talk about the goals of conservatives or liberals. On a higher level of generality, though, one has to operate with certain assumptions that do not have objective reality but are taken as givens, such as utilitarian principles.

It is not meaningful to teach creativity at the elementary school level using SOS problems. One can get problems out of puzzle books, though. Most of them have only one right answer such as if three men take six hours to dig one hole, how long will it take two men to do it? That is reasoning rather than creativity. It is worse than that. It is rote memorizing once one knows what the formula is. The immediate reaction is to think that 3 over 6 somehow equals X, and then solve for X. X equals 4, which is absolute nonsense. If three men take six hours to dig a hole, two men are not going to dig it faster than three. They are not going to dig it in only four hours. One then senses that maybe something is literally upside down. The best way to reason it out is that if 3 men take 6 hours, then if you only had 1-1/2 men it would take twice as long, namely 12 hours. If you had 6 men, it should take half as long, maybe only 3 hours. With 2 men, we should be able to interpolate how long it would take. With one man, it should take 3 times as long as 3 men, which is 18 hours. So we just chop 18 hours in half and we have what it takes 2 men to do, namely 9 hours. The reasoning is simply to figure out from the original information how long does it take one person to do it, then multiply that by however many people the problem asks for. But there is only one right answer.

The creative answer might be that it may take 2 men less than 9 hours, because maybe the 2 men will not talk as much as 3 men would. It may be that it will take them more than 9 hours because they cannot qualify so well as an inspirational group with only 2 people. It may be that it will take more or less than 9 hours because no one said these were 2 out of the original three. Maybe these are 2 out of the 3, but the scrawniest 2 or the brawniest 2. The teacher needs to emphasize the idea of no one right answer. That is a part of the essence of creativity. Or it could be done with any arithmetic problem, especially though probabilities as contrasted to some abstract numbers. It is hard to come to any conclusion other than 4, when asked how much is 2 + 2. The thought problems bring in a human element, i.e., they relate to the real world rather than the world of abstract numbers. A course in arithmetic in which there are no right answers to any of the problems would be conducive to creativity. I have never seen a textbook in arithmetic in which the answer key in the back gives 5 or 10 different possible answers, depending on various circumstances. That is unheard of, but that could be the best kind of arithmetic course, or any kind of course. Arithmetic lends itself better, maybe, because one expects objective reality there since we are not dealing with value judgments. A good course in science might be one that deals with nothing but controversial issues in science on which physicists disagree, or chemists or biologists disagree, including respectable scientists, not crackpot scientists.

One might argue that one cannot talk about how the universe was formed unless one first talks about some elementary astronomy. That is untrue. One may learn a lot more about astronomy by going right to the ultimate of how the universe was formed than by trying to memorize what is the distance between earth and Pluto, or the diameter of the seventh moon of Neptune. Those particular facts are not regularly taught in astronomy, of course, but many trivial are, such as whether the earth revolves around the sun. At one time that was controversial, but it is no longer. It does not make any difference of a practical nature as to how the universe was formed, but it does stimulate creativity. It could stimulate creativity to ask students how can one go about proving that the earth revolves around the sun rather than vice versa. That is a creativity challenge for which people like Copernicus and Kepler won the Nobel prize in astronomy in their day. The ironic thing is that almost nobody who takes a course in elementary astronomy knows the answer to that more interesting question of how does one find out. A creative answer might be that you go up in a rocket far enough away from both the earth and the sun and you watch for about 365 days and see what happens. That alternative was not available, though, to Copernicus. One has to be able to prove that the earth revolves around the sun while one never leaves Warsaw, Poland.

Gallileo in effect went up in a rocket in order to prove that one of Jupiter's moons revolves around Jupiter. He could see in his telescope, watching over a period of months, that the moon did go around Jupiter. He was almost executed for that because the prevailing thought was that everything went around the earth, including the moons of Jupiter. The answer with regard to proving that the earth goes around the sun is that someone noted that the sun is for all practical purposes not moving relative to other objects in space, like stars and planets, but the earth is. Actually, the sun is moving too but the earth is going along with it. The question is not is the sun moving on some straight line out from some universe origin. The question is, is the sun going in a circle around the earth? If it were, then at different times of the year the sun would be in different positions. It just so happens that the sun is in different positions, but that is because the earth is tilted on its axis. The sun is therefore lower in the sky in December-January and higher in the sky in June-July. Or at least, this is the case in Poland and elsewhere in the northern hemisphere. That tends to cause one to think that the sun is moving. I think that the bottom line is that the earth is moving around the sun on a 365-day orbit on an axis that is tilted at a certain angle and rotting every 24 hours on that axis is logically consistent with al kinds of behavior of the sun, moon, planets, and earth. Thus, the proof is not an empirical proof as much as it is a logical internal consistency proof.

No other explanation is logically internally consistent. The idea of the sun revolving around the earth produces inconsistencies.

## 4. EDUCATIONAL POLICY

Educational policy with regard to the idea that education should first encourage creativity, second reasoning skills, and a distant third, factual knowledge. Make that a distant fourth. Somewhere on a higher level should be learning how to read with high reading speed and comprehension and learning how to write. Those are two basic skills that are separate from creativity, reasoning, or factual knowledge. Learning arithmetic could be considered factual knowledge if one memorized multiplication tables. It could be reasoning if one learns how to reason out that 8x2=16. That kind of reasoning is not worth mastering. It is based on the idea that multiplication is basically multiple addition, namely adding 2 to itself 8 times, or adding 8 to itself twice. The best way to do multiplication is with a calculator, namely no memorizing, no reasoning, just know what buttons to hit, at least for the bigger arithmetic problems. For smaller ones, explicit reasoning is rather out of place, just as going through a spreadsheet decision analysis would be out of place in deciding whether to cross the street, or which shoe between your left and right to put on first. There are definitely some things that are so trivial that it does not make any difference. That may not be the case, though, with regard to arithmetic. It depends on the subject matter. In the abstract, saying 2+2=5 causes no harm. In a concrete situation, it may mean the difference between a bridge falling down and staying up. Offhand, I cannot see where which shoe you put on first, though, has any significance. Some things are always trivial regardless of the circumstances.

The other place is in the material that relates to creativity as a possible prerequisite for developing SOS solutions. It sometimes is. The object though is to develop checklists so that one can develop SOS solutions with a minimum of creativity. It is unlikely though that the process can ever be reduced to a checklist that a computer could follow.[2]

## II. COMBINING PESSIMISM AND OPTIMISM

What kinds of attitudes are most likely to bring about a better quality of life for people in developing countries? In that regard, there are three kinds of optimists and three kinds of pessimists. The optimists include:

1. The stultifying optimist who says things are fine now and will be fine in the future.

2. The inspirational optimist who says things are miserable now, but could be fine in the future if we or the relevant people work at it.

3. The middling optimist who says things are neither fine nor miserable now, but there is room for improvement, and that working to bring about the improvements may have some effect.

The pessimists include:

4. The pessimist who says things are miserable now, and they will be miserable in the future regardless what we or the relevant people do.

5. The pessimist who says things are good now, but they are going to be horrible in the future.

6. The middling pessimist who is middling about how good or bad things presently are, but who by definition sees the future as being bad.

Of those six attitudes, the attitude most conducive to progress in developing countries is the second category. The first and third categories are not sufficiently inspirational because they tend to be too satisfied with things as they are. The fourth, fifth, and sixth categories are not sufficiently inspirational because they are too pessimistic as to what the future holds. We could also have a seventh category that combines the inspirational optimist in believing things are miserable but could be greatly improved with hard work, but that people lack the ability or willingness to do the hard work. This is more of a pessimistic category than an optimistic one.

A key element in building developing countries (or improving developed countries) is a favorable attitude toward how much influence one thinks people have over the future. Those who believe that the future is determined by supernatural forces, fate, or other forces beyond human control are in effect a detriment to progressive social change. So are those who believe in the potential of human efficacy, but are pessimistic about the potential being exercised.

A good example of optimism or positive thinking in dealing with developing countries is given in the concluding paragraph of Jan Hogendorn, *Economic Development* (Harper Collins, 1991). A shoe company sent two marketing experts to a poor developing country to determine the prospects for selling shoes there. The country may have been a composite of Bolivia in Latin America, Malawi in Africa, and Bangladesh in Asia.

Both marketing experts observed that a high percentage of the people did not wear shoes. The first marketing expert who had a negative and pessimistic orientation wrote back that the prospects for sales were bad because so few people wore shoes. The second expert who had a positive and optimistic orientation wrote back that the prospects for sales were good because so many people were in need of shoes.

Hogendorn is right in saying that two people can observe exactly the same empirical reality (such as only 20% of the people in the country wear shoes) and arrive at opposite conclusions as to what action should be taken. He may, however, be wrong in implying that mere optimism can get the job done. The best response may have been that the prospects for sales are potentially good if the buying power of the people can be improved so they can afford the shoes that one might reasonably assume they would like to buy. The shoe company, however, may not be in a position to increase the buying power of the people, although relevant public policy-makers and analysts might be. Such policy people might work for the government of the country, an American agency like A.I.D., a global agency like the World Bank, or a policy analysis training program like that of the Policy Studies Organization.

The most correct position might be that without improving the economy, the pessimism of the first expert is correct. With the improvements that can come with effective public policy, the second expert is correct. That synthesis is not a compromise between the two experts. It is a super-optimum perspective whereby with the right public policy, the ownership of shoes in the real or hypothetical country can exceed the best expectations of all the perspectives. [3]

### III. RELATIONS BETWEEN HIGH SOCIETAL GOALS AND SOCIETAL HAPPINESS

One might question whether it is socially desirable to set societal goals substantially higher than one is likely to achieve. The same question might be raised concerning individual goals. Some people say that it is better to set one's goals low and achieve them than it is to set one's goals high and not achieve them. They further argue that happiness is not measured by achievement, but by the size of the gap between goals and achievement.

That philosophy of minimizing the gap has many defects. Carried to its logical extreme, we should all have as our goals in life to be no more than winos, bag people, and other forms of derelicts. Then it would be difficult to fail if we set our sights so low. This is sometimes referred to as happiness by "downward comparisons." See Michalos (1985, 1986). It is epitomized in the idea of telling people who have no shoes that they should be glad to have feet. People who are severely disabled or economically destitute would thus be told how happy or satisfied they should be just to be alive.

Actually it would be quite difficult for most people to achieve the goal of being a derelict. Most people have been socialized into having much higher goals. It might thus be impossible for them to bring their goals drastically down without becoming very unhappy. Doing so would result in a gap between expectations and achievement. Those who do not like a downward comparisons approach to obtaining happiness sometimes reject it on the grounds that it is morally undesirable. See Michalos (1985, 1986). A firmer basis would be to show through logical reasoning and empirical data that downward comparisons do not bring as much happiness as upward achievement.

One might be happy with low goals if everyone else also had low goals. If, however, an individual or a country is highly unusual in having low goals, the individual or country is going to be unhappy unless it can isolate itself from being aware of how well others are doing. This is consistent with the findings reported by Michalos about the importance of deprivation relative to one's reference group.

In feudalistic times, people may have been happy to get through the day without bubonic plague, starvation, or being caught in the middle of a feudalistic war. In modern times, people expect a lot more regarding public policy toward health, poverty, and violent death than people in the dark ages. This is consistent with the idea that one's goals become higher as one's capabilities become greater.

Suppose one person has a goal of earning $100,000 a year, or of producing $100,000 worth of useful goods a year, whichever sounds better. Suppose that person, however, is capable of achieving only $50,000 a year. Suppose further that another person only has in mind to achieve $10,000 a year in the same society and fully succeeds. Not many people would rather be the "successful" $10,000 a year person over the "unsuccessful" $50,000 a year person. In other words, people judge others and themselves in terms of what they achieve more than or as well as the gap between goals and achievement. The gap between goals and achievement may also be quite important to happiness, as Michalos indicates.

The person who has a $100,000 goal is more likely to achieve at the $50,000 level than a person who has only a $50,000 level. There seems to be a natural tendency to not fully achieve goals. This is so because goals are like incentives that stimulate further effort, especially when they are just out of reach, like the carrot that hangs in front of the donkey to make the donkey move forward. This point is in effect saying that high goals are desirable because they stimulate greater productivity and creativity and thereby benefit society, even if individuals with high goals are not happy. Thus high societal goals can be justified pragmatically.

Contrary to the position which recommends setting one's goals low or "realistically" to achieve happiness, there are numerous examples of people who are saddened by having achieved their goals and having lost the excitement of the pursuit. One does not have to be Alexander the Great to want new things to conquer. Business people and others sometimes say that getting an uncontrollable flood of mail is bad, but much worse is getting no mail at all. In other words, people like to have something in their boxes to be done. They do not like having nothing to do as a result of having achieved their goals. What this point is in effect saying is that there is a hill-shaped relation between happiness as an effect and the goals-achievement gap as a cause. That means happiness is low if the gap is either very small or very large. The gap-theory people tend to overemphasize the right side of the hill-shaped curve where happiness goes down as the gap becomes bigger, rather than the left side of the hill-shaped curve where happiness goes down as the gap becomes smaller. The optimum gap is somewhere in the middle.

In management by objectives, it is considered much better to have 50% achievement on a big objective than 100% achievement on a small objective. For example, on a 0 to 100 scale, if a big objective is scored 80, then 50% achievement would be worth 45 points. A specific small objective might be scored 5, and 100% success would receive the full 5 points. Thus in this example, 50% success on a 90-point objective would be nine times as worthy as 100% success on a 5-point objective. One might object to this on the grounds that saying a 45-point achievement is better or more worthy than a 5-point achievement is not the same as saying that it is more happiness-producing. One might further argue there is an implied assumption that achievement is good or worthy for society regardless of the personal happiness of the achiever. That assumption may be true, but what is really being argued is that achievement brings both personal happiness and societal happiness, and that achievement is encouraged by having high but realistically attainable goals.

Applying the same kind of reasoning to societal goals as is expressed in those points, one can say that no goals are too high so long as they are physically possible. Even what is physically impossible may be subject to change. It is thus socially desirable for a society to be an optimizing society, or one that is seeking to achieve the optimum or the super-optimum on various social indicators. That is true with regard to public policies concerning unemployment, inflation, crime, world peace, free speech, poverty, discrimination, health, environment, education, consumers, and government structures/procedures. It is hoped that this chapter will stimulate further ideas along the lines of doing better than the optimum, both with regard to what it means and how to do it.[4]

## IV. RISK TAKING

## A. RELEVANCE TO TECHNOLOGICAL INNOVATION

### 1. RISKING REPUTATION AND RESOURCES

Both the left wing and right wing by definition are deviant types compared to the mainstream middle. There is a certain risk in being a deviant type as contrasted to being a conformist. In the past, political scientists have emphasized that left wing and right wing extremists share a common authoritarianism. We are not talking about extremists in the sense of Nazis on the right and some kind of bloodthirsty communists on the left. We are talking in the context of American politics about people like Norman Thomas Socialists in the 1930s or up to about 1960 when there was some deviance involved in being a Socialist. We are also talking about respectable conservatives like William Buckley and the *National Review.*

What we are really talking about is not the risks involved in being politically deviant. We are talking about the risks involved in devoting time, money, and other resources to undertakings that may turn out to be a big waste. On the other hand, they could turn out to be highly useful, including nuclear energy on the right, or solar energy on the left. The energy field is a good field where great amounts of time and money have been wasted, at least as a matter of hindsight. It is an example, though, where great amounts of money have also been fantastically successful.

### 2. THE ENERGY FIELD

In the energy field, James Watt spent a substantial amount of time inventing a steam engine which revolutionized the world, as contrasted to just tending his horseshoeing, ironworking, or whatever conformist activity he could have done. He may have been a wheelwright (or some other kind of wright) who could have spent the rest of his life making wheels for wagons.

Albert Einstein is an example of someone who spent a substantial amount of his time inventing the idea of getting energy from matter. That could still revolutionize the energy world, although nuclear energy has been somewhat of a disappointment, especially in the United States. It is still greatly increasing in use elsewhere, where the power companies are trusted and have more of a track record for efficiency, credibility, and public interest.

The energy field is also an example where billions of dollars have been wasted as indicated by the Seabrook plant, the Clinton plant, and numerous other plants that represent the worst kinds of monopolistic incompetence. A point that we are trying to make though is that even though they were failures, the risks were worthwhile because the benefits that could have come from success had fantastic potential. Even that is not such a good example because it is a peculiar American problem that nuclear energy is a failure. It is not even considered a failure in the Soviet Union with the Chernobyl incident. They still feel they are getting more benefits than costs from nuclear energy.

## 3. EVENTUAL PAYOFFS

What this may indicate is that virtually all big risks that are persistently pursued eventually do pay off. The fact that they are persistently pursued shows that there is enough feeling that the potential is worth the effort. I cannot think of an example in history where science, engineering, or social science pursued a research-and-development course persistently for at least a couple of generations, and then declared the whole thing a failure. That is even more supportive of the point. The original point is that one has to expect some failures in order to have the successes, maybe even 100 failures for every big success. That is the traditional thinking that ties in with criminal justice about letting 10 guilty people free wrongly in order to have the more important successes of saving one innocent defendant from being convicted.

Super-optimum thinking does not accept that kind of trade-off reasoning. It emphasizes that one can simultaneously decrease the guilty going free and the innocent being convicted through more effective procedures. It also does not accept the idea that with large-scale projects there has to be long run failures. What is accepted is that if one is looking for a cure for a disease, one should expect to find that a few hundred drugs or combinations of drugs do not work before one finds the drug that does work. The important thing is the idea that through persistent effort, one will find the drug that does work. One nice thing about that proposition is it is incapable of being disproved, because one would have to live to infinity to see if there was ever an example of a disease for which no drug could ever be found. One does not have to live to infinity. Just living to 1989 tends to indicate that there is no such thing as a bacteria-caused disease for which no drug could ever be found. It looks as if in time, there may be no such thing as a virus-caused disease for which there is no cure or preventative. In fact, we may be on the verge of declaring that there is no genetically caused disease for which genetic engineering could not be used to prevent the disease. That could include genetic engineering which changes the aging process to get rid of diseases related to aging, such as cancer, heart disease, and diabetes.

## 4. COLD FUSION

The reaction to the cold-fusion experiments at Utah State University in 1989 represents a good example of how not to react to risk-taking and experimentation. Scientists generally reacted by criticizing the lack of carefulness in conducting the experiment. Perhaps they should have prefaced their remarks by commending the researchers for trying to be innovative with regard to a potentially highly important subject. Doing so would help communicate the message that a type 1 error situation would be far worse than a type 2 error. A type 1 error would involve a failure to develop the cold-fusion energy idea when it could have succeeded. A type 2 error would involve the less important error of wrongly developing the idea when for the time being one finds that it does not work.

## B. A BETTER SYSTEM OF LIABILITY

### 1. GOALS

We want to encourage people to take chances. That doesn't mean taking chances in the sense of tying to race through a red light before it changes, it means taking chances in developing new potentially useful products, such as new contraceptives.

On the other hand, we want people who are injured whether it be auto cases or product liability, to be compensated. Although better yet, we want the injuries to be prevented.

### 2. COMPARING INDUSTRIES

We can't necessarily apply the same rules in product liability as in auto cases. The auto accidents can be reduced by better cars, better roads, better drivers. Product liability is very broad in covering numerous types of products. Auto accidents have a lot in common. They all involve a road, a car, and a driver.

This is definitely a trade-off problem that lends itself well to an SOS application, especially in the pharmaceutical field where people are so afraid of things like thalidomide babies that we are now suffering from all kinds of diseases ,including AIDS, that could be lessened if the pharmaceutical companies were given more leeway to experiment. It is also a good example of where kneejerk liberalism is not so good. The kneejerk liberal wants to automatically hold the vulturous pharmaceutical companies liable whenever somebody gets hurt as a result of a defective drug. The pharmaceutical companies are vultures in the sense that they live off of sick people and have the highest margin of profit of any industry in the world. They sell pills that cost them a penny to make for $5 apiece. It is, however, cutting off one's healthy body to satisfy one's head, or some such thing, to try to punish the companies by wrecking their incentive to develop new products that could save people form diseases and that could especially save unwanted pregnancies.

A big award might be somebody gets hit by a locomotive while driving through a railroad crossing and becomes a quadriplegic. Amtrak gets sued successfully for over $1 million. This does not dampen research on how to build bullet trains in Japan. For one thing, the bullet trains do not go through the railroad crossings. They have special tracks that never cross highways. The above example is not such a good example though since it involves suing the railroad rather than a car owner. It is the same idea, though, of the liberals applauding because the deep pocket pays, and the conservatives thinking that is terrible. Neither side is especially concerned with the effect it has on technological innovation. It maybe encourages the building of safer trains or cars. In the case of pharmaceuticals, it encourages doing nothing, out of fear that it's impossible to be perfectly safe.

## 3. POSSIBLE SOLUTIONS

The solution with regard to the pharmaceuticals and maybe with regard to other product liability is that for the first five years of any new product, the manufacturer is subject to liability only for negligence and not for strict no-fault liability. One tricky problem in that is that although at first glance it sounds like it would help manufacturers not to be strictly liable even when they're not at fault, at second glance being liable for negligence may cost them more which is why the insurance companies want to switch to no fault. It would cost them more because they have to pay a 1/3 fee to a lawyer who doesn't exist in a strict liability case. It would also cost them more because strict liability has limits on what can be collected whereas negligence law is unlimited. We would not want to go to the opposite extreme of exempting them from any liability whatsoever, or even saying that they only will be liable if it's gross negligence and not ordinary negligence.

What may be needed is simply well-placed subsidies where the government agrees that if the pharmaceuticals will, for example, experiment with contraceptive skin implants, the government will guarantee that it will pay whatever damages occur. The government guarantees Savings and Loans and has gotten a lot less out of that than out of guaranteeing pharmaceutical damages. Liberals might think it's outrageous for the government to guarantee pharmaceutical damages. Some of the free market conservatives might think it's an interference with the free market. The newer thinking on well-placed subsidies, though, might recognize that society will be better off if its tax-paying dollar is invested in that way.

That is an SOS approach rather than even the Ralph Nader approach of talking in terms of roads, drivers, and cars. The Ralph Nader approach on product liability is strict liability. More applicable to existing products whose dangers are more known than to new products. Nader may take the liberal shortsighted pro-consumer approach rather than the more farsighted SOS approach which asks what is this going to do for the well-being of society rather than what is this going to do for the injured consumer. The two do not conflict. If the government pays the injured consumer and encourages the developing of new pharmaceuticals, then both sides exceed their best expectations. The injured consumer would collect a lot more a lot faster through a government guarantee and there would be a lot more innovative activity if the potential innovators were not so fearful of liability. The subsidy could not only remove the fear of liability but also help to cover other deterring expenses such as the fact that doing the research may take years to pay off and may never pay off.

Product liability is the most important kind of liability in terms of the expanded GNP and not auto accident cases. Although the two are related in the sense that a good deal of auto safety could be improved through well-placed subsidies. We could have had airbags a lot sooner if they were subsidized rather than relying solely on the auto manufacturers to make them. That is another example of misplaced liberalism. The liberals want the manufacturers to pay the whole cost. As a result, they force a 20-year delay in the adoption of a safety device and cost thousands of lives that otherwise could have been saved. Table 5-1 summarizes this example.

TABLE 5-1. ALTERNATIVES FOR PRODUCT LIABILITY

| Criteria<br><br>Alternatives | C GOAL<br>Stimulate Innovation of Production | L GOAL<br>Safety & Compensation | N TOTAL<br>(Neutral Weights) | L TOTAL<br>(LIberal Weights) | C TOTAL<br>(Conservative Weights) |
|---|---|---|---|---|---|
| C Alternative<br>Common Law Defenses | 3 | 2 | 10 | 9 | 11* |
| L Alternative<br>Strict Liabiltiy | 2 | 5 | 14 | 17* | 11 |
| N Alternative<br>C. L. Defenses w/Exeptions or Comparative Negligence | 3 | 3 | 12 | 12 | 12 |
| SOS Alternative<br>Strict Liability after 3 years of Marketing | 4 | 4 | 16 | 16** | 16** |

NOTES:

1. Common law defenses enable manufacturers to escape liability by arguing (1) they did not sell directly to the consumer, (2) contributory negligence by the consumer, (3) third party partially responsible, and (4) implicit waiver of the right to sue.

2. Strict liability means the manufacturer is liable for damages to the consumer if the product injured the consumer, regardless of the above common law defenses.

3. Comparative negligence means the consumer collects even if the consumer is partly negligent, as long as the part is less than 50%.

4. The SOS Alternative as mentioned here provides for strict liability only after three years of marketing in order to stimulate product innovation and provide a time period for debugging product defects. A better SOS Alternative might be to have the government be an insurer for the first three years so as to provide better compensation to injured persons while freeing product innovators from liability if they exercise reasonable care.

## V. SOCIALIZATION AND PUBLIC POLICY

### A. IN GENERAL

Risk takers get generated from about age 0 to 5 in little children depending on whether they are allowed to take chances or treated in such a way that they never come in contact with anything that might hurt them. There is certainly a need for encouraging more experimentation on the part of children within reason. More rebelliousness, more of the kind of trying out to see what will happen if you push your food off the highchair onto the floor without being punished for doing so, to see if the bowl will break or not. That does not necessarily mean that you jump off the third story porch to see if your head will break.

The socialization matter could be discussed across every field of public policy. If one is going to have a super-optimum society, then it is important what kinds of attitudes children have with regard to discrimination, poverty, world peace, crime, education, consumer-merchant relations, labor-management relations, free speech, and fair procedure. One could even say that the key purpose, or a key purpose of public policy is to provide for a socialization environment in which children have socially desired attitudes on every field of public policy. If that is done properly, then a good deal of the problems of what policies to adopt will take care of themselves because the need for public policy will be lessened. If children, for instance, are imbued with more of the idea of judging each other in terms of their individual characteristics rather than in terms of ethnic characteristics, then we have less need for public policies dealing with racism because there is likely to be a lot less racism.

Liberals have a lot of trouble with talking about socialization because it sounds like brainwashing people. It can be done in a brainwashing way, or it can be done in a way that encourages children to think things out for themselves to some extent. It is one thing to have a child parrot back some kind of catechism about thou shalt not discriminate against blacks or Hispanics. It is another thing to use approaches similar to Sesame Street or any kind of child teaching that involves the children being involved in working out and deducing what is the right thing to do instead of being told what it is and to memorize some appropriate words that they do not understand.

### B. SPECIFIC POLICY PROBLEMS

If we go down the list of public policy problems we could talk about appropriate attitudes and then later worry about how instilling those attitudes can be best implemented in a way that constitutes self development rather than useless brainwashing, which does not even succeed in washing anybody's brain in the sense of making them into equalitarians or work-oriented people, or what have you.

On the matter of employment, this raises the attitude of the work ethic, meaning where people enjoy the work they do and do not look forward to the end of the work day or the end of their careers when they retire. One might say that depends on what kind of job one has, implying that the problem is mainly in the stimulus, not the response. If people are oriented toward doing constructive work as a satisfying way of spending time, indeed as the most satisfying way of spending time, then they are likely to find constructive work for them to get themselves into. In other words, the attitude leads to the enjoyable work. The enjoyable work does not seek out people with work-oriented attitudes.

On the matter of consumer-merchant attitudes, it is important to get across to little children that in business transactions one seeks to provide quality and reasonable quantity when one is on the selling end and that it should be expected. We could talk about the opposite attitude on each of these. The opposite attitude on the work ethic is for people to have as their goal to not have to work at all, to be independently wealthy, win a lottery and just loaf away the rest of their lives. The opposite on the consumer-merchant attitude is that a good seller is one who makes a profit who maybe cons the buyer into thinking the buyer is getting quality. The person who is oriented toward a profit-making orientation by providing a low quantity in return for a high price is a detriment to society as contrasted to the Japanese philosophy of making big profits by providing high quality and high quantity in return for profitable prices.

On labor relations, it is the same kind of attitude. In fact, we might find that on many of these, the Japanese socialization makes a lot more sense but maybe not so much on civil liberties like due process equal protection, and free speech where they have a miserable record. In labor relations the Japanese philosophy is you do not make money by paying low wages, having relatively cheap working conditions. Instead, you make money by motivating workers partly with high wages and lots of fringe benefits ,including recreation facilities and teamwork. The idea of expecting as a worker or as a future employer to be working together rather than in conflict is an important attitude with regard to a society doing well.

On environmental matters, little children can easily acquire a respect or a disregard for the idea of conservation. That comes in under both environment, energy, and land use. The American attitude has traditionally been one of waste rather than conserving. Conserving at a child's level can simply mean throwing away litter. However, one does not want to get across the idea of over-emphasis on individual responsibility. That may be difficult to deal with at the pre-school level, though. One cannot so easily communicate to a child that it would do a lot more good if society were to do things to encourage the existence of non-biodegradable litter than by putting up signs saying throw the litter in the wastebasket. Preschoolers do not understand the concept of government and public policy. It is meaningful for them to understand individual responsibility. Individual responsibility is not in conflict with collective responsibility. It can maybe even lead to thinking in more collective terms later when they understand what the collectivity is all about. At the preschool level, they cannot be expected to have much understanding of how to deal with water pollution or air pollution, although there is not reason why parents cannot indicate their own negative attitudes if they have them toward air pollution and water pollution.

On the matter of poverty, little kids do run into other little kids that are poorer or richer than they are. The traditional America attitude is to look down upon those who are poorer and to be jealous of those who are richer. There might be something to be said for the fundamentalist idea of hating the way of doing things and loving the sinner. It doesn't maybe seem so meaningful to expect little children to love poor people and love rich people but to hate the idea that society makes for such big disparities. That is too abstract. The key attitude toward poverty is to instill the idea that it is wrong for some people to go without food or shelter or decent clothing and that some day maybe the child who is being socialized will be in a position to do something about it. The idea of doing something about rich children in a negative way is not in conformity with super-optimum solutions as contrasted to more traditional class-conflict thinking. The SOS thinking says there is nothing wrong with having lots of rich people so long as there are no deprived people below a minimum level. The more traditional class conflict thinking objects to rich people as something objectionable in itself.

On the matter of racism, parents are the main source of racism in children by their racist examples. Studies show that racist children are that way by about age 4 or 5 and it has nothing to do with their peer group contacts or elementary school or high school, although those contacts may be reinforcing, especially if those contacts also have racist parents. On this matter of socialization, we are not just talking about parental socialization, we are talking about the socialization that can come through nursery schools, preschools, public television, all with regard to values that most people pay lip service to even if they do not practice them. Very few people are going to openly object to an integrated preschool program that seeks to encourage respect for other ethnic groups, even if the people themselves do not have respect for other ethnic groups. As of the 1980s, people are embarrassed to admit to racist attitudes, whereas they were highly open as recently as the 1960s. In fact, as recently as the 1960s people would have been embarrassed in many parts of the country not to be racist. The term racist did not exist, but terms like nigger-lover and jew-lover would turn a non-racist into being ostracized by the community.

On the matter of <u>criminal justice</u> it is important to instill basic ideas of due process, meaning that when people are accused of wrongdoing they should have an opportunity to defined themselves. They should be told what they have done wrong. They should have an opportunity to call upon others to defend them. The person who is doing the accusing should not be the same person who decides whether they are guilty or not. On the matter of criminal behavior. There we need a broader notion of wrongdoing and it needs to be treated with a very negative attitude, including traditional criminal behavior, negligent behavior that causes injuries to others, and exploitative behavior that is now grounds for at least civil if not criminal action.

<u>Free speech</u> is extremely important. On that, children need to be encouraged to speak up and object to what they are told to do. There are people with authoritarian minds who would object to that kind of childhood training. They may be in the process of being as embarrassed by those attitudes as is the case with racist attitudes. One generation ago, authoritarianism was much more accepted than it is now. One generation ago there were no free speech rights in the U.S., although there was a free speech clause in the First Amendment. But not until the 1930s and the 1950s was it made applicable to the states or even made applicable in any significant way in the federal government. And really not until the 1960s did people have any constitutional right to speak out vigorously against government policy.

Attitudes toward <u>world peace</u>. The idea of going to war needs to become almost as unthinkable as the idea of robbing banks or murdering people. There is a movement in that direction to some extent, but little kids still play with war toys, although it is more on an individual basis than one country versus another. It is still not as bad as it formerly was, The U.S. has been moving away from being an oppressive world bully ever since the early 1900s. Although Vietnam was a contrary example, but maybe the final lesson that no such war could ever be fought again by the U.S., as occurred when the Reagan administration sought to repeat Vietnam in Nicaragua. It is important to get across to children the need to resolve disputes through peaceful means rather than through violence.

At the same time, there is a need to get across the idea of being capable of defending one's self.

There are a number of policy problems that are basically variations on poverty policy. For example, little children can have the attitude that it is highly undesirable for some people to go without food, shelter, or adequate clothing, and also adequate health care. Health care for those who cannot afford it is the most important health policy issue. Another health policy issue is developing cures and preventatives for various diseases. That gets back to the work ethic and risk taking as applied to health policy. The work ethic and risk taking cuts across all policy fields in the sense of encouraging children to work to solve problems including finding cures for diseases.

Reforming government structures is a bit abstract, but it can have its concrete aspects. Basically, in the world of the preschool child it means decision making through democratic means where children participate in making decisions in their preschool environments at nursery school. The most important government structure is democracy with its emphasis on majority rule and universal participation. Democracy also means minority rights, especially free speech to convert the majority. That is a separate point.

## C.  PRESCHOOL EDUCATION

In addition to elementary, secondary, higher, OJT, and adult education, there is a need for school of education people to show more interest in preschool education. That subject is not being adequately covered by people in child psychology, sociology of the family, social work, or other disciplines which have an interest in preschool children. The emphasis in schools of education has been on elementary and secondary. That only covers from about age 5 to age 18, although people need to learn from age 10 to the average life span of 70-80. Possibly more important, the years form age 0 to 5 may shape one's attitudes for learning in life such that a little extra educational effort could have a big subsequent payoff.

Table 5-2 presents an SOS analysis of the subject of preschool education. The conservative alternative is to provide no government support or government interference. The liberal alternative is to provide a substantial amount of government support and possibly a paternalistic concern of the tender psyches of preschoolers. The neutral compromise is in between on support and concern.

A key conservative goal is to decrease tax expenses. A key liberal goal in this context involves government subsidies especially oriented toward

TABLE 5-2.  EVALUATING POLICIES TOWARD PRESCHOOL EDUCATION

| Criteria<br><br>Alternatives | L GOAL<br>Civil<br>Liberties | C GOAL<br>Productivity | N GOAL<br>Peaceful<br>Dispute<br>Resolution | C GOAL<br>-Tax<br>Expenditures | L GOAL<br>Do Something<br>for the Poor | N TOTAL<br>(Nuetral<br>Weights) | L TOTAL<br>(Liberal<br>Weights) | C TOTAL<br>(Conservative<br>Weights) |
|---|---|---|---|---|---|---|---|---|
| C Alternative<br>No Government<br>Support | 3 | 3 | 3 | 4 | 2 | 30 | 28 | 32* |
| L Alternative<br>A Lot of<br>Government<br>Support | 3 | 3 | 3 | 2 | 4 | 30 | 32* | 28 |
| N Alternative<br>In Between | 3 | 3 | 3 | 3 | 2 | 28 | 27 | 29 |
| SOS Alternative<br>Package | 5 | 5 | 5 | 2 | 4 | 42 | 44** | 40** |

NOTES: (Table 5-2)

1. The conservative position is not too enthusiastic about spending large amounts of federal money on preschool education including daycare education, Headstart, or subsidized public television. The liberal position is more enthusiastic about such expenditures.

2. Instead of arguing over the quantity of money to spend, there is a need for more concern over the content of preschool education. If the content could simultaneously promote widely accepted conservative and liberal values then both conservatives and liberals might feel that their best expectations have been more than satisfied.

3. As part of the SOS package, there is a need for developing modules whereby teachers could discuss with students such matters as (1) whether it is all right to disagree with the teacher, (2) whether it is all right to let children play with certain toys, depending on whether the child is black or white, a boy or girl, or has other characteristics, and (3) how to handle a situation where someone thinks a child has stolen something. Those modules can get at free speech, equal treatment under law, and due process without using such abstract concepts, rather than concrete solutions.

4. As part of the SOS package, widely accepted conservative values can also be the basis of other modules. Teachers could discuss with students such matters as (1) how does one decide whether one wants to be a doctor, a teacher, a policeman, or some other useful occupation, (2) how does one deal with a bully or someone who tries to encourage other children to do bad things, and (3) how can one be a good American in helping one's country. Those modules can get at the value of a productive work ethic, protecting others from abuse, and being patriotic in a modern context.

doing something for the poor such as the Headstart Program. A key liberal goal in other contexts is to promote civil liberties, and a key conservative goal is to promote productivity, with neutrals especially liking peaceful dispute resolution.

The conservative alternative does well with conservative weights for the goals since it does so well on saving tax money, at least in the short run. The liberal alternative does well with liberal weights since it does well on doing something for the poor, at least in the short run.

The SOS package does involve the expenditure of money, but to help create preschool facilities for both the poor and the middle class. Preschool facilities in this context can mean subsidizing learning modules and teachers as part of day care centers. A requirement for receiving such subsidies would be that the day care centers do not discriminate on the basis of race or religion and they the provide tuition waivers for those who cannot afford the tuition but who otherwise qualify.

The learning modules to be developed with grants from the National Institute for Education might emphasize (1) having a productive work ethic which should please conservatives, (2) encouraging non-violent dispute resolution, which should please neutrals, and (3a) allowing differing ideas, (3b) opportunities to defend oneself when accused, and (3c) rewards on the basis of merit. Those last three cover free speech, due process, and equal treatment under law which should please liberals and civil libertarians.

## VI.  BALANCING POSITIVE AND NEGATIVE DISCRETION

Negative discretion refers to looking upon discretion as being something undesirable that has to be restricted, or it would be abused. Positive discretion involves looking upon discretion as something potentially desirable, since it allows for more effective public policy than if public policy is straightjacketed by inflexible rules.

### A.  THE 30% TAX CUT AS TOO LITTLE DISCRETION

A good example of avoiding the granting of discretion and winding up with highly ineffective policy is the 30% across-the-board tax cut. during the Reagan Administration  It involved no governmental discretion. Everybody rich or poor, individual or cooperation received a 30% tax cut. There was no possibility of abuse by the IRS or any government agency. The result was a waste of about one-third of a trillion dollars that served virtually no useful purpose in increasing societal productivity.  The original thinking was that this would somehow cause lots of money to go into retooling the steel industry or the auto industry and other industries. Instead it went into real estate, luxury goods, and high CEO salaries.

The current liberal thinking (and to a considerable extent conservative thinking as well) is that subsidies and tax breaks have great potential, but they need strings attached. They need to be focused. That means giving some government agency the authority to say that there shall be a 50% tax cut to the steel industry if it will switch from traditional blast furnaces to oxygenated steel making. The same agency should have the authority to say there will be no subsidy or tax break to the shoemaking industry to develop some new kind of high-heeled shoe that is not likely to be very internationally competitive. Conservatives and some liberals have traditionally objected to giving any kind of government agency that kind of discretion on the grounds that it will result in great abuses.

The middling position or super-optimum position is to allow a lot more discretion than a flat 30% across-the-board tax cut allows, but with guidelines that are specified by Congress and further enforced by judicial review. One can also have a special government agency (like the Japanese have) that consists of bipartisan experts on how to deal with well-placed subsidies and tax breaks. The agency would have representatives from business, labor, and consumers so as to minimize its possible bias and provide a diversity of viewpoints. That provides a combination of non-straightjacketing guidelines and of setting up a specialized government agency that has specialized expertise and has a balance of ideological viewpoints. The guidelines and the type of agency together can make the granting of discretion less subject to abuse.

## B. SOME HUD SUBSIDIES AS TOO MUCH DISCRETION

The Department of Housing and Urban Development is an example of the opposite of the 30% across-the-board tax cut in the Reagan administration. HUD was given virtually unlimited discretion as to who would get subsidies for different kinds of housing development projects. The discretion was badly abused in the worst partisan sense of favoring Republican contributors. It was even worse than that by favoring outright graft and bribery. It included favoritism toward one's own law firm, which is one of the worst kinds of conflict of interest.

The remedy might be a specialized agency like the independent regulatory agencies that would operate with more visibility, more expertise, and more congressional control. Such an agency should be in charge of housing subsidies or housing stimulation, and not leave it up to a massive bureaucracy such as HUD. It should especially not be left up to a political appointee. The head of HUD is a political member of the president's cabinet. If there were an independent agency called the Housing Stimulation Commission, each member of that five-member commission would have a fixed appointment. The members would not be subject to removal by the president, except by Congress by way of impeachment. Each member would have to be appointed by the president and approved by Congress. Guidelines could specify that three of the five members would be of the president's political party and two of the other political party in order to provide bipartisan balance. The commission would do nothing but decide on housing subsidies and tax breaks. It would have no responsibility for day-to-day administration. That could be left to HUD. The routine activities do not need much discretion.

For example, the commission could decide that it makes sense to allocate a big subsidy for rent supplements and nothing for public housing construction. The bookkeeping on the rent supplements gets done by lower level bureaucrats. The bookkeeping simply involves processing individual applications from poor people to determine how much they can afford to apply for rent. It then involves providing a supplement between that figure and the going rate for minimum level housing for a given family size. Even that kind of discretion can be abused, but not a lot of harm occurs as a result. It can be abused by somebody being denied a rent supplement who should get one, or being given one that is smaller than they are entitled to. That can be handled through the Legal Services Corporation or other legal aid program. The real abuse is throwing $100 million almost literally down a rathole or at some Republican real estate operator, who after getting the money goes bankrupt in building whatever housing was promised. He really does not go bankrupt. The money may have been siphoned into his personal account. Only the shadow real estate firm goes bankrupt. A poor person getting a $100 per month housing supplement is not going to run away with the $100 and lose the housing. The bureaucrat is not going to be able to so easily steal the poor person's $100.

The big discretion needs to be in the hands of special commissions like the Japanese Ministry of International Trade and Investment which exercises tremendous discretion. They decide that a billion dollars should be devoted to developing computer-operated factories, rather than spending Japanese investment money on developing consumer items (like television sets or cameras), on which the profit margin is too small compared to what it can be from computerized factories. One could say that is not the same thing as deciding which business firm will get the one billion dollar contract. Indirectly it is the same because there are not that many business firms making computerized factories. The possible abuse is partly limited because even in the formerly monopolistic Japanese economy, there is encouragement of competition among the Japanese automobile companies, the computer companies, and camera-making companies. Competition does keep some of the abuses in line, especially abuses that involve favoritism. In order for all the firms in a given industry to get together and pressure the government agency to favor their industry, they would have to operate reasonably above-board and offer good arguments for why their industry can do more for the Japanese GNP than some other industry can. The possibility of a total industry or even a part of the industry seeking to bribe the MITI seems to have not occurred. It is within the realm of possibility that it could occur, and that would be unfortunate. But the cost of a bad decision due to bribery is relatively small compared to all the bad decisions or non-decisions that are due to inaction as a result of having no such agency at all.

## C.  OPPOSITE TRENDS

Regarding federalism, there is an increase in the power of the national government and the state-local governments going on simultaneously. It is not an increase of one level of government at the expense of the other. Likewise chief executives, legislatures and courts are simultaneously exercising more responsibility for policy problems.

There is also an increase with regard to governmental activity in general, while at the same time an increase in the amount of delegation by the government to the private sector. That delegation includes various forms of privatization such as rent supplements, turning over the management of state prisons to the private sector, or various activities in government buildings like janitorial and watchman services that are now commonly done by private companies rather than government employees.

At the same time while there is a move toward more discretion in the awarding of subsidies and tax breaks, there is also a move toward less discretion when it comes to sentencing with the sentencing guidelines that now exist. That is not inconsistent. We do not want judges to have wide discretion regarding who goes to prison and for how long. We know that leads to decisions that are biased regarding race, economic class, sex, and other characteristics of defendants including age, rural-urban, and north-south. Subsidies and tax breaks are not so much an individual recipient matter, but a corporate matter. There we do not see prejudiced decision-making so much, although HUD is an example of bias favoring Republican real-estate people over Democratic real-estate people. Prejudice can exist in subsidies and in sentencing, although more easily in sentencing. The more important point is that the benefits outweigh the costs in limiting sentencing discretion, but the costs may outweigh the benefits in having no discretion regarding subsidies.

## D. CRITERIA FOR GRANTING DISCRETION

Criteria have been developed for the division of labor between branches of government, levels of government, and between the public and private sectors. We should develop criteria for when to give relatively broad discretion to government people and when to give relatively narrow discretion.

One of the criteria might be to give narrow discretion when individuals are involved, as contrasted to corporate entities. The reason is that when decision-makers relate to individuals, they have in front of them someone who is black or white, rich or poor, male or female. When decision-makers relate to corporations, they do not think that this is a male corporation or a female one, or a black or white one. Those concepts apply a lot less to corporations than they do to individuals.

When it is discretion to give punishment, we want the discretion more limited than when it is discretion to give rewards. We are more concerned about the wrong person being punished than we are about the wrong person being rewarded. It is a much worse mistake to wrongly execute someone than it is to wrongly give a subsidy to some real estate firm.

We are willing to give more discretion when the previous non-discretion situation has resulted in a lot of hardship or missed opportunities, and the new discretion situation will lessen than. Although this introduces the possibility of some abuses or favoritism that did not formerly occur.

An example is moving away from the rule that says everybody who is arrested for a misdemeanor, no matter how minor, must be brought to the police station and booked, as contrasted to being given a summons to appear in court. The summons to appear in court may work just fine in the case of two people who get into a fist fight in a bar. Bringing them in to the police station wastes the time of the police officer, the offenders, and the witnesses. If the police officer is satisfied the parties will not continue to fight, they can be given a summons to appear in court. This assumes they are not transients passing through the community.

Some liberals who do not trust the police argue that the police will abuse the discretion. They may give summonses to two white brawlers but not to two black brawlers, or especially not to a black who hits a white. The counter-argument though is that under the present system, everybody goes to the police station if they are going to be arrested. The discretionary system relieves the inconvenience to some people, including the police department which gains nothing from wasting so much police time. The general public, in the meantime, has less police protection, while the policeman spends an hour or two in the booking procedure.

We need to know what existed before and what we are changing to. In the case of sentencing, the previous arrangement was wide open discretion with numerous abuses. We have moved to sentencing guidelines to reduce that. In the arrest situation, the previous arrangement was virtually no discretion once a decision was made that a crime had been committed and that the person who did it was reasonable known. There is still discretion as to whether there would be an arrest, just as in a traffic violation a police officer could give a warning or a summons. Once the decision had been reached, though, that a wrong had been committed and who the wrongdoer was, then there was no discretion. A summons to appear had to be issued in a traffic matter and a booking arrest had to occur in a misdemeanor matter. Thus in the arrest situation, we are moving away from too little discretion toward some flexibility. In the sentencing situation, we are moving away form too much discretion toward some flexibility. Judges still have discretion, especially since they can generally still grant probation. The prosecutors still have tremendous discretion as to what charges they will bring, if any.

We don't want to go too far in the opposite direction. We still need restrictions on discretion. What we seem to have though, especially in liberal thinking but also in conservative thinking too, is too much emphasis on avoiding the errors that a government person who has discretion will abuse it, rather than the error which occurs as a result of allowing no discretion at all and thereby forcing bad decisions.

### E. THE EXAMPLE OF REQUIRING OVERLY PRECISE ADDRESSES

This business of how to deal with government discretion was triggered by a relatively mundane matter of whether the post offices should require people to give street addresses no matter whom they write to. More specifically, the U.S. Post Office requires people at the University of Illinois and other universities (or tries to require them) to inform outsiders who write letters to the University of Illinois to use street addresses. The reason for doing so has nothing to do with being able to find the University of Illinois. The Champaign and Urbana post offices know where it is. It has nothing to do with being able to find small units within the University of Illinois since the U.S. Post Office does not deliver to the small units. They deliver only to the central receiving station, and university employees then carry the mail to the individual units.

It is an example of laying down a rule with no discretion, regardless whether it makes any sense in individual cases. The Post Office would argue that if they make an exception for the University of Illinois, they would have to make an exception for other major universities. Then there would be problems as to what is a major university and what is a minor university. The situation could be handled by leaving it to each local post office to decide whether they have any trouble finding the University of Illinois without a street address versus some small college of podiatry in Chicago that the Chicago post office does not know so well where it is at. There is almost a kneejerk reaction that if each individual post office were given the discretion to decide who should have street addresses and who should not, then this discretion would somehow be abused.

The counter-argument to that is there is virtually no harm at all if there is some slight abuse in the sense that one post office tells a university that it should use street addresses when it really should not have to in light of how other post offices are operating. In the previous situation all the universities were being wrongly told to use overly-precise addresses. The opposite kind of abuse is not so likely to occur where the post office tells some minor college that it does not need to use street addresses when it really does. The minor college is probably going to want to voluntarily use street addresses in order to get its mail. People at the University of Illinois consider the street address a silly symbolism that is absolutely nonfunctional. One quick way to test how dumb it is, is to mail a letter to the University of Illinois or to some specific individual, like Stuart Nagel, 361 Lincoln Hall, University of Illinois, 572 Nonsense Street, Urbana, Illinois, 61801, and see if it gets returned to sender as undeliverable. It just might out of spite.

These problems need to be analyzed in terms of the benefits minus costs of one alternative versus the benefits minus costs of the alternative that allows for more discretion or less discretion. The post office loses nothing by allowing local postal discretion to leave off the street addresses for major recipients. On the other hand, requiring the street addresses does mean that universities all across the country had to change all their letterheads at some expense. That is only a one shot thing, though. It becomes a continuing problem when one has to be constantly sensitive to what address is given orally over the telephone, or in contexts other than just referring to the letterhead. It also becomes a cost if partly out of spite the post office delays delivering important mail because it does not have a street address which they do not need.

The post office address business may be a rather small matter compared to executing people and to giving out million-dollar subsidies. It does illustrate on a simple level the problems of having no discretion at all and thereby generating silly and costly results, versus allowing some discretion to operate a government agency in a more meaningful and cost-effective way.

There may be too much emphasis on limiting discretion of people in government, thereby making for bureaucratic inflexibility. We need to think more about how to expand the discretion of people in government without getting undue abuses along with it. That is where the criteria approach is important and being able to distinguish between different kinds of situations that merit more or less discretion is important. The discretion chapter of my book on *Public Policy: Goals, Means, and Methods*, emphasizes the limiting of discretion because the chapter was primarily concerned with sentencing discretion. As a result, that chapter is too narrowly focused, since it is not seeing the big picture. The chapter also deals with pretrial release, delay in the courts, and convicting defendants. All those situations involve individuals, rather than business firms. They also involve punishments, rather than subsidies. We need a new perspective on the subject of dealing with discretion as a means for achieving public policy goals.

## F. THE EXAMPLE OF NEW PHARMACEUTICALS

The pharmaceutical industry could be used as a good illustrative example. In the past, the emphasis has been on having all kinds of restrictions on new pharmaceuticals out of fear that some of them might be unsafe or ineffective. The newer liberalism is a need for more balance in the direction of encouraging the development of new pharmaceuticals that can prevent and cure disease, even with a somewhat greater risk of unsafe or ineffective drugs.

The unsafe criterion seems a bit ridiculous when dealing with people who are terminal AIDS or cancer patients. The ineffective criterion also seems a bit ridiculous if the drug is really working because it is believed in. Forcing it to be withdrawn from people on whom it is working obviously forces it to be ineffective. The so-called ineffective drugs also seem ridiculous to prohibit if they are being used by terminal cases for which there are not effective drugs available.

Encouraging the development of vaccines, cures, and better contraceptives means giving the FDA or a different agency more discretion as to what it will subsidize or award tax breaks to. As of now, there is no such positive program for developing vaccines and cures. The closest thing is the National Institute of Health which gives grants for research, but then almost completely to universities, rather than commercial pharmaceutical companies.

A good example of a law that produces ridiculous results because it does not allow for common sense discretion is the Delaney law that says if any food or drug is found to have even a .000000000001 level of carcinogen, it must be prohibited. The law specifically says any trace level, no matter how small. This fails to consider whether the benefits might outweigh the costs. This is an example of only considering the cost or dangers and ignoring the benefits, even ignoring the low probability that the cost will occur.

That is the law that resulted in taking off the market all the cranberries a few years ago because one small piece of cranberry had something in it that violated the law. Since then, apparently some discretion has been allowed because the same result did not occur with green grapes from Chile. The explanation though is that the grapes had cyanide, and the cranberry had carcinogen. One would not expect to find cyanide in all grapes since it is not a natural element. The carcinogen in the cranberry, though, was probably not a natural element either. It probably came from some pesticide, herbicide, or chemical fertilizer. It was not necessarily used in all cranberries and could also be handled more selectively if discretion were allowed.

## G.  BEING FLEXIBLE TO ADOPT AN SOS SOLUTION

People sometimes recognize a solution where everybody is going to come out ahead, but the solution cannot be adopted because it violates some rule. They then sometimes have the flexibility of mind to bend the rule. Many examples can be given. They tend to be rather earthy, rather than anything in the realm of public policy. One example of interest to political scientists was the International Political Science Association luncheon for officers of related associations in Rio de Janeiro in 1982. The Hindu president of the Indian Political Science Association along with everybody else was served the very best Brazilian beef for the occasion. The waiter brought it to him with great pride. The Indian president asked what it was. The waiter said this is our very best Brazilian beef. The Indian president said, what did you say it was? The waiter then said, "This is Argentine chicken." The Indian president said, "Wonderful!" and ate it with great relish. Everybody came out ahead. No scene was created. The president enjoyed his meal, and the waiter was not fired.

A student wanted to get into a pre-law course I was teaching. He was told by the undergraduate adviser that the class had closed and nobody could be added to it. No exceptions could be made. I told him to go back and register for independent study. He would be required as part of his independent study to come to every class session of the pre-law course, take notes, take the exams, and receive for independent study whatever grade he got in the pre-law course. He went back to get the approval of the undergraduate adviser. She probably sensed what was going on. She gave him the papers to sign up for the independent study course, and repeated her regrets that it would be impossible to get into the pre-law course.

Another example was Mike McCarroll, the Director of Lexington Books. He emphasized how important it was to get permissions for every quotation that was used. Once some publishing firm that he worked for was sued for not handling the permissions properly. They had to withdraw a book on which they had done a lot of advertising. I started to mention that I would like to use material in my own book that had previously appeared in one of the Lexington PSO books. I was not able to get the message out to him. He sensed what I was going to ask for, and he cut me off by in effect saying that I could do it if I do not ask his permission. If I ask my permission he will have to say no. Just do not tell him anything about it, and everybody will probably come out ahead.

That is a common occurrence, although it can be abused. That was in effect the policy of President Reagan to a considerable extent. He sought to save himself from having to make decisions which might have to be negative given what the law provides but that he wanted to see done anyhow because he considered them to be the equivalent of super-optimum solutions. He therefore gave instructions to people like Poindexter to make sure that Reagan did not know very much about what Oliver North was doing. Poindexter was probably telling the truth in saying Reagan did not know exactly what North was doing.

The key point is not the desirability of Reagan's or McCaroll's behavior, but that there are two kinds of psychology involved here. One is the inflexible person who goes out of his way to come up with flimsy reasons why new ideas or super-optimum solutions cannot be adopted. The other is the more flexible person who goes out of his way to avoid what might be firm rules, but who wants to keep them from getting in the way of new worthwhile ideas that may even be super-optimum solutions.

We do have to worry about both kinds of people. One is someone refusing to exercise discretion where it should be exercised. The other is someone exercising discretion where the rules and maybe even the spirit say it should not be exercised. These cannot be evaluated in the abstract. One has to know what the subject matter is. We do not want judges abusing discretion when it comes to sentencing people to prison or to be executed. We do want discretion to be exercised by policy-makers when it comes to innovative ways of developing new technologies, new cures for disease, illiteracy, poverty, and other public policy problems. That is where the idea of positive discretion comes in.

## VII. PSYCHOLOGY OF BENEFITS, COSTS, AND EFFICIENCY

### A. UNDUE COST SENSITIVITY

In the <u>ultimate extreme of cost sensitivity,</u> one obviously gets nothing done because one does not exert any costs at all. One is then totally ineffective, but one has saved a lot of money. That is the ultimate absurdity of cost sensitivity. It is analogous to the ultimate absurdity of keeping one's goals low in order to be happy, which means having no goals at all, which means being the equivalent of a wino.

A key point is that <u>each incremental penny or minute that is put into any project is likely to lower the efficiency given the pervasive principle of diminishing returns.</u> If one works about one minute a day, or say one hour a day, one may get ten units of work done. Each subsequent hour means less units per hour. Maybe the next hour is only nine units and the one after that is eight units, and so on. If one quits the minute the output to input ratio goes down, then one quits after the first time unit. The criterion of success is not how many units does one get done in an hour or for a dollar, but how many units does one get done, period. Thus a successful Japanese firm that captures 100% of the market may require a great deal of effort to do so. The American firm that captures 1% of the market with very little effort may be much more efficient. If the market is 100 units, maybe they are able to capture one percent of the market, or one unit with a minute of effort, or by just existing with even zero effort. To capture the 100 units, the Japanese firm may require 1,000 minutes or effort units. There is no question in people's minds that a Japanese firm that captures 100% of the market is the better firm.

Like many of the traditional principles of decision-making, especially in policy analysis, what sounds like things that make sense may really have a conservative ideological bias behind them, such as Pareto's standards of optimality. They protect the rich from progressive income taxes and from any redistribution of income. Likewise, the traditional efficiency principles by emphasizing cost to the taxpayer have that ulterior motive. The idea of being opposed to government spending, at least with regard to domestic projects, is definitely not a completely bipartisan idea. It is bipartisan in the sense that if one can buy ten units of something for $1, then why wastefully spend $1.50 for it. It is conservative, though, to say let us only buy one unit of it so that we only have to pay a penny if the "it" is education, health care, an antipoverty program, or almost any other domestic program as contrasted to defense expenditures where almost the opposite efficiency criteria apply.

It is important to think in terms of equity so that the benefits are fairly distributed and the costs are fairly distributed. It is also important to think of efficiency in the above sense of not spending more for something when you can get it for less. The evil is in saying, especially with a double standard, let us always have less of something in order to save money. It is never explicitly put in those terms. The magic words are "easing the burden on the taxpayer," or the big magic word is "efficiency." In that sense, efficiency means hold back on achievement, suffer opportunity costs, in order to save on some kind of dollar cost or time expenditure. It can have an adverse effect on individual achievement. We are primarily concerned with societal achievement. If we are concerned with individual activity, the basic business principle that one has to spend money to make money has to be applied to individual and society. One has to expend possibly great amounts of effort in order to achieve. One has to tolerate a great deal of waste in order to have success.

A good academic world example is almost any Nobel Prize winner. By any standard of an objective achievement, they have done well. They are probably the most inefficient, wasteful people in the academic world though. A good example is the Curies, who are the only husband and wife team that ever won the Nobel Prize. They also won a Nobel Prize for an especially revolutionary development, namely the basis for atomic energy and whole new concept of matter, namely radioactive matter. Every person who mouths efficiency as a goal should see the movie about the Curies. It shows how they wasted 30 years of their lives doing nothing that produced anything of any value. The lived in poverty and did not even have furniture in their house because they had to use every bit of floor space for plates on which various chemicals and rocks were being subjected to experiments. They got very little sleep. By any objective standard they were extremely inefficient. An efficient way to do what they did would be to somehow think things out in advance before getting started so that on the first try they would succeed. By the time they possibly were ready, they might have been dead of old age. They plunged in without knowing what they were doing, without even knowing exactly what they were looking for. They were very inefficient with regard to how they conducted their experiments. They just tried everything somewhat randomly.

Other good examples, though that is the best one, have to do with the discovery of cures for various diseases, such as the book by Ehrlich on how the first cure for syphilis was found, which was horribly inefficient. The people who achieve those results, though, are not criticized for how much time they wasted, What counts is the end product. Both Curies also died of cancer, which was certainly an inefficient cost. One could argue that they should have done a little bit more experimenting with regard to the side effects on human health before trying to find radium. They would then have been more efficient in the sense of not suffering that cost. Neither of them died very young. They might have died of cancer anyhow.

The important thing is to get away form the psychology of trying to have low cost, low time expenditure, either as an absolute or as a ratio-to-benefits. That should be no criterion whatsoever.

## B. THREE KEY CRITERIA

1. <u>Effectiveness</u>, meaning does it reduce crime, pollution, or illiteracy. Or does it raise law compliance, cleanliness of the air and water, and education levels. And does it raise it a lot versus a little.

2. We could use the word <u>efficiency</u>, but it has such a bad connotation in this context. We need a different word to get at the question of could it have been achieved with less cost, not at a better benefit/cost ratio. Meaning, could we have still raised compliance a lot without especially non-monetary costs like infringements on civil liberties, as well as monetary costs like expenditures for patrol cars rather than a more "efficient" monitoring system.

3. Are the benefits of reduced crime, reduced pollution, etc., being received by people across various groups or only <u>disproportionately certain groups?</u> and are the costs being paid across groups in terms of ability to pay, or disproportionately being paid especially by those who have the least ability to pay?

## C. TWO KINDS OF EFFICIENCY

There are <u>two kinds of efficiency</u>, and they need separate names.

1. The traditional efficiency is the <u>ratio between output to input</u>, or benefits to costs. It is the bad kind of efficiency because it can be achieved by decreasing benefits, i.e., by having very little output or very little achievement. It could be referred to as benefit/cost efficiency.

2. The other kind of efficiency, which is less talked about, is the efficiency that says if we want 100% of the market, zero crime, or zero pollution, what is the cheapest way of getting it? That could be referred to as cost-effectiveness efficiency, because we start out with a high minimum benefits level. And then we say, what is the lowest cost in order to achieve that high minimum benefits level?

In the past we have put down <u>cost-effectiveness efficiency because it is</u> <u>sequential rather than simultaneous</u>. It has two steps. Step one is to determine the desired achievement level. Step two is to find the lowest cost for getting there. A simultaneous approach seeks to maximize benefits minus costs and uses percentaging or 1-5 scales, or some other method, to make the benefits and costs commensurate. Even that kind of efficiency, which is a third kind, is no good. We could easily give an example of where it unduly hampers. Table 5-3 shows three projects of Alternative 1, Alternative 2, and Alternative 3. Alternative 3 gets 100 benefit units, at an expenditure of 120 cost units. Alternative 1 gets 50 benefit units.

TABLE 5-3.  USING BENEFITS AND COSTS IN MEASUREMENT

|  | Assets Before | B | C | B/C | B-C | Assets After |
|---|---|---|---|---|---|---|
| Alternative 1 | 20 | 50 | 20 | 2.5 | 30 | 50 |
| Alternative 2 | 20 | 10 | 5 | 2.0 | 5 | 25 |
| Alternative 3 | 80 | 100 | 80 | 1.25 | 20 |  |
|  |  |  | Assets Before |  |  | Assets After |
| Alternative 1 |  |  | 80 |  |  | 110 |
| Alternative 2 |  |  | 80 |  |  | 85 |
| Alternative 3 |  |  | 80 |  |  | 100 |

One question this immediately raises is whether we need a cost constraint in talking about cost effectiveness efficiency. It may be that the lowest cost for achieving 100 units is a very high cost, such that one would be taking a loss. It may be that it would still be worth it. That is nonsense, though, if the costs are measured in the same units as the benefits. It can never be worth it to make $100 where one has to spend $120 to make $100. We can definitely add the qualification that if the benefits and costs are measured in the same units or can be measured in the same units that we do not spend more in costs than we gain in benefits. The typical situation, though, involves dollar costs and non-dollar benefits.

The more typical situation is not should we refuse to spend $120 to get a little girl out of a well when the monetary value of a little girl is maybe substantially less than the $120. Those things are done for the non-monetary value. The key cost to consider is the opportunity cost. It does not make much sense to spend a great deal of money achieving some worthwhile goal when that money could be spent elsewhere achieving something that is objectively much more valuable. The girl in the well situation is so emotional that one cannot use that as an example in talking about public policy. We do not have public policy on getting little girls out of wells. It is an individual incident. There is no law that requires that it must be done, there is no public policy at all on the subject. It is strictly a matter of individual discretion. The more analogous example would be spending a great deal of money fighting AIDS when a much smaller amount of money could save a lot more lives if spent on heart disease, cancer, or something else. Even then, even though it does not involve just a single individual, it still involves a highly emotional subject where the decision that is reached is based to a considerable extent on the intensity of feeling rather than some democratic vote or rather than some kind of benefit-cost calculations.

## D. THREE TYPICAL SITUATIONS

Table 5-3 shows three typical situations. It does not include little girls in wells, but three alternatives. One wins on benefit/cost ratio, one wins on benefits minus costs, and one wins on benefits achieved. alternative number 1 is clearly the most profitable in the sense of benefits minus costs. Alternative number 2 is clearly the most efficient in the sense of benefits divided by costs. Alternative number 3 is clearly the most effective in terms of benefits achieved. It is alternative number 3 that we are now arguing in favor of, whereas in the PPG book we only dealt with Alternatives 1 and 2, and argued in favor of Alternative 1.

## E.  WHAT REALLY COUNTS

What really counts is <u>how much one's assets minus liabilities have</u> <u>improved before and after deciding between the alternatives.</u> We are not dealing with any liabilities here, it is just assets.  In all three cases we must have at least 80 units, otherwise we could not do Alternative 3.  For the moment, forget about Alternative 3 and say we must have at least 20 units or we could not do Alternative 1.  If we just talk about assets before, and assets after, then under Alternative 1 we start out with 20 units and we wind up with 40 units because our 20 units have generated a 30-unit profit.  With Alternative 2 we start out with 20 units.  We invest 5.  We have 15 left over.  The investment of 5 produces a return of 10, including the 5 that is invested.  Thus we wind up with 25.  The 15 that we had in the mattress that we did not use and the 10 we get back at the end of the year. Alternative 2 is clearly inferior to Alternative 1.  In both cases we started out with 20 units in the beginning.  Under Alternative 1 we wind up with 50 units in the end, and only 25 units in the end under Alternative number 2.

If we now add Alternative 3 and think in terms of all three alternatives starting out with 80 units, then after the decisions have been made Alternative 1 has 60 units in the mattress that it did not use or 50 units of benefit for 110 altogether.   This logically follows since it generated 30 units of profit over the 80 to begin with.  Alternative 2 starts with 80, spends 5, and has 75 left over plus 10 in new income for 85, or 80 plus 5 units of profit.  Alternative 3 starts with 80, makes 20 units of profit, has nothing in the mattress since it spent the whole 80, and winds up with 100.  Alternative 3 thus winds up with less than Alternative 1, and by the criteria of assets before and assets after is a loser to Alternative 1 just like Alternative 2 is a loser to Alternative 1 because both are less profitable than Alternative 1.

The sense in which Alternative 3 is better is that we now have 100 units of education benefits, anti-crime benefits, anti-pollution benefits, or whatever it is.   One could argue that with the profit made from Alternative 1, Alternative 1 could not buy 100 anti-crime units or whatever on a second round.  This is in effect saying to do the most profitable thing first in order to get the capital to do what might be the most useful thing.  But why wait for the second round if one has the capital to do the most useful thing right away?  The answer to that might be that if we wait until the second round we can invest 100 of 110 to achieve whatever anti-crime or pollution goal we are seeking and have 10 units left over, which we do not have if we spend the whole 80 on the first round.  What this amounts to then, is a time-discount problem.  The extra 10 units a year from now will not do us much good if we have suffered some unrecoverable loss as a result of tolerating the crime, pollution, or illiteracy during that time period. In other words, it boils down to whether having the benefits now is worth losing out on the $10 later. It is a simple investment problem. One could put some money in the bank and draw, say 6% interest that would produce an extra $6 a year from now, or spend the $100 right now and get some benefits that if monetized would be worth more than $6 a year from now.

The key thing is that Alternative 3 may be the best of the three alternatives, depending on the circumstances. Alternative 2, which is traditional efficiency, is clearly the worst. It has nothing going for it other than that it scores highest on traditional efficiency calculations. Even profit maximization tends to be concerned with getting high benefits or high income. That is the idea of spending money to make money. Whereas traditional efficiency takes a cautious approach that says not to spend money unless it is a bargain. The kind of entrepreneurs that we want to develop are those who are not looking for bargains but are willing to take risks and take losses and be wasteful in return for the eventual discovery of their version of radium.

In that sense, this ties back in with the psychology of risk and the psychology of positive discretion. The SOS psychology chapter has lots of parts to it, but they are all related. It also ties in with the psychology of optimism-pessimism. This is not inconsistent with the previous portions of the chapter. It is quite consistent. But it deals with a different angle, namely the idea not that effectiveness should be preferred over efficiency, or that equity should be preferred over efficiency, but that efficiency in the traditional benefit/cost ratio sense is more likely to be an evil than a good by hampering goal achievement.

An additional point is not brought out in this set of three examples. That is the point that relates to looking at the cost column. We have four columns here. The cost column gets looked to in two ways. One way is where we have a cost constraint that says we cannot spend more than a certain amount, like not more than 5, which means that Alternative 2 would have to be chosen. That kind of cost constraint is generally a fiction. If the investment is worthwhile enough, such as Alternative 1 or 3, money can be borrowed. Additional people can be hired to provide additional time units.

The other kind of consideration is looking down the cost column and picking out the lowest cost where everything in the benefits column is equal As previously mentioned, if we had three alternatives, all of which produced 100 units of benefit, we definitely would want to take Alternative 2 that only costs 5 units of cost. That is not the case. They each produce different benefit amounts. Converting the benefit column and the cost column into a benefit/cost ratio results in picking the worst alternative, not the best.  Converting the benefits column and the cost column into a benefits minus cost difference requires expressing the benefits and the costs in the same units.  That is not so difficult.  It does result in a better choice, especially in light of the before and after criterion.  It has the defect, though, in that it may not produce enough benefits.  At the same time. we do not want to say to simply pick the alternative that is the highest on benefits regardless of cost.   As previously mentioned, if the costs exceed the benefits that would not make sense, just as we do not want to pick the alternative that is lowest on cost regardless of the benefits.

## F.  PSYCHOLOGY OF EFFICIENCY

Cost-effectiveness efficiency makes sense but not benefit/cost efficiency, and maybe not even benefits minus costs efficiency where one needs a certain amount of benefit achievement or where the time discounting is such that the extra profit later will not offset the delay of having to wait for it.

## G.  MISCELLANEOUS POINTS

If one uses the benefits/costs ratio as a standard, then there is no question whatsoever that the best thing one could ever do on any policy problems is to do nothing.  This is clearly a justification for a do-nothing policy.  No matter how great the benefits might be, if one divides by a cost of 0, the quotient is infinity.  One cannot do better than infinity.  There is no bigger number.

One reason that cost effectiveness was previously put down besides the argument that it was an escape form having to measure benefits and costs in the same units is that it was given such a bad image by the Reagan administration.  That notion of cost effectiveness meant that as a first step one would determine what is the absolute minimum amount of benefits necessary in order to satisfy a safety net criterion.  In a context of welfare, that would mean what is the minimum in the way of welfare benefits that need to be paid in order to prevent food riots or race riots, like in 1967.  Anything more than that would be a waste of money.

There is nothing inherent in a two-step process of determining the benefits first and then seeking the minimum costs to achieve those benefits that says that Step 2 has to arrive at safety net benefits.  Step 1 could arrive at very high benefits and then in step 2 one asks what is the least expensive way of achieving them.  There is nothing inherent in cost effectiveness analysis that says that the effectiveness criterion has to be low or at a safety net level.

With regard to the idea of thinking low in terms of both benefits and costs, that logically follows from the Reagan administration's concern for keeping the costs down. The low benefits in that sense do not lead to low costs. It is the <u>desire for low costs that lead to low benefits</u>. One aspect of SOS analysis that is especially important in this context is the idea of finding alternatives in which the benefits are up and the costs are down. The Reagan administration, like traditional decision analysts and policy analysts, was constantly thinking at least in this context of a trade-off that in order to get costs down, benefits had to come down. They were not thinking of not applying some of the SOS analysis ideas that were applied to dealing with the deficit to dealing with more across-the-board kinds of thinking.

## VIII.  THE PSYCHOLOGY AND LEGAL OBLIGATION OF HELPING OTHERS

The American legal system is the only major legal system where people have no obligation to come to the aid of other people and where, if they dare to do so, they strongly risk the possibility to be held liable for having negligently done so.

The situation differs in West Europe operating under the Napoleonic code, and East Europe using communist values, in Moslem countries, Buddhist countries, Catholic Latin America, or pre-literate Africa. Everywhere, if a person who is capable of swimming watches somebody drown in 3 feet of water, he or she may go to prison for criminal malfeasance in failing to act. Such observers may surely be subject to a damages suit.

In the United States, they have no obligation to help. If they do jump in the water and try to save the person and fail to succeed, then they may get sued. In the United States, people are penalized for helping. Everywhere else they are penalized for not helping.

This shows up in the Reagan and Bush administrations with all its signs around about immediately reporting lying, cheating, fraud. No signs saying immediately report sins of omission on the part of your superiors. Just if somebody has stolen some paper clips, call a hotline on them.

It reflects to a considerable extent the time period in about the 1500s with regard to Protestantism and the rise of capitalism. The Catholic church has always believed in salvation by deed. If one allows somebody to drown even if the law doesn't penalize you, God will. The Protestant Reformation changed that partly for capitalistic reasons. Business people did not want to be held to any standards of having to be nice to consumers or workers. Martin Luther gave them the stamp of God's approval to charge interest, to overcharge consumers, to employ child labor, to do all the things that helped England become a capitalistic power when France and Italy were running behind the times but doing a little better with regard to business ethics. The United States has inherited those values form England. England has changed, though, as a result of Labour Party and socialistic influences. The United States stands along in that regard as being the most unethical country with regard to how it deals with sins of omission. Some of these policy problems thus go a lot deeper than just how one handles multidimensionality. And deeper than what can be offered in a preschool socialization module.

American values are changing though. They are not totally stagnant. Some states are changing their rules about sins of omission. They are passing good Samaritan laws that at least say one cannot be sued for trying to save somebody's life when the person would have died without the attempt. There is not state, though, that makes it an obligation. The exception is medical malpractice where the failure to prescribe something that should have been prescribed may be both a sin of omission and the basis for a damage suit, or lawyer malpractice or other kinds of malpractice. Governmental malfeasance is included, although that is almost totally unheard of. A prosecutor who fails to persecute a homicidal maniac is not liable for any of the maniac's subsequent victims. In a layman's sense, it would be malpractice for the prosecutor not to have prosecuted, or malfeasance, or nonfeasance, or misfeasance. In the eyes of the law, the prosecutor has 100% discretion as to who to prosecute. But the prosecutor could commit sins of commission where the prosecutor goes after his wife's lover in a trumped-up case. Then the prosecutor might even get disbarred. But not if he refuses to accept a complaint against a homicidal maniac on grounds that boys will be boys, or whatever.

## FOOTNOTES

1. For literature on generating goals to be achieved in public policy and public administration, see Martin Wachs (ed.), *Ethics in Planning* (New Brunswick, N.J.: Rutgers Center for Urban Policy Research, 1985); Duncan MacRae, Jr., *The Social Function of Social Science* (New Haven, CT.: Yale, 1976); Ronald Cohen (ed.). *Justice: Views from the Social Sciences* (New York: Aldine, 1982). For literature on determining relations between goals and alternatives, see David Hoaglin et al., *Data for Decisions: Information Strategies for Policymakers* (Cambridge, Mass.: ABT Associates, 1982); Michael Carley, *Social Measurement and Social Indicators: Issues of Policy and Theory* (London: George Allen & Unwin, 1981); Jerome Murphy, *Getting the Facts: A Fieldwork Guide for Evaluators and Policy Analysis* (Santa Monica, Ca.: Goodyear, 1980); and S. Nagel, "Information Sources in Decision-Support Systems" in Jack Rabin and Edward Jackowski (eds.), *Handbook of Information Resource Management* (New York: Marcel Dekker, 1988).

2. For literature on improving creativity in general, see the following items:

(1) Sam Baker, <u>Your Key to Creative Thinking: How to Get More and Better Ideas </u>(New York: Harper & Row, 1962).

(2) David Campbell, <u>Take the Road to Creativity and Get Off Your Dead End </u>(Greensboro, NC: Center for Creative Leadership, 1977).

(3) H. W. Gabriel, <u>Techniques of Creative Thinking for Management</u> (Englewood Cliffs, NJ: Prentice-Hall, 1970).

(4) Paul Hare, <u>Creativity in Small Groups </u>(Beverly Hills, CA: Sage 1981).

(5) Arthur Koestler, <u>The Art of Creation</u> (New York: Macmillan, 1964).

(6) Harold Lasswell, <u>The Future of Political Science </u>(Chicago: Atherton, 1963). See the two chapters on "Cultivation of Creativity."

(7) Fred Lichtgarn, <u>Basic Components of Creativity </u>(Cupertino, CA: Aim Publications, 1979).

(8) Gerard Nierenberg, <u>The Art of Creative Thinking </u>(New York: Simon & Schuster, 1982).

(9) Alex Osborn, Applied Imagination: Principles and Procedures of Creative Problem Solving (New York: Scribner's, 1963).

(10)Albert Rothenberg, The Emerging Goddess: The Creative Process in Art, Science, and Other Fields (Chicago: University of Chicago Press, 1979).

(11)Morris Stein and Shirley Heinze, Creativity and the Individual: Summaries of Selected Literature in Psychology and Psychiatry (New York: Free Press, 1960).

(12)Calvin Taylor and Frank Barron (eds.), Scientific Creativity: Its Recognition and Development (New York: Wiley, 1963).

(13)Gerald Zaltman, Robert Duncan, and Jonny Holbek, Organizations and Innovation (New York: Wiley, 1973).

(14)Milan Zeleny, Multiple Criteria Decision Making (New York: McGraw-Hill, 1982). See the chapter on "Invention of Alternatives and Conflict Dissolution."

3.   Hogendorn in effect says that if one has to choose between just those two perspectives, then the second more optimistic one is better. That may be so, but one does not have to choose between just those two perspectives if one is trying to decide what to do about the lack of shoes in a given country. Also one might note that the first more pessimistic perspective is more accurate if everything else is held constant. If the people do not wear shoes, then it is a bad place in which to try to sell shoes. The people either do not wear shoes because they do not need them or because they cannot afford them. Either reason makes this a bad market.

Hogendorn is also in effect saying that optimistically perceiving the situation is a step in the right direction. As an abstract principle, that might be true. In this concrete situation, however, that kind of optimism does not go very far since the shoe company is in no position to either change the people's need for shoes or their ability to buy them. The example might have been more relevant to a book on economic development policy if the two experts were working for a policy-analyzing government agency, policy institute, or university, rather than working for a shoe company.

4.   For a discussion of the extensive literature on the relation between happiness and the gap between goals and achievement, see Alex Michalos, "Multiple Discrepancies Theory," 16 Social Indicators

Research 347-414 (1985) and "What Makes People Happy?" Unpublished paper presented at the Conference on the Quality of Life in Oslo, Norway (1986). The emphasis in most of that literature is on individual happiness based on comparing individuals, rather than on comparing societal happiness across nations.

# CHAPTER 6

## INSTITUTIONALIZING SOS ANALYSIS

It is one thing to talk about the desirability of super-optimizing policy analysis. It is another thing to talk abut establishing or improving a set of institutions for more effectively arriving at super-optimum solutions in public policy analysis. The discussion below is also applicable to institutionalizing improved policy analysis that seeks to find the best alternative, combination, or allocation among various alternatives without necessarily arriving at super-optimum solutions.

Table 6-1 is entitled, "Institutions for Policy Studies Activities." There are five activities listed on the columns, consisting of training, research, funding, publishing, and associations. There are three basic institutions listed along the rows, consisting of universities, independent institutes or private-sector entities, and government agencies. There are also three basic concepts on the lower rows, consisting of trends, examples from developing nations, and SOS solutions for synthesizing the work of the three basic institutions on each of the five policy analysis activities.

## I. FIVE POLICY ANALYSIS ACTIVITIES
## AND THREE INSTITUTIONS

The first column deals with <u>training</u>. The cells within each column emphasize what each institution can do best on the activity that is associated with the column. On the matter of training, universities are best on career preparation. That includes university programs in public policy, public administration, political science, or another social science where the program is geared toward training practitioners or academics who will spend a substantial amount of their time evaluating alternative public policies or other forms of policy analysis. Government agencies are especially good at on-the-job training. An example would be a training program within the Department of Housing and Urban Development to teach policy analysts or other HUD employees how to evaluate applications for urban development grants or alternative public housing proposals. Independent entities refer to those which are neither universities nor government agencies. They can include the American Society for Public Administration conducting pre-conference workshops designed to upgrade the skills of governmental decision-makers, or the American Bar Association conducting continuing legal education (CLE) Programs. The abbreviation CPE for continuing policy education programs is used in the table.

The second column deals with <u>research</u> activities. The universities are especially oriented toward generalized or basic research. They are also most appropriate if one wants to emphasize innovative creativity. In-house government research is especially effective for more specific tasks from an insider's perspective. It is research that has a good chance of being adopted, just as OJT training has a good chance of leading to a higher job. The independent institutes range form high-quality policy institutes like the Brookings Institution and the American Enterprise Institute to institutes that are sometimes referred to as the beltway bandits who specialize in good packaging but possibly shallow substance at high prices. The independent institutes do well on complying with time and subject-matter specifications.

The third column is concerned with <u>funding</u> activities. Much of the policy training and research at universities is funded internally through legislative appropriations, alumni contributions, and student tuition, but also from government grants and foundations. The independent sector can include policy institutes and also funding sources like the Ford Foundation. Both may benefit from endowments. Most independent institutes, however, rely on soft money, and they usually do better financially on business training and research than on governmental training and research. The government agencies tend to

TABLE 6-1. INSTITUTIONS FOR POLICY STUDIES ACTIVITIES

| Activities<br><br>Institutions & Concepts | 1. Training<br><br>(3 Tracks) | 2. Research<br><br>(3 Tracks) | 3. Funding<br><br>(For Training & Research) | 4. Publishing<br><br>(Books & Journals) | 5. Associations<br><br>(Mutual Interactions) |
|---|---|---|---|---|---|
| A. Universities | Career preparations | Generalized or basic research | 1. Career training<br>2. Basic research | 1. University presses<br>2. Scholarly Journals | Scholalrly associations |
| B. Independent Institutions & Private Sector | Continuing policy education (CPE) | Intermedi-ate or mid-level research (Evaluation research) | 1.Continuing education<br>2.Mid-level research | 1. Commercial publishing<br>2. Commercial journals | Interest groups |
| C. Government Agencies | Job-specific (OJT) | Task specific (Program evaluation) | 1. Job-specific<br>2. Task-specific | 1. Internal reports<br>2. Internal periodicals | Government agencies |
| D. Trends | 70's schools<br>80's texts<br>90's CPE | 70's centers<br>80's texts<br>90's CPE | 70's up<br>80's down<br>90's ? | 70's new<br>80's plateau<br>90s " | 70's new<br>80's plateau<br>90s " |
| E. Developing Nations | e.g.<br>A. Beijing U.<br>B. NSA<br>C. Ministry | e.g.<br>A. Zambia U.<br>B. CAFRAD<br>C. UN Commission | e.g.<br>A. MUCIA<br>B. Ford Found<br>C. AID & World Bank | e.g.<br>1. Macmillan<br>2. PSO journals | e.g.<br>A. EROPA<br>B. UNUSA<br>C. PRC |
| F. SOS Solutions | All | All | All | All | All |

rely almost exclusively on taxes to fund their training and research activities. They could rely more on the willingness of many academics to governmental training and research. The government agencies tend to participate in training and research activities for only the out-of-pocket cost, in view of the interest of policy academics in insightful experiences and in making a worthwhile contribution.

The fourth column relates to publishing as a policy studies activity, including both books and journals. Universities provide university presses, which publish some policy-relevant books, although they tend to be concerned with more abstract matters or more geographically-narrow matters. Some universities publish relevant scholarly journals, such as the Policy Studies Journal and the Policy Studies Review which have been published at various universities since they began. The private sector publishes policy-relevant books series, such as those published by Greenwood, Macmillan, JAI Press, Marcel Dekker, Lexington, Sage, and others. Many of the relevant journals are commercially published, such as the Journal of Policy Analysis and Management, which is published by Wiley Publishers. Government agencies do relevant publishing in the form of internal reports and internal periodicals. The Government Accounting Office does both.

The fifth column deals with associations as forms of mutual interaction and networking. People at universities tend to be associated with scholarly associations, such as the American Political Science Association or the Policy Studies Organization. The private sector tends to be organized into interest groups that take a strong interest in public policy, such as the various trade and professional associations. The private sector also includes public-interest groups like Common Cause or more partisan groups like the Americans for Democratic Action. People from government agencies often belong to specialized associations which might emphasize public works, criminal justice, or education. They also join more general practitioner groups which also include academics like the American Evaluation Association or the American Society for Public administration.

## II. TRENDS, DEVELOPING NATIONS, AND SOS

On the matter of trends:

1. Training in the 70's emphasized the development of new schools like the Kennedy School of Government at Harvard or the Graduate School of Public Policy at Berkeley. The 80's emphasized the development of new public policy textbooks, starting with books by Edward Quade and by Stokey and Zeckhauser. the 90's may see more

emphasis on continuing policy education with the upgrading of skills through workshops and OJT, as in other industries.

2. Research in the 70's emphasized the establishment of research centers like the American Enterprise Institute. The 80's saw an outpouring of books form such centers, as well as other sources such as the Policy Studies Organization. The 90's may see more research and publishing that is relevant to providing materials for continuing policy education, rather than so much emphasis on textbooks and trade books.

3. Trends in funding included being upward in the 70's when money was more readily available for policy research from the Carter administration, but downward in the 80's when it was less available from the Reagan administration. The 90's may see an increase in policy analysis funding as part of the peace dividend and the increased interest in industrial policy and the role of the government in stimulating the marketplace.

4. There were new journals in the 70's including PSJ, PSR, and JPAM. There has been leveling-off in the 80's, although at a high level. That is likely to continue in the 90's.

5. Associations tend to be related to journals. The 70's saw new policy associations established, such as PSO, APPAM, and AEA. There has been a leveling-off in the 80's and 90's. One upsurge, though, has been the expansion of policy associations toward being more cross-national. The Policy Studies Organization has thus established regional PSO's in Asia, Africa, East Europe, and Latin America.

The above analysis has tended to use American examples. We could discuss each of the five activities in terms of examples from developing nations, such as:

1. Policy analysis training in China as elsewhere involves universities, independent institutes, and government agencies. Beijing University has an excellent program in foreign policy and international relations. National School of Administration is a semi-independent training institute which as links with People's University and also the government. A good example of in-house government training is the Ministry of Machinery and Electronics which has its own training campus.

2. One can use Africa to illustrate the role of universities, institutes, and government agencies in research. Zambia University in the Political Science Department does policy-relevant research on electoral reform and other matters. The African Training and Research Center in Administration for Development (CAFRAD) is a policy institute which does excellent research and publishing on African policy problems. A relevant government agency might be the UN Economic Commission on

Africa, or the Commonwealth Secretariat. Both also encourage relevant conferences and research.

3. Funding for training and research in developing nations includes university programs like the Midwest University Consortium for International Affairs (MUCIA). Good examples of the semi-private sector funding training and research are the Ford, the Asia, and Rockefeller Foundations. Important government agencies include the Agency for International Development and the World Bank. Both have recently taken an increased interest in the importance of democratic institutions and systematic public policy analysis.

4. There are a number of book publishers who have specialized series that deal with developing nations, such as Macmillan, M. E. Sharpe, and Kumerian. There are many journals that specialize in developing nations, such as the Journal of Commonwealth and Comparative Politics, the Journal of Asian Studies, the Journal of Development Studies, African Affairs, and the Latin American Research Review.

5. An example of a scholarly association concerned with developing nations is the Eastern Regional Organization of Public Administration. It is the Asia regional organization for the International Association of Schools and Institutes of Administration. A relevant interest group is the UNUSA. It is an American organization that supports the activities of the United Nations including activities directed toward economic, social, technological, political, and legal development. An example of a government agency in a developing nation context might be the PRC Ministry of Foreign Affairs, which seeks to bring students to China from developing nations of Africa and elsewhere in Asia.

The last row of the table addresses the question of what is a super-optimum way of resolving the division of labor between universities, independent private institutes, and government agencies, in dealing with policy training, research, funding, publishing, and associations. One could say that emphasizing the private sector is the conservative way. Emphasizing government agencies is the liberal way. Emphasizing universities is relatively neutral, although some universities are governmental and some are private. The super-optimum solution is not a compromise that involves giving more to the neutral position. That would defeat the purpose of getting the separate benefits of each type of institution. Rather, the SOS solution seeks to expand the policy activities of universities, independent institutes, and government agencies all simultaneously. There is plenty of room for that kind of three-way expansion, given the need for better policy analysis in order to have better public policies and a better quality of life in industrial and developing nations. That means more and better policy training, research, funding, publishing, and associations through universities, independent institutes, and government agencies. [1]

### III. APPENDIX: ALLOCATING $100 MILLION TO POLICY ANALYSIS ACTIVITIES AND INSTITUTIONS

The allocation budget of $100 million comes from page 27 of The African Capacity Building Initiative: Toward Improved Policy Analysis and Development Management in Sub-Saharan Africa (The World Bank, 1991). The exact quote is, "Financial resources will be needed to implement capacity building action programs....an ACB fund will be created initially of $100 million."

Training and research are given greater <u>weight</u> than funding, publishing, and associations since the second set of activities mainly serve to facilitate the first set of activities. The $100 million is allocated to the five activities in proportion to their weights.

Going down each activity separately, each institution is scored using <u>relative scoring.</u> Such scoring involves first deciding which institution is (relatively speaking) the least important of the three types of institutions. It is given an anchor score of 1. One then scores the middling institution as being twice as important s the base and half as important as the most important institution unless a more precise scoring system is needed and is available.

Those relative scores are then converted to <u>part/whole percentages</u> by adding down to determine the total of each column. Then divide the score in each cell by the total score of the column. The decimal equivalents of those part/whole percentages are then multiplied by the total allocated to each activity in order to determine the dollar allocations for each type of institution on each activity.

The total dollar allocations for each type of institution are determined by adding across the five separate allocations. The total allocation percentages for each institution are determined by adding across the weighted percentages and dividing by the sum of the weights.

All dollar amounts in the table are million dollar amounts. Due to <u>rounding</u> to the nearest million dollars, the percentages may sometimes add to slightly more or less than 100%. The dollar amounts may also add to slightly more or less than $100, $28, or $14. Table 6-2 summarizes this example.

This allocation analysis is not meant to be final. it is meant to be a <u>stimulus to thinking</u> systematically about how (on a relatively high level of generality) $100 million might best be allocated to various activities and institutions for improving African capacity building, especially with regard to systematic public policy analysis.

TABLE 6-2. ALLOCATING WORLD BANK FUNDS TO POLICY ANALYSIS ACTIVITIES AND INSTITUTIONS

| Activities (On Columns) / Institutions (On Rows) | 1. Training (3 Tracks) W=2 | 2. Research (3 Tracks) W=2 | 3. Funding (For Training & Research) W=1 | 4. Publishing (Books & Journals) W=1 | 5. Associa-tions (mutual Interactions) | Allocations (Across Each Row) |
|---|---|---|---|---|---|---|
| L Universities | Career preparation<br><br>4<br><br>(14%=$16) | Generalized or basic research<br><br>4<br><br>(56%=$16) | 1.Career training 2.Basic research<br><br>4<br><br>(56%=$8) | 1. University presses 2.Scholarly journals 1<br><br>1<br><br>(14%=$2) | Scholarly associations<br><br>4<br><br>(56%=$8) | (50%=$50) |
| C Independent Institutes & Private Sector | Continuing policy education (CPE)<br><br>1<br><br>(14%=$4) | Intermediate or mid-level research (Evaluation research)<br><br>1<br><br>(14%=$4) | 1. Continuing education 2.Mid-level research<br><br>1<br><br>(14%=$2) | 1. Commercial Publishing 2. Commercial journals 4<br><br>4<br><br>(56%=$8) | Interest groups<br><br>2<br><br>(28%=$4) | (22%=$22) |
| N Government Agencies | Job-specific (OJT)<br><br>2<br><br>(28%=$8) | Task-specific (program evaluation)<br><br>2<br><br>(28%=$8) | 1.Job-specific 2.Task specific<br><br>2<br><br>(28%=$4) | 1.Internal reports 2.Internal periodicals<br><br>2<br><br>(28%=$4) | Government agencies<br><br>1<br><br>(14%=$2) | (26%=$26) |
| Totals (Down Each Column) | 7<br>(100%=$28) | 7<br>(100%=$28) | 7<br>(100%=$14) | 7<br>(100%=$14) | 7<br>(100%=$14) | 7<br>(100%=$100) |

BUDGET=100 MILLION

This allocation analysis may not lend itself to an <u>SOS allocation</u> since all the goals are ideologically neutral. None of the goals are re;atively conservative or relatively liberal. The the alternativeinstitutions receive only one set of allocation percentages and amounts, rather than a conservative and liberal set that need to be exceeded. One relatively conservative or relatively liberal. Thus the alternative Table can say that emphasizing universities is relatively liberal, and emphasizing private sector institutes is relatively conservative, with government agencies in the middle. One needs ideological goals as well as alternatives, however, in order to have an ideological controversy subject to a super-optimum solution as contrasted to an optimum solution. The latter finds the best allocation in light of the goals, alternatives, and relations with only one set of weights. The SOS solution finds and alternative that does better than the conservative alternative with conservative weights, and simultaneously does better than the liberal alternative with liberal weights. [2]

## FOOTNOTES

1. On institutionalizing policy analysis (including training, research, funding, publishing, and networking institutions, see John Crecine, *The New Educational Programs in Public Policy: The First Decade* (JAI Press, 1982); Ilene Bernstein and Howard Freeman, *Academic and Entrepreneurial Research: The Consequences of Diversity in Federal Evaluation Studies* (Russell Sage, 1975); Carolyn Mullins, *A Guide to Writing and Publishing in the Social and Behavioral Sciences* (Wiley, 1977): UNESCO, *International Organizations in the Social Sciences* (UNESCO, 1981); and S. Nagel, the *Policy Studies Handbook* (Lexington-Heath, 1980).

2. For additional literature on the subject of capacity building regarding policy analysis institutions in developing nations, see Edward Jaycox, *The African Capacity Building Initiative: Toward Improved Policy Analysis and Development Management in Sub-Saharan Africa* (The World Bank, 1991); Mohan Kaul and Gelase Mutahaba, *Enhancement of Public Policy Management Capacity in Africa* (Commonwealth Secretariat and African Association for Public Administration and Management, 1991); Vasant Moharir, "Capacity Building Initiative for Sub-Saharan Africa," in J. Pronk (ed.), *Sub-Saharan Africa: Beyond Adjustment* (Netherlands Ministry of Foreign Affairs, 1990). For additional literature on the subject of allocating scarce resources among alternative activities, see S. Nagel, "Allocating Scarce Resources," in *Decision-Aiding Software: Skills, Obstacles and*

*Applications* (Macmillan, 1991); and S. Nagel, "Super-Optimum Solutions and Allocation Problems," in *Policy Analysis Methods, Process, and Super-Optimum Solutions* (Greenwood, 1992).

## SOS METHODS AND PROCESSES

## RELATED BIBLIOGRAPHY

Agnew, John (ed.), Innovation Research and Public Policy (Syracuse, N.Y.: Syracuse University, 1980).

Alperovitz, Gar, and Jeff Faux, Rebuilding America: A Blueprint for the New Economy (New York: Pantheon, 1984).

Baker, Sam, Your Key to Creative Thinking: How to Get M ore and Better Ideas (New York: Harper and Row, 1962).

Ball, Michael, Michael Harlow, and Maartje Martens, Housing and Social Change in Europe and the USA (London: Routledge, 1988).

Bawden, Lee, and Felicity Skidmore (eds.), Rethinking Employment Policy (Washington, D.C.: Urban Institute, 1989).

Butler, Stuart, Enterprise Zones: Greenlining the Inner Cities (New York: Universe Books, 1981).

Campbell, David, Take the Road to Creativity and Get Off Your Dead End (Greensboro, N.C.: Center for Creative Leadership, 1977).

Carley, Michael, Social Measurement and Social Indicators: Issues of Policy and Theory (London: George Allen and Unwin, 1981).

Clark, Mary, Ariadne's Thread: The Search for New Modes of Thinking (New York: St. Martin's, 1989).

Cohen, Ronald (ed.), Justice: Views form the Social Sciences (New York: Aldine, 1982).

Dermer, Jerry (ed.), Competitiveness through Technology: What Business Needs form Government (Lexington, Mass.: Lexington-Heath, 1986).

Dobel, Patrick, Compromise and Political Action: Political Morality in Liberal and Democratic Life (Savage, Md.: Rowman and Littlefield, 1990).

Easton, Allan, Complex Managerial Decisions Involving Multiple Objectives (New York: Wiley, 1973).

Etzioni, Amitai, An Immodest Agenda: Rebuilding America Before the 21st Century (New York: McGraw Hill, 1983).

Etzioni, Amitai, The Moral Dimension: Toward a New Economics (New York: The Free Press, 1988).

Fisher, Roger, and William Ury, Getting to Yes: Negotiating Agreement Without Giving In (New York: Houghton-Mifflin, 1981).

Flemming, Roy, Punishment Before Trial: An Organizational Perspective of Felony Bail Processes (New York: Longman, 1982).

Folbert, Jay, and Alison Taylor, Mediation: A Comprehensive Guide to Resolving Conflicts Without Litigation (San Francisco: Jossey-Bass, 1984).

Gabriel, H. W., Techniques of Creative Thinking for Management (Englewood Cliffs, N.J.: Prentice-Hall, 1970).

Gass, Saul, et at. (eds.), Impacts of Microcomputers on Operating Research (Amsterdam: North-Holland, 1986).

Goldberg, Stephen, Eric Green, and Frank Sander (eds.), Dispute Resolution (Boston: Little, Brown, 1984).

Gove, Samuel, and Thomas Stauffer (eds.), Policy Controversies in Higher Education (Westport, Conn.: Greenwood, 1986).

Gray, Barbara, Collaborating: Finding Common Ground for Multiparty Problems (San Francisco: Jossey-Bass, 1989).

Hall, Andy, Pretrial Release Program Options (Washington, D.C.: National Institute of Justice, 1984).

Hare, Paul, Creativity in Small Groups (Beverly Hills, Calif.: Sage, 1981).

Hoaglin, David, et al., <u>Data for Decisions: Information Strategies for Policymakers</u> (Cambridge, Mass.: ABT Associates, 1982).

Holzer, Marc, and Arie Halachmi, <u>Public Sector Productivity: a Resource Guide</u> (New York: Garland, 1988).

Holzer, Marc, and S. Nagel (eds.), <u>Productivity and Public Policy</u> (Beverly Hills, Calif.: Sage, 1984).

Humphreys, Patrick, and Ayleen Wisudha, <u>Methods and Tools for Structuring and Analyzing Decision Problems</u> (London: London School of Economics and Political Science, 1987).

Hwang, Ching-Lai, and Kwangsun Yoon, <u>Multiple Attribute Decision Making: Methods and Applications</u> (Berlin: Springer-Verlag, 1981).

Jandt, Fred, <u>Win-Win Negotiating: Turning Conflict Into Agreement</u> (New York: Wiley, 1985).

Jones, Robert (ed.), <u>Programming the Process: An Examination of the Use of Computers in Dispute Resolution</u> (Washington, D.C.: National Institute of Dispute Resolution, 1988).

Kash, Don, <u>Perpetual Innovation: The New World of Competition</u> (New York: Basic Books, 1989).

Kelly, Rita (ed.), <u>Promoting Productivity in the Public Sector: Problems, Strategies, and Prospects</u> (New York: St. Martin's, 1988).

Koestler, Arthur, <u>The Art of Creation</u> (New York: Macmillan, 1964).

Kressel, Kenneth, and Dean Pruitt (eds.), <u>Mediation Research: The Process and Effectiveness of Third-Party Intervention</u> (San Francisco: Jossey-Bass, 1989).

Lasswell, Harold, <u>The Future of Political Science</u> (Chicago: Atherton, 1963).

LeBoeuf, Michael, <u>The Productivity Challenge: How to Make it Work for American and You</u> (New York: McGraw Hill, 1982).

Levine, James, Michael Musheno, Dennis Palumbo, Criminal Justice: A Public Policy Approach (New York: Harcourt, Brace and Javanovich, 1980).

Lichtgarn, Fred, Basic Components of Creativity (Cupertino, Calif.: Aim Publications, 1979).

Lindsey, Lawrence, The Growth Experiment: How the New Tax Policy in Transforming the U.S. Economy (New York: Basic Books, 1990).

MacRae, Duncan, The Social Function of Social Science (New Haven, Conn.: Yale, 1976).

Magaziner, Ira, and Robert Reich, Minding America's Business: The Decline and Rise of the American Economy (New York: Harcourt, Brace, 1982).

Michalos, Alex, "Multiple Discrepancies Theory," *16 Social Indicators Research* 347-414 (1985).

Mole, Veronica, and Dave Elliot, Enterprising Innovation: An Alternative Approach (London: Frances Pinter, 1987).

Moore, Christopher, The Mediation Process: Practical Strategies for Resolving Conflict (San Francisco: Jossey-Bass, 1986).

Murphy, Jerome, Getting the Facts: A Fieldwork Guide for Evaluators and Policy Analysis (Santa Monica, Calif.: Goodyear, 1980).

Nagel, S., and M. Mills, Multi-Criteria Methods for Alternative Dispute Resolution: With Microcomputer Software Applications (Westport, Conn.: Greenwood-Quorum, 1990).

Nagel, S., and M. Mills, "Microcomputers, P/G%, and Dispute Resolution," *2 Ohio State Journal on Dispute Resolution* 187-223 (1987).

Nagel, S., and M. Mills (eds.), Systematic Analysis in Dispute Resolution (Westport, Conn.: Greenwood-Quorum, 1991).

Nagel, S., Applying Microcomputers to Dispute Resolution (Champaign, Ill.: Decision Aids, Inc., 1987).

Nagel, S., Decision-Aiding Software: Skills, Obstacles and Applications (London: Macmillan, 1990).

Nagel, S., Developing Nations and Super-Optimum Policy Analysis (Chicago: Nelson-Hall, 1991).

Nagel, S., Evaluation Analysis with Microcomputers (Greenwich, Conn.: JAI Press, 1989).

Nagel, S., Higher Goals for America: Doing Better That the Best (Lanham, Md.: University Press of America, 1989).

Nagel, S., "Information Sources in Decision-Support Systems" in Jack Rabin and Edward Jackowski (eds.), Handbook of Information Resource Management (New York: Marcel Dekker, 1988).

Nagel, S. (ed.), Applications of Decision-Aiding Software (London: Macmillan, 1991).

Nierenberg, Gerard, The Art of Creative Thinking (New York: Simon and Schuster, 1982).

Nyhart, Don (ed.), Computer Models and Modeling for Negotiation Management (Cambridge, Mass.: MIT Conference Proceedings, November, 1987).

Osborn, Alex, Applied Imagination: Principles and Procedures of Creative Problem-Solving (New York: Scribner's, 1963).

Osborn, Alex, Applied Imagination: Principles and Procedures of Creative Problem-Solving (New York: Scribner's, 1963).

Palda, Kristian, Industrial Innovation: Its Place in the Public Policy Agenda (Toronto: The Fraser Institute, 1984).

Rabin, Jack, and Edward Jackowski (eds.), Handbook of Information Resource Management (New York: Marcel Dekker, 1988).

Raiffa, Howard, The Art and Science of Negotiation (Cambridge, Mass.: Harvard, 1982).

Raskin, Marcus, The Common Good: Its Politics, Policies, and Philosophy (New York: Routledge and Kegan Paul, 1986).

Roberts, Paul, The Supply Side Revolution (Cambridge, Mass.: Harvard University Press, 1984).

Rothenberg, Albert, The Emerging Goddess: The Creative Process in Art, Science, and Other Fields (Chicago: University of Chicago Press, 1979).

Ruby, Lionel, Logic: An Introduction (Chicago, Ill.: Lippincott, 1950).

Saaty, Thomas, Decision Making for Leaders: The Analytical Hierarchy Process for Decisions in a Complex World (Belmont, Calif.: Wadsworth, 1982).

Sabine, George, A History of Political Theory (New York: Holt, 1950).

Salamon, Lester (ed.), Beyond Privatization: The Tools of Government Action (Washington, D.C.: Urban Institute, 1989).

Sato, Ryuzo, and Gilbert Suzawa, Research and Productivity: Endogenous Technical Change (Boston: Auburn House, 1983).

Sawhill, Isabel (ed.), Challenge to Leadership: Economic and Social Issues for the Next Decade (Washington, D.C.: Urban Institute, 1988).

Stein, Morris, and Shirley Heinze, Creativity and the Individual: Summaries of Selected Literature in Psychology and Psychiatry (New York: Free Press, 1960).

Sternlieb, George, and David Listokin (eds.), New Tools for Economic Development: The Enterprise Zone, Development Bank, and RFC (New Brunswick, N.J.: Rutgers University, 1981).

Susskind, Lawrence, and Jeffrey Cruikshank, Breaking the Impasse: Consensual Approaches to Resolving Public Disputes (New York: Basic Books, 1987).

Taylor, Calvin, and Frank Barron (eds.), Scientific Creativity: Its Recognition and Development (New York: Wiley, 1963).

Thomas, Wayne, Ball Reform in America (Berkeley, Calif.: University of California Press, 1976).

Titus, Harold, Ethics for Today (New York: American Book Company, 1947).

Ury, William, Jeanne Brett, and Stephen Goldberg, <u>Getting Disputes Resolved: Designing Systems to cut the costs of Conflict</u> (San Francisco: Jossey-Bass, 1988).

Wachs, Martin (ed.), <u>Ethics in Planning</u> (New Brunswick, N.J.: Rutgers Center for Urban Policy Research, 1985).

Walker, Samuel, <u>Sense and Nonsense About Crime: A Policy Guide</u> (Pacific Grove, Calif.: Brooks/Cole, 1989).

Winslow, Robert, <u>Crime in a Free Society</u> (Encino, Calif.: Dickenson, 1977).

Zaltman, Gerald, Robert Duncan, and Jonny Holbek, <u>Organizations and Innovation</u> (New York: Wiley, 1973).

Zeleny, Milan, <u>Multiple Criteria Decision Making</u> (New York: McGraw-Hill, 1982).

## SOS PUBLICATIONS

Super-optimum solutions are ways of dealing with public policy problems that can enable conservatives, liberals, and other major viewpoints to all come out ahead of their best initial expectations simultaneously. This is a bibliography of published and forthcoming books and articles on the subject of SOS solutions. It is preliminary in the sense that the field is quite new and rapidly developing. This list is reasonable up to date as of April 1, 1991. The items are authored or edited by Stuart Nagel unless noted otherwise. Nearly all of these items have been already published, completed for publication, or virtually completed. Most of them are available on request for the cost of photocopying.

## A. BOOKS

### 1. AUTHORED BOOKS

1. *The Bill of Rights and Super-Optimum Solutions* (SOS Group, 1991).

2. *Developing National and Super-Optimum Policy Analysis* (Nelson-Hall, 1991). Translated into Chinese, 1990-91.

3. *Higher Goals for America: Doing Better than the Best* (University Press of America, 1989).

4. *Legal Process Controversies and Super-Optimum Solutions* (Greenwood-Quorum, 1992). Also known as SOS-Law.

5. *Multi-Criteria Methods in Alternative Dispute Resolution: With Microcomputer Software Applications* (Greenwood-Quorum, 1990).

6. *Policy Analysis Methods, Process, and Super-Optimum Solutions* (University of Michigan Press, 1991). Also know as SOS-Methods.

7. *Public Policy Substance and Super-Optimum Solutions* (Macmillan, 1992). Also know as SOS-Substance.

8. *Super-Optimum Policy Analysis* (SOS Group, 1991). Also know as Short SOS.

9. *The Super-Optimum Society* (1992).

## 2. EDITED BOOKS

1. *Applications of Super-Optimum Solutions* (Greenwood, 1992).

2. *Global Policy Problems and Super-Optimum Solutions* (1992).

3. *International Dispute Resolution through Win-Win or SOS Solutions* (1992).

4. *Super-Optimum Solutions* (Symposium issue of *Public Budgeting* and Financial Management, 1991).

## B. ARTICLES

### 1. METHODS AND PROCESS

1. "Airport Location, the USSR, and Super-Optimum Solutions," by Oleg Larichev, in S. Nagel (ed.), *Applications of Super-Optimizing Analysis* (Greenwood, 1992).

2. "Arriving at Super-Optimum Solutions," in M. Holzer (ed.), *Handbook of Public Productivity* (Marcel Dekker, 1991). Also in *Research Annual on Public Policy Analysis and Management* (JAI Press, Volume 6, 1992).

3. "Economic and Public Policy: On the Relevance of Constitutional Economic Advice," by Robert Haveman, in S. Nagel (ed.), *Super-Optimum Solutions* (*Symposium issue of *Public Budgeting and Financial Management*, 1991).

4. "Formulating and Implementing Super-optimum Solutions," International Institute of Administrative Sciences Annual Meeting (1991)

5. "Group Decision-Making, Negotiation, and Super-Optimum Solutions, "ORSA/TIMS Annual Meeting (1991).

6. "Microcomputers, P/G%, and Dispute Resolution," 2 *Ohio State Journal on Dispute Resolution* 187-221 (1987).

7. "SOS Analysis in Education and Training in Public Policy," International Association of Schools and Institutes of Administration Annual Meeting (1991).

8. "SOS Causation," in *Evaluative and Explanatory Reasoning* (Quorum Books, 1991).

9. "SOS Evaluation," in *Evaluative and Explanatory Reasoning* (Quorum Books, 1991).

10."Super-Optimum Analysis and Policy Studies," 18 *Policy Studies Journal* 507-513 (1990).

11."Super-Optimum Solutions and Public Controversies," *Futures Research Quarterly* (1990). Also in *Research Advances in Social Science and Computers*, David Garson (ed.), (JAI Press, Volume 3, 1992), and *Social Science, Law, and Public Policy* (University Press of America, 1991).

12."Teach Yourself Super-Optimizing with P/G%," in *Teach Yourself Decision-Aiding Software* (University Press of America, 1991).

13."Two Super-Optimum Solutions in a Cutback Mode," by Robert Colembiewski, in S. Nagel (ed.), *Super-Optimum Solutions* (Symposium issue of *Public Budgeting and Financial Management*, 1991).

## 2. PUBLIC POLICY AND SUBSTANCE

1. "Abortion, Birth Control, and Public Policy," by Rhonda Peek and Mark Loenig in S. Nagel (ed.), *Applications of Super-Optimizing Analysis* (Greenwood, 1992).

2. "Abortion Policy and Super-Optimum Solutions," in Hector Correa (ed.), *Public Policy and Unwanted Pregnancies* (Greenwood, 1991).

3. "Arms Control, Super-Optimum Solutions, and Decision-Aiding Software," 1 *The Peacebuilder* 10-11 (1990).

4. "Doing Better than the Best in Pharmaceutical Drugs," by Edward Glavinskas in S. Nagel (ed.), *Applications of Super-Optimizing Analysis* (Greenwood, 1992).

5. "Doing Better Than the Optimum," 21 *Social Indicators Research* 193-220 (1989).

6. "Education Policy and Multi-Criteria Decision-Making," in Walberg (ed.), *Analytic Methods for Education Productivity* (1991).

7. "Global Policy Studies and Super-Optimum Solutions," International Political Science Association Annual Meeting (1991).

8. "Governmental Structures and Super-Optimum Solutions," in Ali Farazmand (ed.), *Handbook of Developing Nations* (Marcel Dekker, 1991).

9. "Higher Goals for Public Policy," 9 *Policy Studies Review* 835-842 (1990).

10. "The New Patriotism," (1992).

11. "Optimum Budget Allocation for Alternative Energy Development in Japan," by Akiko Yuimoto in S. Nagel (ed.) *Applications of Super-Optimizing Analysis* (Greenwood, 1992).

12. "A Policy Analysis on the Issues of Bilingual Education in the United States," by Grace Ching-hsia Li in S. Nagel (ed.), *Applications of Super-Optimizing Analysis* (Greenwood, 1992).

13. "Public Policy Substance and Super-Optimum Solutions," (Submitted to *Journal of Public Policy*).

14. "Women and Children in Poverty: a Policy Analysis," by Sue Campbell Clark in S. Nagel (ed.), *Applications of Super-Optimizing Analysis* (Greenwood, 1992).

### 3. LEGAL POLICY CONTROVERSIES

1. "Doing Better Than Zero Crime," 15 *The Key* 7 (summer, 1989).

2. "The Drug War: There Has to Be a Better Way," by Patrick Walls in S. Nagel (ed.), *Applications of Super-Optimizing Analysis* (Greenwood, (1992).

3. "The History, Development, and Alternatives to the Exclusionary Rule," by Kevin Young Joon Pak in S. Nagel (ed.), *Applications of Super-Optimizing Analysis* (Greenwood, 1992).

4. "Humor, Mediation, and Super-Optimum Solutions," by John W. Cooley in S. Nagel (ed.), *Applications of Super-Optimizing Analysis* (Greenwood, 1992).

5. "Legal Process Controversies and Super-Optimum Solutions," *Judicature* (1992).

6. "Multi-Criteria Dispute Resolution through Computer-Aided Mediation Software," 7 *Mediation Quarterly* 175-189 (1989).

7. "Plea Bargaining," by Al Pena in S. Nagel (ed.), *Applications of Super-Optimizing Analysis* (Greenwood, 1992).

8. "Super-Optimum Mediation," by John Cooley in S. Nagel (ed.), Super-Optimum Solutions (Symposium Issue of *Public Budgeting and Financial Management*, 1991).

9. "Super-Optimum Mediation in Adjudicating Disputes," 7 *Journal of Management Science and Policy Analysis* 157-162 (1990).

10. "Super-Optimum Mediation in Rule-Making Controversies,": 6 *Journal of Management Science and Policy Analysis* 70-78 (1989).

11. "Super-Optimum Solutions to Procedural Controversies," in *Computer-Aided Judicial Analysis: Predicting, Prescribing, and Administering* (Quorum Books, 1991).

12. "Using Decision-Aiding Software to Aid in Finding Super-Optimum Solutions," in *Decision-Aiding Software and Judicial Decision-Making* (ABA Judicial Administration Division Annual Meeting, 1991).

13. "What's New and Useful in Legal Analysis Technology?" International Bar Association Annual Meeting (1991).

## 4. DEVELOPING NATIONS

1. "Agriculture, Pesticides, and SOS," by Nancy Robinson in S. Nagel (ed.), *Applications of Super-Optimizing Analysis* (Greenwood, 1992).

2. "Global Policy Analysis: Specific Problems and Cross-Cutting Issues," in S. Nagel (ed.), *Global Policy Studies* (Macmillan, 1990).

3. "Improving Developmental Policy Analysis," by King Chow in S. Nagel (ed.), *Super-Optimum Solutions* (Symposium Issue of *Public Budgeting and Financial Management*, 1991).

4. "Improving Public Policy Toward and Within Developing Countries," in Public Administration and Decision-Aiding Software: Improving Procedure and Substance (Greenwood, 1990).

5. "The Israeli-Palestinian Conflict: A Social and Political Solution," by Gideon Doron in S. Nagel (ed.), *Applications of Super-Optimizing Analysis* (Greenwood, 1992).

6. "The Law of Developing Nations and Super-Optimum Solutions," in *Advances in Developmental Policy Studies* (JAI Press, 1991).

7. "Philippine Policy Problems and Super-Optimum Solutions," in *Philippine Journal of Public Administration* (1991).

8. "Super-Optimizing Analysis and Chinese Policy Problems," in *Public Administration, Public Policy, and the People's Republic of China* (Macmillan, 1991).

9. "U.S. Military Bases in the Philippines," in *Applications of Super-Optimizing Analysis* (Greenwood, 1992).

10."Urban, Regional, and National Development in China," by Tong Dao-Chi in S. Nagel (ed.), Applications of Super-Optimizing Analysis (Greenwood, 1992).

# Subject Index

Abuses of discretion, 174
Academic
    competition, 121
    honors, 129
    world, 118
Accuracy of juries, 56
Acquitting the innocent, 57
Addresses, 171
Administrative feasibility, 41
Adopting SOS solutions, 4
Adoption of policies, 71
Advocacy, 21
Agriculture Department, 127
Airlines, 62
Allocation, 195
Alternatives, 15
American productivity, 105
Analysis, 21
Arriving at SOS solutions, 2, 15
Arrow diagram, 18
Assets, 97
    minus liabilities, 181
Associations, 192
Astronomy, 146
Auto accidents, 153
Automation, 108
Automobile industry, 21

Benefits 3, 23, 175
    increasing, 58
Bipartisan growth, 96

Bond, 51
Budget deficit, 98
Business
    conservatives, 25
    firms, 9, 20
By-products, 64

Capacity building, 197
Capital punishment, 45
Capitalistic ownership, 134
Causal
    analysis, 71
    arrows, 18
Causes of conflict, 45
Child care, 20
Childhood socialization, 9
China, 39
Civil liberties, 163
Combining alternatives, 3, 43
Commission, sins of, 174
Commitments, 141
Common law defenses, 156
Comparative negligence, 156
Compensation, 156
Competence, 7
Competent personnel, 85
Competition, 111, 117, 118, 123
    business firms, 9
    political parties, 8
Competitiveness, 107
Compliance information, 29

Compounding effect, 107
Compromise, 19
    position, 15
Computer-aided mediation, 33
Computer-assisted instruction,
    58
Condominium arrangement, 57
Conflict, source, 3
Conservative, 39
Conservatives, 15, 85,125
Consolidation, 126
Constraints, 182
Consumer
    prices, 115
    problems, 93
    merchant relations, 159
Consumption, 17
Contracting out, 131
Convicting the guilty, 57
Cooperation, 117
Cost
    constraints, 182
    cutting, 60
    reduction, 58
    effectiveness, 178
Costs, 3, 23, 175
Counsel for poor clients, 56
Creativity, 66, 143
Credit union, 27
Crime reduction, 90
Criminal
    cases, 54
    justice, 93, 161
Cultural conservatives, 25


Debt, 97
Decision-making, 22, 109
Defendant, 27
Defense, 17
    spending, 92, 102
Deficit, 15
Delaney Law, 171
Desired behavior, 90
Developing nations, 133, 191, 209
Diminishing returns, 175
Disabled people, 25

Discretion, 168
Discrimination, 49
Disruption to society, 24
Domestic
    programs, 17
    spending, 92
Drug
    medicalization, 49
    problem, 47


Economic
    competition, 133
    development, 27
    growth, 111
    process, 1, 9
Education, 93
    Department, 126
    preschool, 162
Educational policy, 147
Effectiveness, 38, 178
    measure, 16
Efficiency, 38, 175, 177
    measure, 16
Elderly people, 25
Electricity, 119
Employment, 64, 93, 159
Energy Department, 126
Energy field, 151
Energy sources, 104
Entrepreneurs, 111
Environmental
    incentives, 93
    matters, 159
    policy, 126
    Protection Agency, 127
Equity, 38, 176, 177
Executions, 49
Expanded-pie solutions, 22
Expanded resources, 2, 15, 66
Expectations, 31
Exporting, 41


Facilitators, 141
Facilitators, 8
Fact-learning, 143

Farmers, 25
Farming methods, 41
Federal Aviation
    Administration, 61
Federalism, 168
Flexibility, 173
Flight controllers, 62
Food
    and Drug Administration,
    173
    prices, 59
    stamps, 42
Free speech, 131, 161
Funding, 7, 190
Fusion energy, 153

Generating policies, 139
Goals, 66
    higher, 2
    raising, 22
    setting, 2
Government
    agencies, 191
    monopoly, 118
    reform, 162
    spending, 18
Great Society legislation, 81
Grievance procedures, 28
Gross national product, 16
Growth, 89
    perspective, 95
Gun control, 49

Happiness, 149
Helping others, 184
Higher
    education, 44, 130
    goals, 2
Holding rate, 51
Housing, 31, 93
    and urban development, 166
    for the poor, 34

Imagination, 8, 85
Immigrant opportunities, 24
Immigrants, 111
Implementation, 110
    of policies, 71
Implementing SOS solutions, 6
Importing technology, 41
Incentives, 89, 99, 103
Independent institutions, 191
Industrial
    nations, 133
    policy, 101
Inertia in innovation, 56
Inflation, 90
Information systems, 90
Innovation, 66, 123
Innovative risk-taking, 10
Inspiration, 148
Institutionalizing analysis, 189
Institutions, 8
Intellectual liberals, 25
Intergenerational
    conflict, 33
    effect, 127
International
    competitiveness, 127
    trade, 98
Invention-necessity, 94
Investment, 17, 101

Jails, 51
Japanese productivity, 105
Judicial reform, 48
Jury
    accuracy, 69
    size, 53, 68
Juveniles, 37

Labor
    costs, 108
    force, 23
    relations, 159
    shortage, 22
    management disputes, 31
Learning improvement, 59

Legal
  obligations, 183
  policy, 208
Liability, 153
Liberals, 15, 39, 85, 125
Litigation, 23
  costs, 29

Management by objectives, 150
Market share, 105
Marketing, 156
Marketplace, 37, 121
Mediation, 67
Mediators, 4
Mental blocks, 91
Methods, 18, 205
Migrant labor, 25
Ministry of International Trade,
  167
Mixed economy, 135
Monetary incentives, 90
Monopolies, 115
Monopoly, 118
Mothers of preschool children,
  25
Multi-criteria
  decision-making, 142
  methods, 31
Multiplier effect, 106
Murder reduction, 47

National
  productivity, 9
  purity, 24
Nativism, 24
Natural monopolies, 123
Necessity-invention, 94
Negative discretion, 165
Net worth, 181
Networking, 197
Neutral, 39
Nobel Prize, 118, 176
Note taking by juries, 55
Nuclear energy, 104

Omission, sins of, 174
On-the-job training, 20
One-five scale, 30
Opportunity costs, 10
Opposition parties, 132
Optimism, 10, 147
Optimum society, 92
Output-input ratio, 177
Ozone layer, 91

Package of alternatives, 3, 68
Part/whole percentages, 195
Partisan battles, 108
Payoffs, 152
Peaceful dispute resolution, 163
Personnel, 7
Pessimism, 10, 147
Pharmaceuticals, 172
Physical blocks, 91
Plaintiff, 27
Plutonium energy, 91
Police protection, 129
Policy analysis, 18, 113, 190
  institutions, 8
  methods, 8
Political
  competition, 133
  facilitators, 8
  feasibility, 41
  parties, 8, 129
  process, 1, 12
Pollution, 64
Positive
  competition, 124
  discretion, 165
  psychology, 139
Post Office, 118, 170
Poverty, 159, 162
  gap, 92
Prejudice, 168
Preschools education, 162
Pretrial release, 68
Price
  constraints, 136
  supplement, 42

Prisons, 168
Private
    police, 130
    schools, 129
    sector, 66
    universities, 43
    public orientation, 118
Privatization, 168
Procedural changes, 54
Process, 105
    of super-optimizing, 1
    political, 13
Product liability, 153
Production, 157
Productivity, 9, 15, 89, 99, 103, 163
    increase, 66
Profit maximization, 105
Profits, 108
Proportional representation, 131
Prosperity, 133
Psychology, 135, 175
    sociology of SOS solutions, 2
Public
    housing, 37
    policy, 158
    schools, 128
    sector, 66, 137
    universities, 43
Publishing, 192
Pulling factors, 142
Pushing factors, 140

Quality indicators, 130
Questioning by juries, 55

Racism, 23, 160
Raw scores, 16
Reagan Administration, 78
Reaganomics, 95
Reasoning powers, 143
Redefining problems, 53
Redistricting, 132
Reforming government, 162
Registration of voters, 132

Regulation, 155
Relative scoring, 195
Release on recognizance, 48
Releasing rate, 51
Rent supplements, 37, 130
Representatives, 73
Reputation, risking, 151
Research, 190
Resolving disputes, 35
Resources, 25
    expanding, 2
Revenge factor, 5
Rewards, 142
Rightdoing, 90
Risk-taking, 151
Rural well-being, 41

Safety, 156
Salaries, 59
Salary rewards, 129
School vouchers, 130
Schools, 92
Seed money, 136
Sensitivity, 175
Sequencing, 85
    principles, 33
Settlement costs, 28
Single-member districts, 131
Skills upgrading, 37, 115
Social psychology, 137
Socialistic ownership, 134
Socialization, 10, 49, 158
Societal
    goals, 91, 149
    happiness, 149
Solar energy, 114
SOS
    adoption, 56
    allocation, 197
    analysis, 125, 189
    awareness, 58
    prediction, 72
    solution, 15
    solutions, 1, 13
    table, 15
Source of conflict, 3, 45

Speech, free, 161
Spending, 17
Spiral, upward, 100
Staffing, 109
Standard of living, 133
State-owned schools, 44
Strict liability, 156
Strings attached, 6, 75, 102
Stullifying, 147
Subsidies, 9, 16, 92
Substance, public policy, 207
Success, SOS, 76
Sufficient money, 85
Summons to appear, 169
Super-optimizing, 1, 112, 194
Super-optimum, 194
    solution, 15, 66
    thinking, 153
Supply-side economics, 95
Suspicion, 5
Systematic analysis, 18

Tariffs, 101, 114
Tax
    breaks, 9, 15
    cuts, 165
    reduction, 60
Taxes, 17
Teachers, 129
Teaching creativity, 144
Technological innovation,
    93, 151
Technologies, new, 21
Telephoning, 119
Tenants, 37
Third-party benefactor, 3, 34
Timing, 75
Trade, international, 98

Tradeoff
    attitude, 100
    reasoning, 153
Traffic violations, 170
Training, 190
    for juries, 55
Trends, 192
Turnout of voters, 132

Unanimity, 57
Unemployment, 20, 90
Union
    liberals, 15
    wages, 24
Universities, 191
Upping the ante, 3
Upward spiral, 18, 100
Urban well-being, 41

Vested
    jobs, 5, 75
    property, 5, 75
Videotaping, 54
Violent competition, 123
Voter registration, 92
Vouchers for housing, 37

Wages, 107
Waste, 176
Weights, 16, 195
Workers, 25, 111
Working style, 141
Workplace, 117
Wrongdoers, 64
Wrongdoing, 90

Zero-sum thinking, 99